CHAPTER FiVE

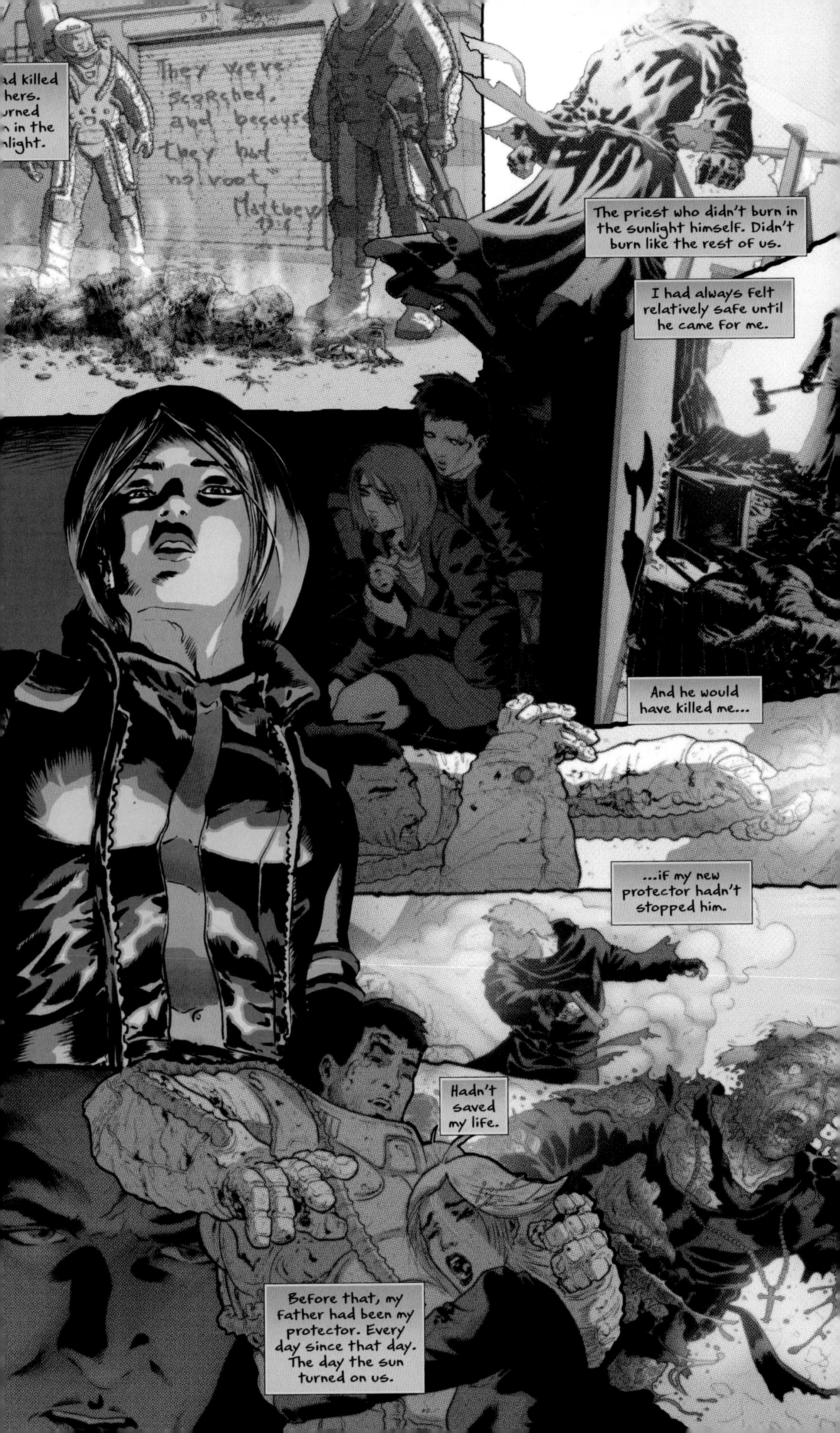
ad killed hers. urned n in the nlight.
The priest who didn't burn in the sunlight himself. Didn't burn like the rest of us.
I had always felt relatively safe until he came for me.
And he would have killed me...
...if my new protector hadn't stopped him.
Hadn't saved my life.
Before that, my father had been my protector. Every day since that day. The day the sun turned on us.

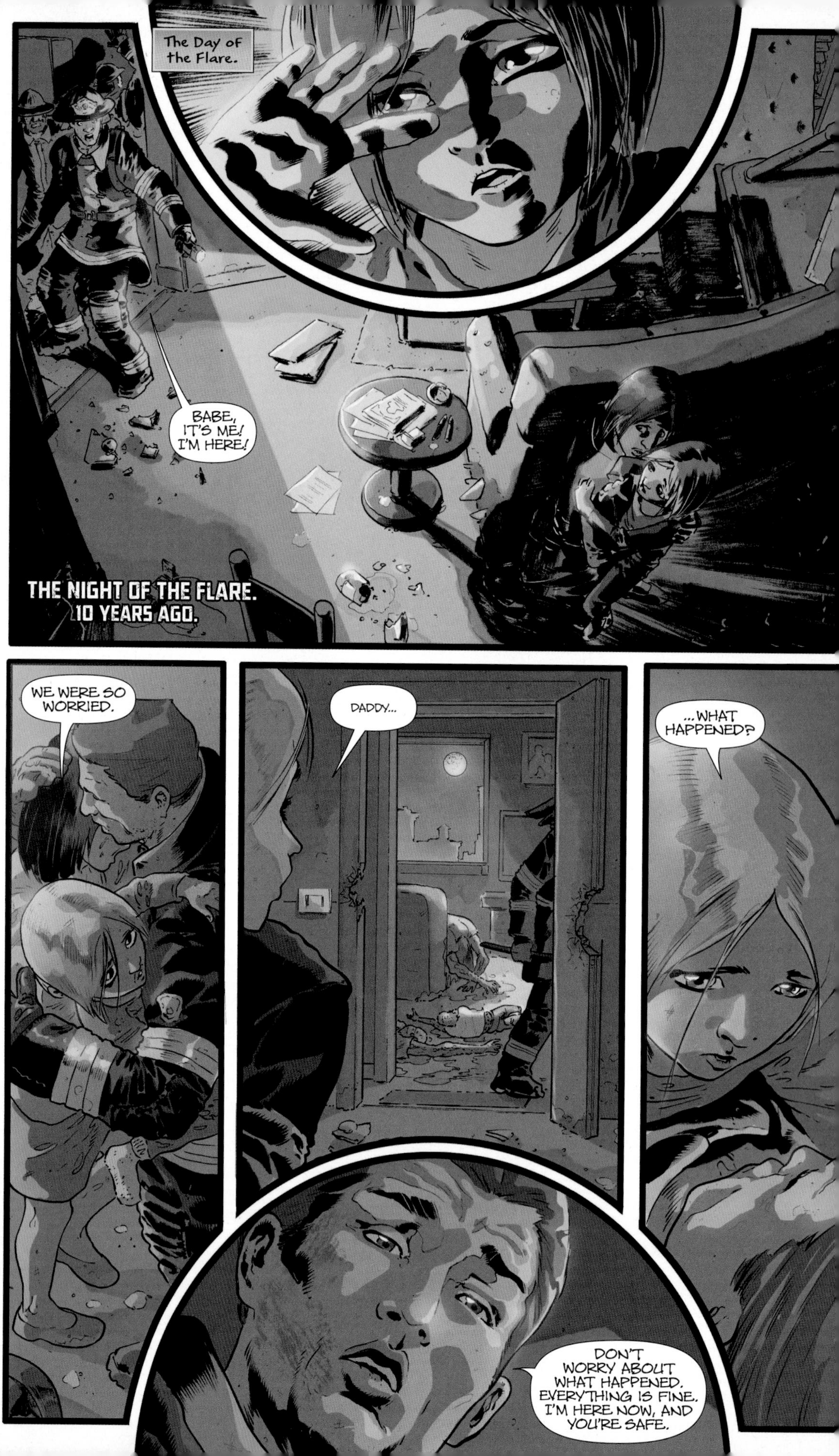
The Day of the Flare.
BABE, IT'S ME! I'M HERE!
THE NIGHT OF THE FLARE. 10 YEARS AGO.
WE WERE SO WORRIED.
DADDY...
...WHAT HAPPENED?
DON'T WORRY ABOUT WHAT HAPPENED. EVERYTHING IS FINE. I'M HERE NOW, AND YOU'RE SAFE.

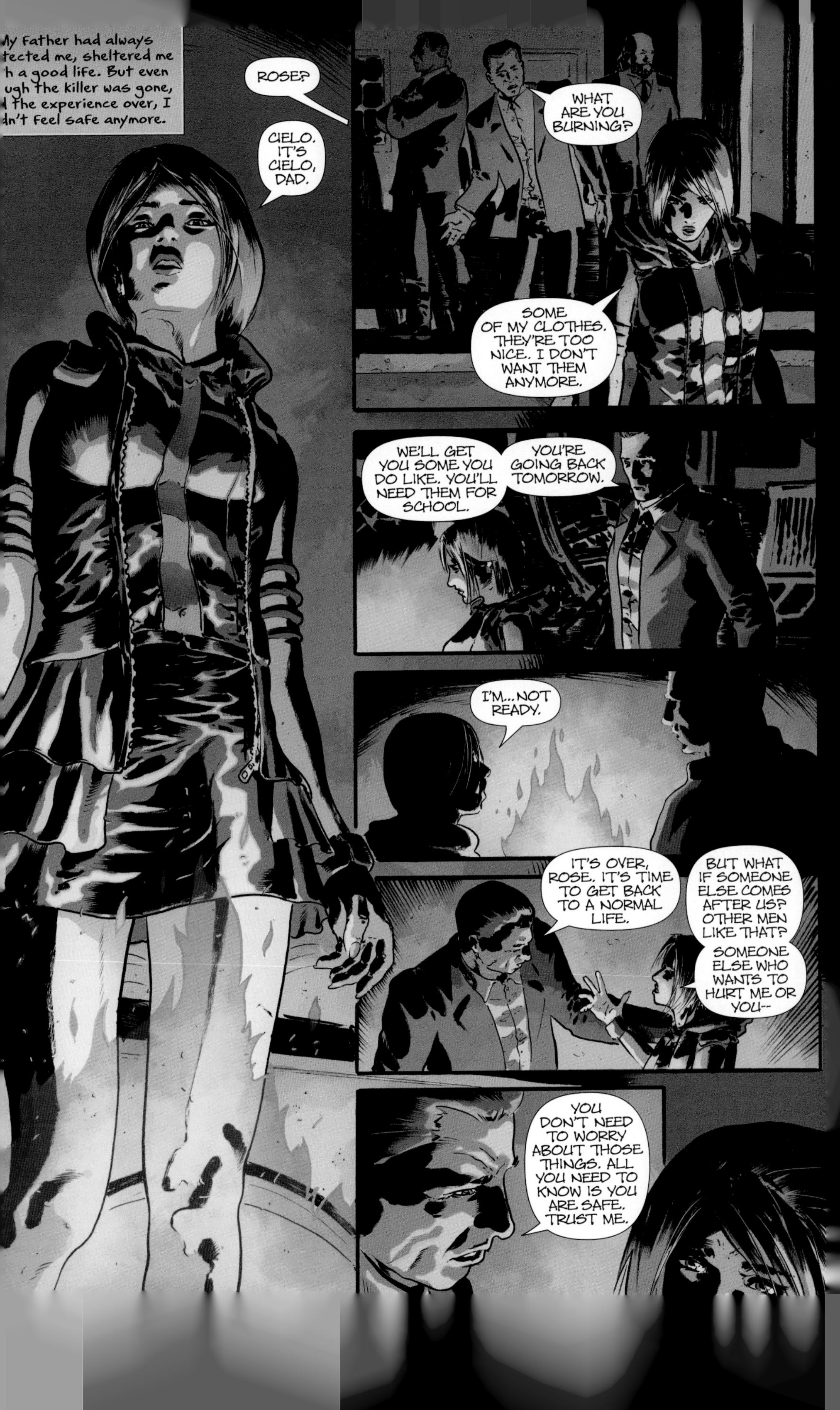

My Father had always
tected me, sheltered me
h a good life. But even
ugh the killer was gone,
the experience over, I
dn't feel safe anymore.
ROSE?
CIELO. IT'S CIELO, DAD.
WHAT ARE YOU BURNING?
SOME OF MY CLOTHES. THEY'RE TOO NICE. I DON'T WANT THEM ANYMORE.
WE'LL GET YOU SOME YOU DO LIKE. YOU'LL NEED THEM FOR SCHOOL.
YOU'RE GOING BACK TOMORROW.
I'M...NOT READY.
IT'S OVER, ROSE. IT'S TIME TO GET BACK TO A NORMAL LIFE.
BUT WHAT IF SOMEONE ELSE COMES AFTER US? OTHER MEN LIKE THAT?
SOMEONE ELSE WHO WANTS TO HURT ME OR YOU--
YOU DON'T NEED TO WORRY ABOUT THOSE THINGS. ALL YOU NEED TO KNOW IS YOU ARE SAFE. TRUST ME.

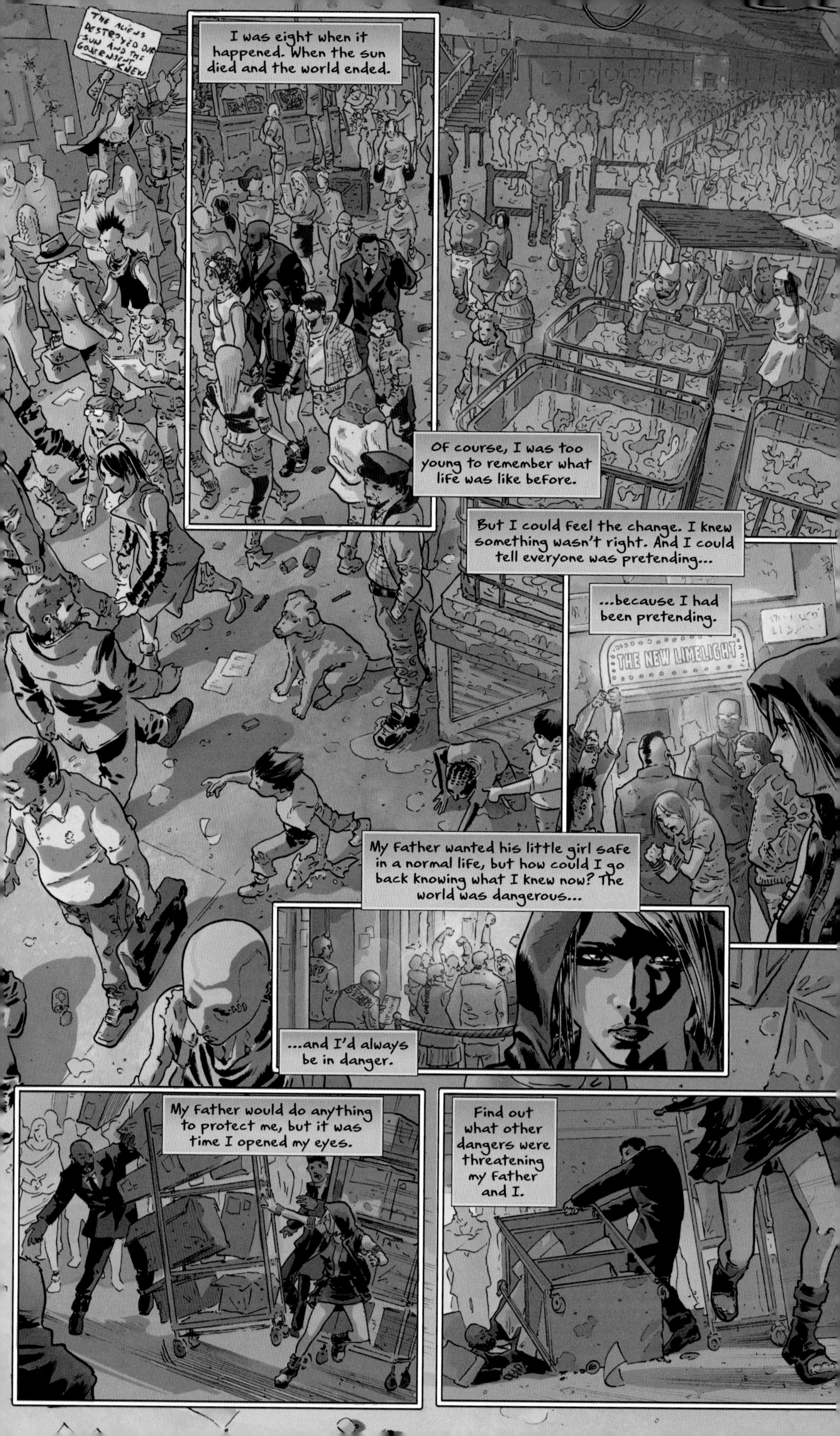

THE ALIENS DESTROYED OUR SUN AND THE GOVERNMENT KNEW
I was eight when it happened. When the sun died and the world ended.
Of course, I was too young to remember what life was like before.
But I could feel the change. I knew something wasn't right. And I could tell everyone was pretending...
...because I had been pretending.
THE NEW LIMELIGHT
My father wanted his little girl safe in a normal life, but how could I go back knowing what I knew now? The world was dangerous...
...and I'd always be in danger.
My father would do anything to protect me, but it was time I opened my eyes.
Find out what other dangers were threatening my father and I.

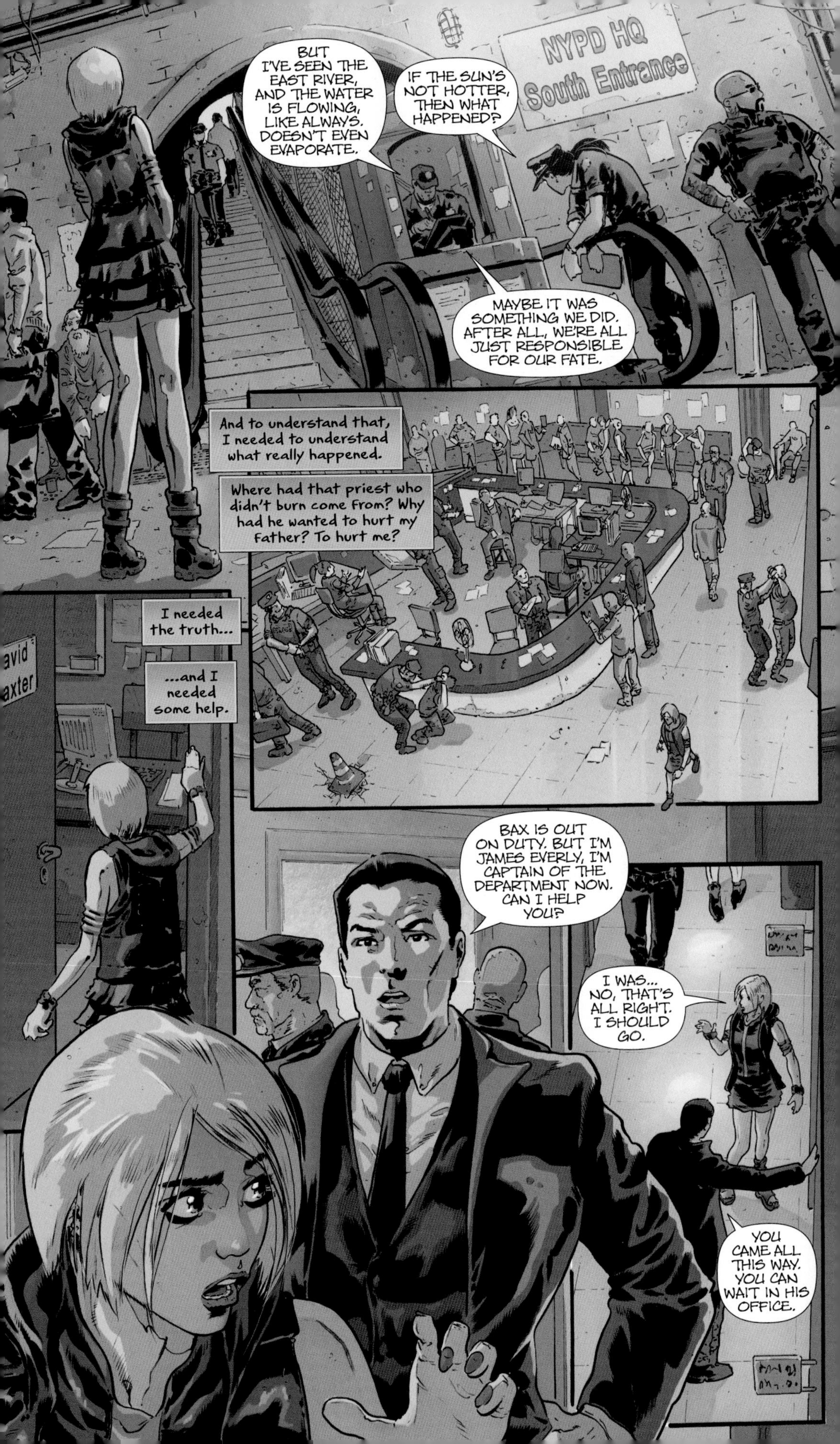
NYPD HQ
South Entrance
BUT I'VE SEEN THE EAST RIVER, AND THE WATER IS FLOWING, LIKE ALWAYS. DOESN'T EVEN EVAPORATE.
IF THE SUN'S NOT HOTTER, THEN WHAT HAPPENED?
MAYBE IT WAS SOMETHING WE DID. AFTER ALL, WE'RE ALL JUST RESPONSIBLE FOR OUR FATE.
And to understand that, I needed to understand what really happened.
Where had that priest who didn't burn come from? Why had he wanted to hurt my Father? To hurt me?
I needed the truth...
...and I needed some help.
avid
axter
BAX IS OUT ON DUTY. BUT I'M JAMES EVERLY, I'M CAPTAIN OF THE DEPARTMENT NOW. CAN I HELP YOU?
I WAS... NO, THAT'S ALL RIGHT. I SHOULD GO.
YOU CAME ALL THIS WAY. YOU CAN WAIT IN HIS OFFICE.

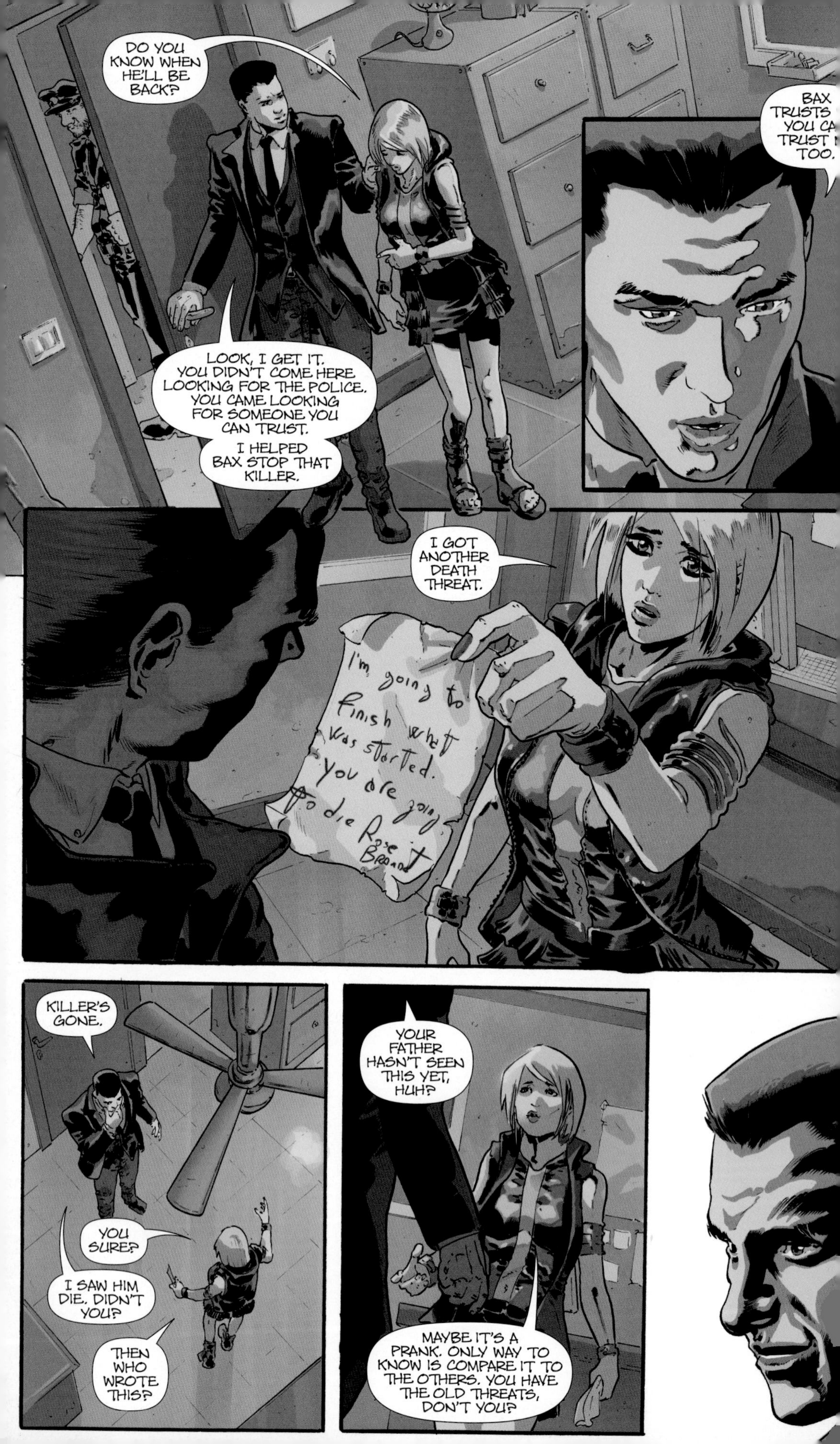

DO YOU KNOW WHEN HE'LL BE BACK?
LOOK, I GET IT. YOU DIDN'T COME HERE LOOKING FOR THE POLICE. YOU CAME LOOKING FOR SOMEONE YOU CAN TRUST.
I HELPED BAX STOP THAT KILLER.
BAX TRUSTS YOU CA TRUST TOO.
I GOT ANOTHER DEATH THREAT.
I'm going to finish what was started. you are going to die Rose
KILLER'S GONE.
YOU SURE?
I SAW HIM DIE. DIDN'T YOU?
THEN WHO WROTE THIS?
YOUR FATHER HASN'T SEEN THIS YET, HUH?
MAYBE IT'S A PRANK. ONLY WAY TO KNOW IS COMPARE IT TO THE OTHERS. YOU HAVE THE OLD THREATS, DON'T YOU?

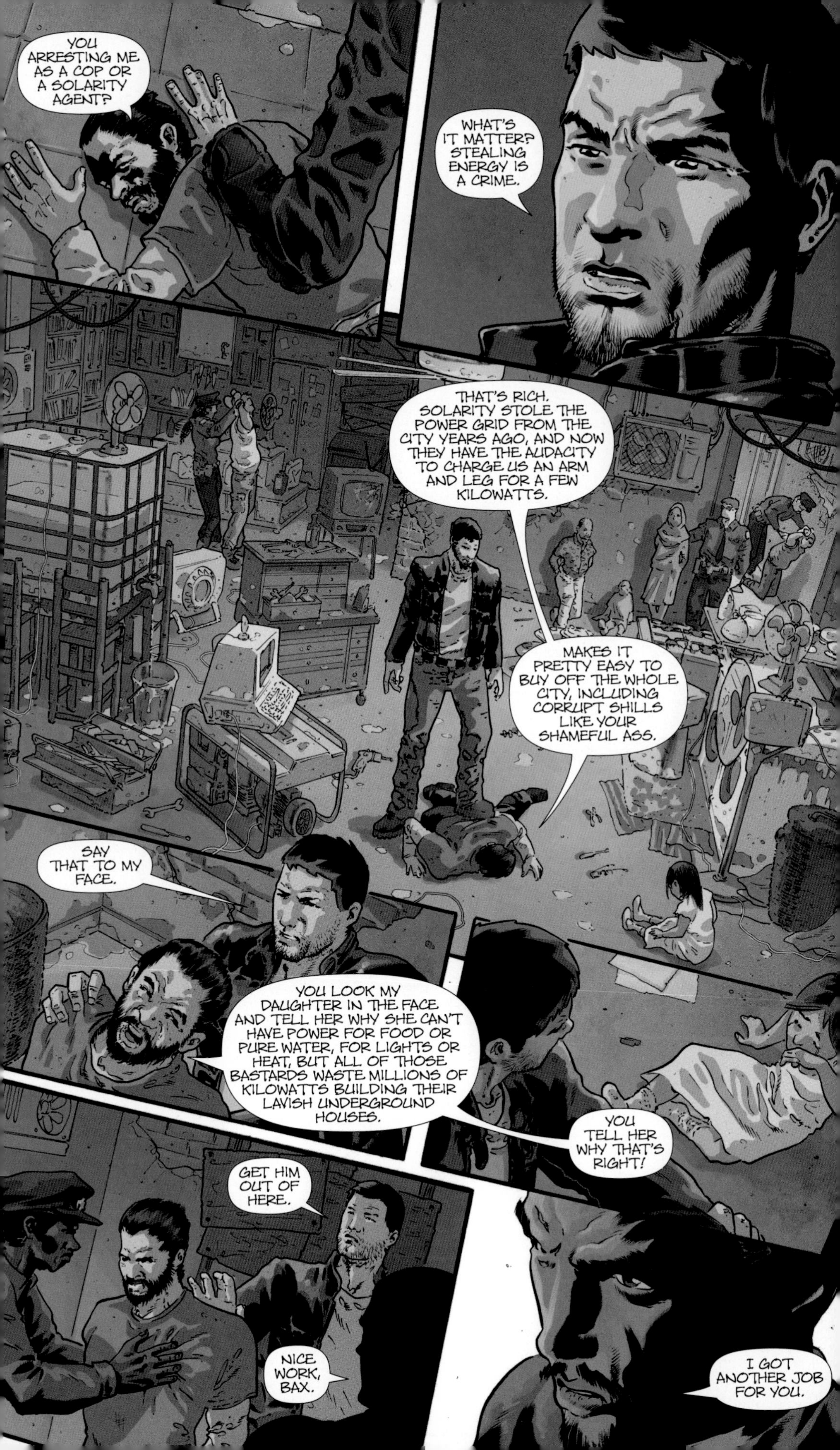
YOU ARRESTING ME AS A COP OR A SOLARITY AGENT?
WHAT'S IT MATTER? STEALING ENERGY IS A CRIME.
THAT'S RICH. SOLARITY STOLE THE POWER GRID FROM THE CITY YEARS AGO, AND NOW THEY HAVE THE AUDACITY TO CHARGE US AN ARM AND LEG FOR A FEW KILOWATTS.
MAKES IT PRETTY EASY TO BUY OFF THE WHOLE CITY, INCLUDING CORRUPT SHILLS LIKE YOUR SHAMEFUL ASS.
SAY THAT TO MY FACE.
YOU LOOK MY DAUGHTER IN THE FACE AND TELL HER WHY SHE CAN'T HAVE POWER FOR FOOD OR PURE WATER, FOR LIGHTS OR HEAT, BUT ALL OF THOSE BASTARDS WASTE MILLIONS OF KILOWATTS BUILDING THEIR LAVISH UNDERGROUND HOUSES.
YOU TELL HER WHY THAT'S RIGHT!
GET HIM OUT OF HERE.
NICE WORK, BAX.
I GOT ANOTHER JOB FOR YOU.

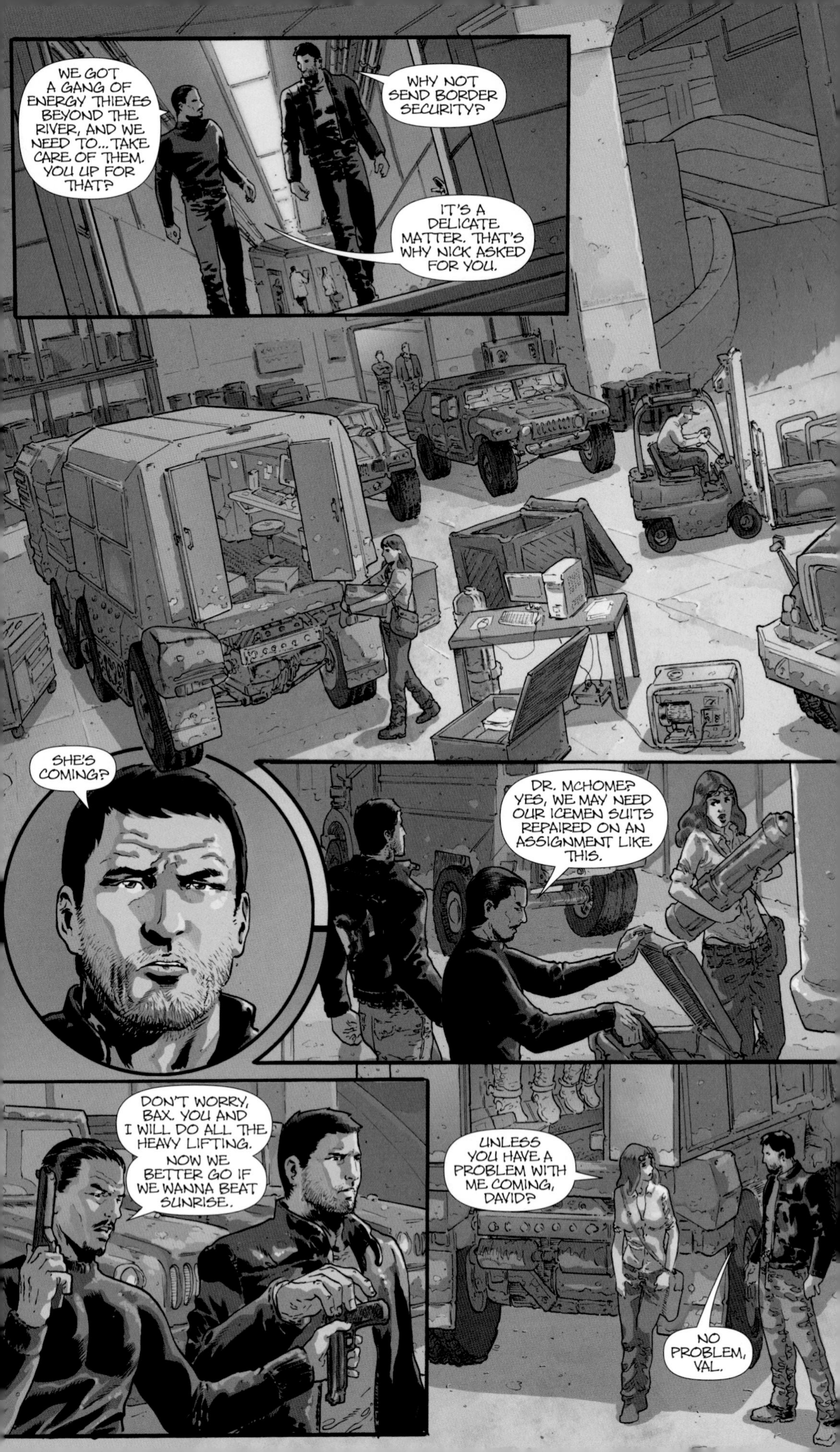
WE GOT A GANG OF ENERGY THIEVES BEYOND THE RIVER, AND WE NEED TO... TAKE CARE OF THEM. YOU UP FOR THAT?
WHY NOT SEND BORDER SECURITY?
IT'S A DELICATE MATTER. THAT'S WHY NICK ASKED FOR YOU.
SHE'S COMING?
DR. MCHOME? YES, WE MAY NEED OUR ICEMEN SUITS REPAIRED ON AN ASSIGNMENT LIKE THIS.
DON'T WORRY, BAX. YOU AND I WILL DO ALL THE HEAVY LIFTING.
NOW WE BETTER GO IF WE WANNA BEAT SUNRISE.
UNLESS YOU HAVE A PROBLEM WITH ME COMING, DAVID?
NO PROBLEM, VAL.

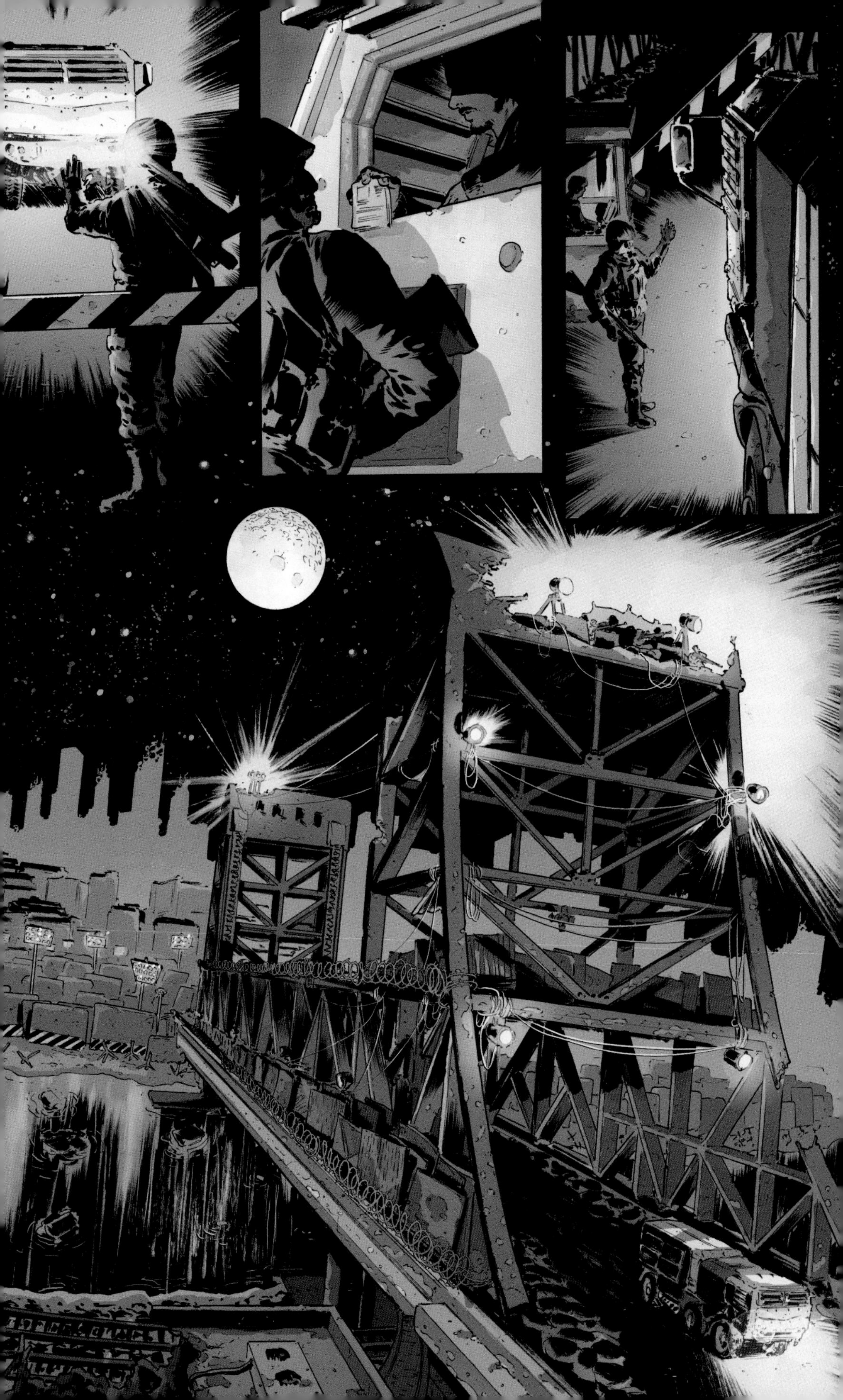

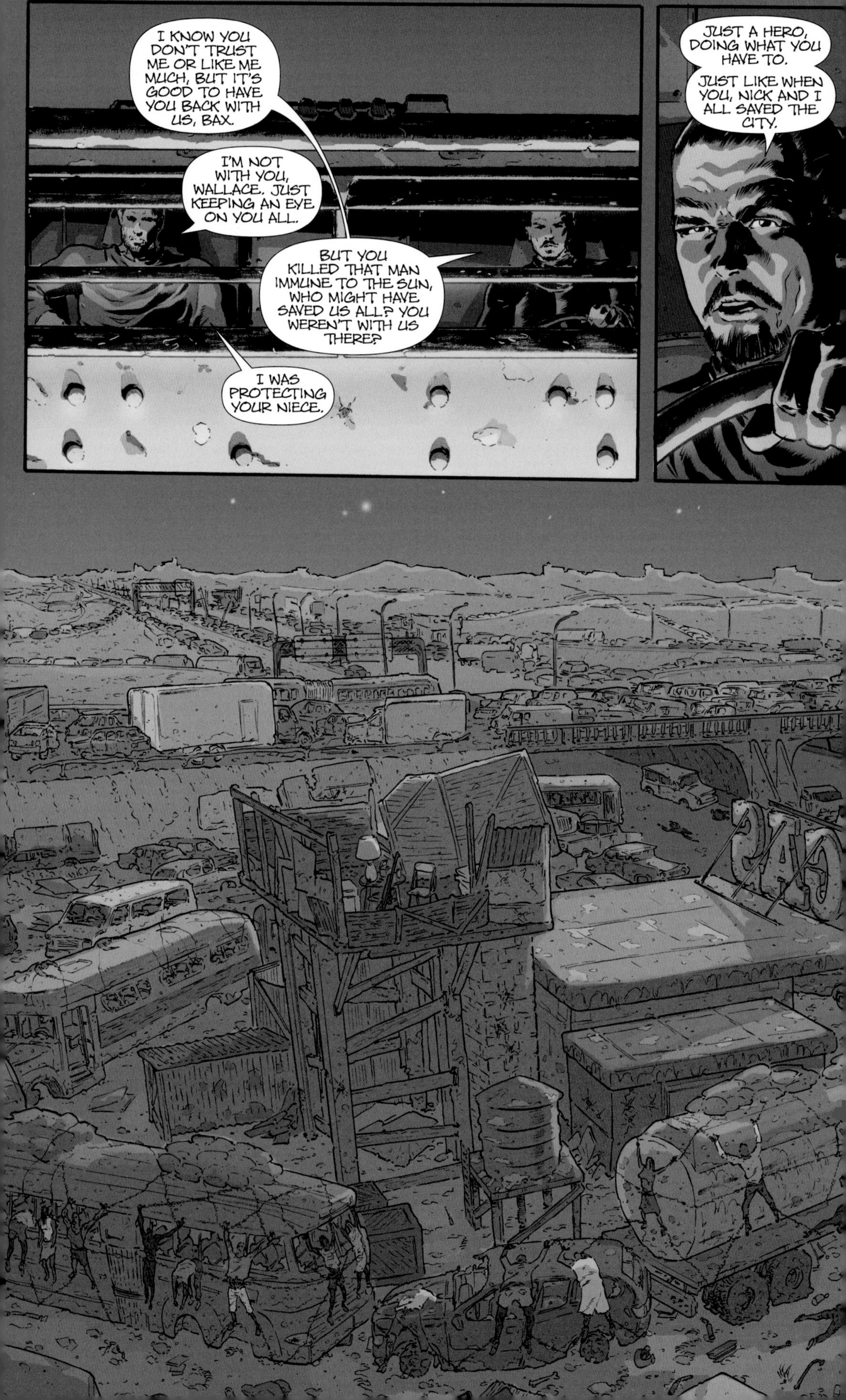
I KNOW YOU DON'T TRUST ME OR LIKE ME MUCH, BUT IT'S GOOD TO HAVE YOU BACK WITH US, BAX.
I'M NOT WITH YOU, WALLACE. JUST KEEPING AN EYE ON YOU ALL.
BUT YOU KILLED THAT MAN IMMUNE TO THE SUN, WHO MIGHT HAVE SAVED US ALL? YOU WEREN'T WITH US THERE?
I WAS PROTECTING YOUR NIECE.
JUST A HERO, DOING WHAT YOU HAVE TO.
JUST LIKE WHEN YOU, NICK AND I ALL SAVED THE CITY.

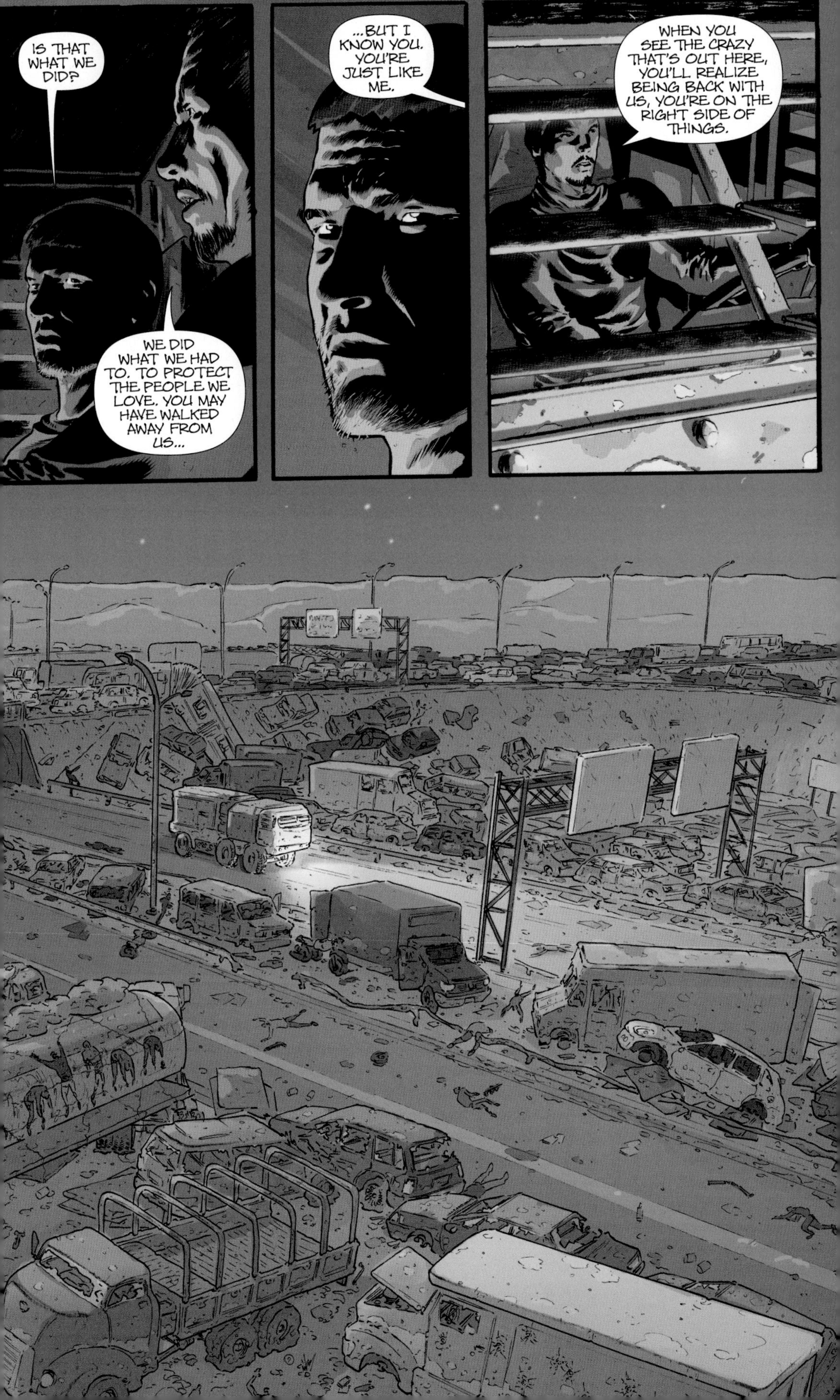
IS THAT WHAT WE DID?
WE DID WHAT WE HAD TO. TO PROTECT THE PEOPLE WE LOVE. YOU MAY HAVE WALKED AWAY FROM US...
...BUT I KNOW YOU. YOU'RE JUST LIKE ME.
WHEN YOU SEE THE CRAZY THAT'S OUT HERE, YOU'LL REALIZE BEING BACK WITH US, YOU'RE ON THE RIGHT SIDE OF THINGS.

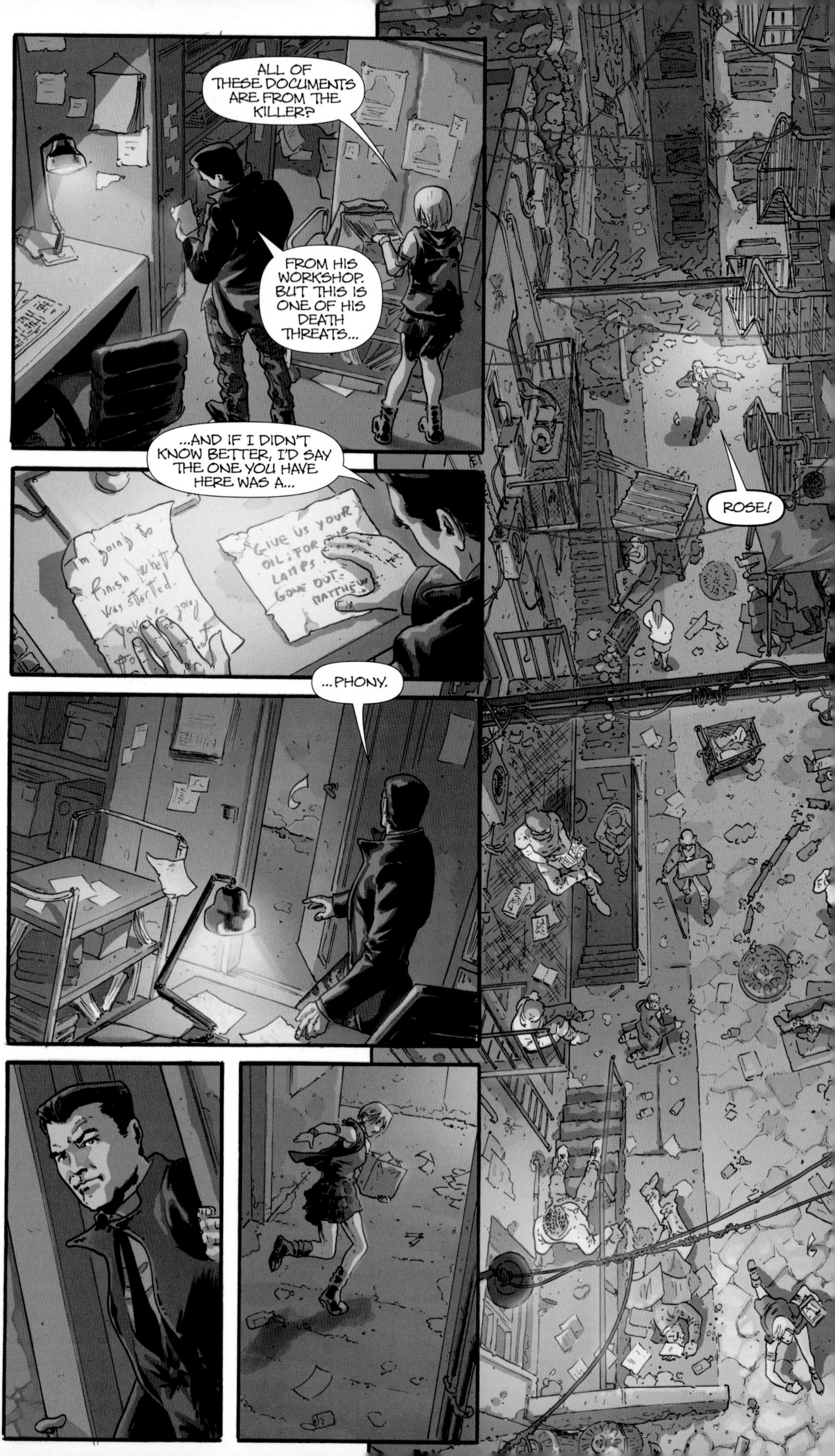
ALL OF THESE DOCUMENTS ARE FROM THE KILLER?
FROM HIS WORKSHOP. BUT THIS IS ONE OF HIS DEATH THREATS...
...AND IF I DIDN'T KNOW BETTER, I'D SAY THE ONE YOU HAVE HERE WAS A...
I'm going to finish what was started.
...PHONY.
ROSE!

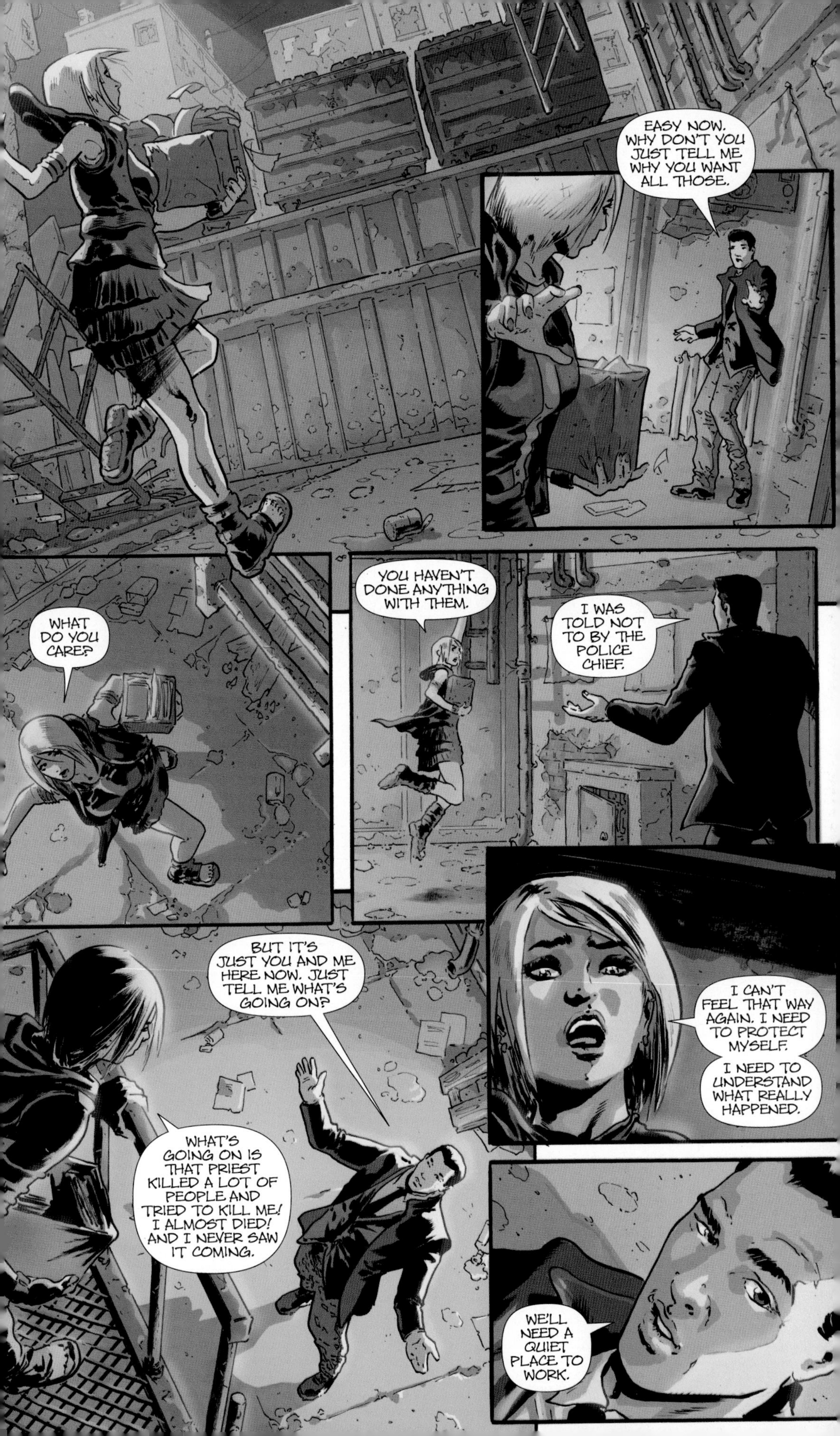
EASY NOW. WHY DON'T YOU JUST TELL ME WHY YOU WANT ALL THOSE.
WHAT DO YOU CARE?
YOU HAVEN'T DONE ANYTHING WITH THEM.
I WAS TOLD NOT TO BY THE POLICE CHIEF.
BUT IT'S JUST YOU AND ME HERE NOW. JUST TELL ME WHAT'S GOING ON?
WHAT'S GOING ON IS THAT PRIEST KILLED A LOT OF PEOPLE AND TRIED TO KILL ME! I ALMOST DIED! AND I NEVER SAW IT COMING.
I CAN'T FEEL THAT WAY AGAIN. I NEED TO PROTECT MYSELF.
I NEED TO UNDERSTAND WHAT REALLY HAPPENED.
WE'LL NEED A QUIET PLACE TO WORK.

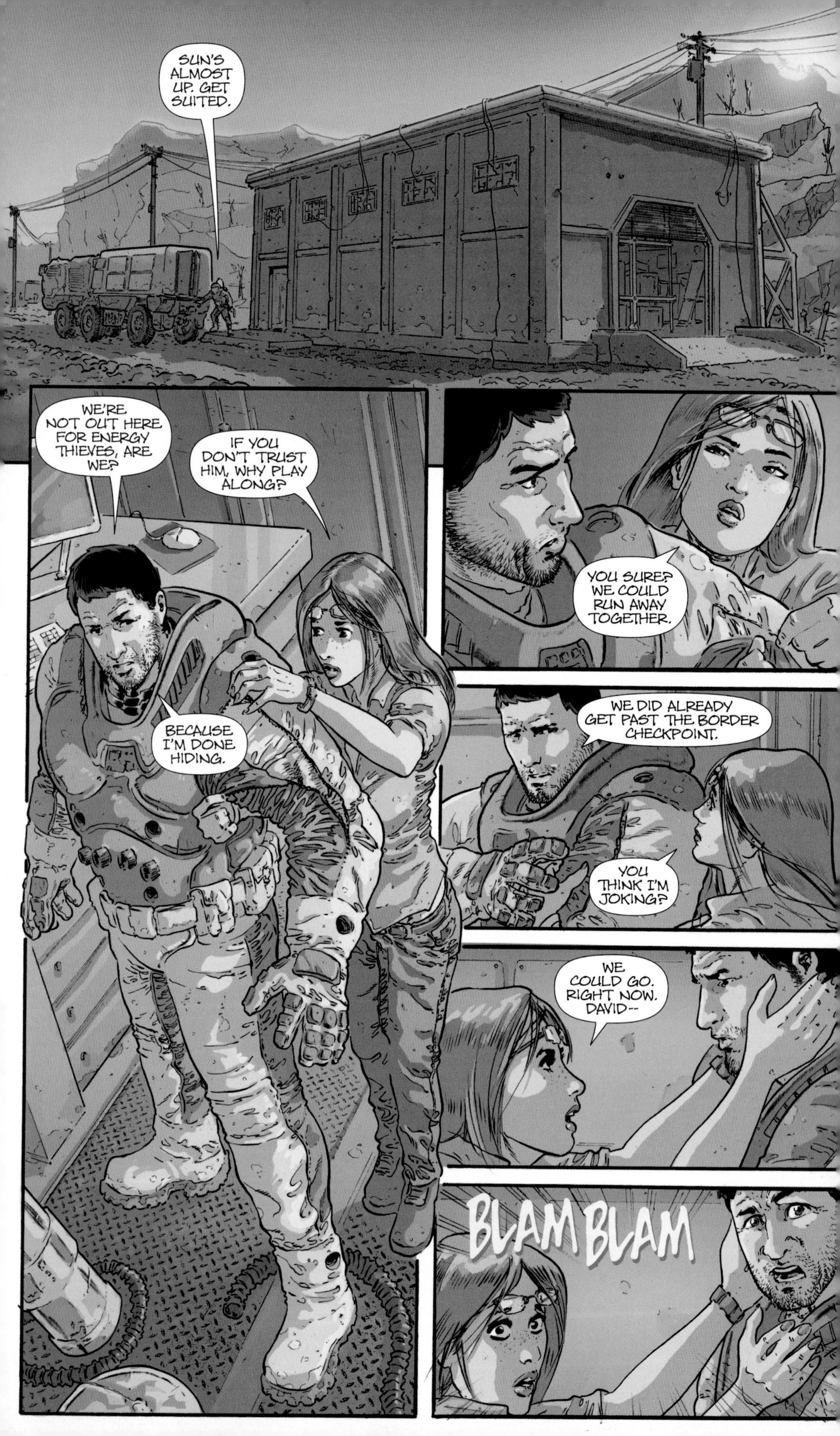
SUN'S ALMOST UP. GET SUITED.
WE'RE NOT OUT HERE FOR ENERGY THIEVES, ARE WE?
IF YOU DON'T TRUST HIM, WHY PLAY ALONG?
BECAUSE I'M DONE HIDING.
YOU SURE? WE COULD RUN AWAY TOGETHER.
WE DID ALREADY GET PAST THE BORDER CHECKPOINT.
YOU THINK I'M JOKING?
WE COULD GO. RIGHT NOW. DAVID--
BLAM BLAM

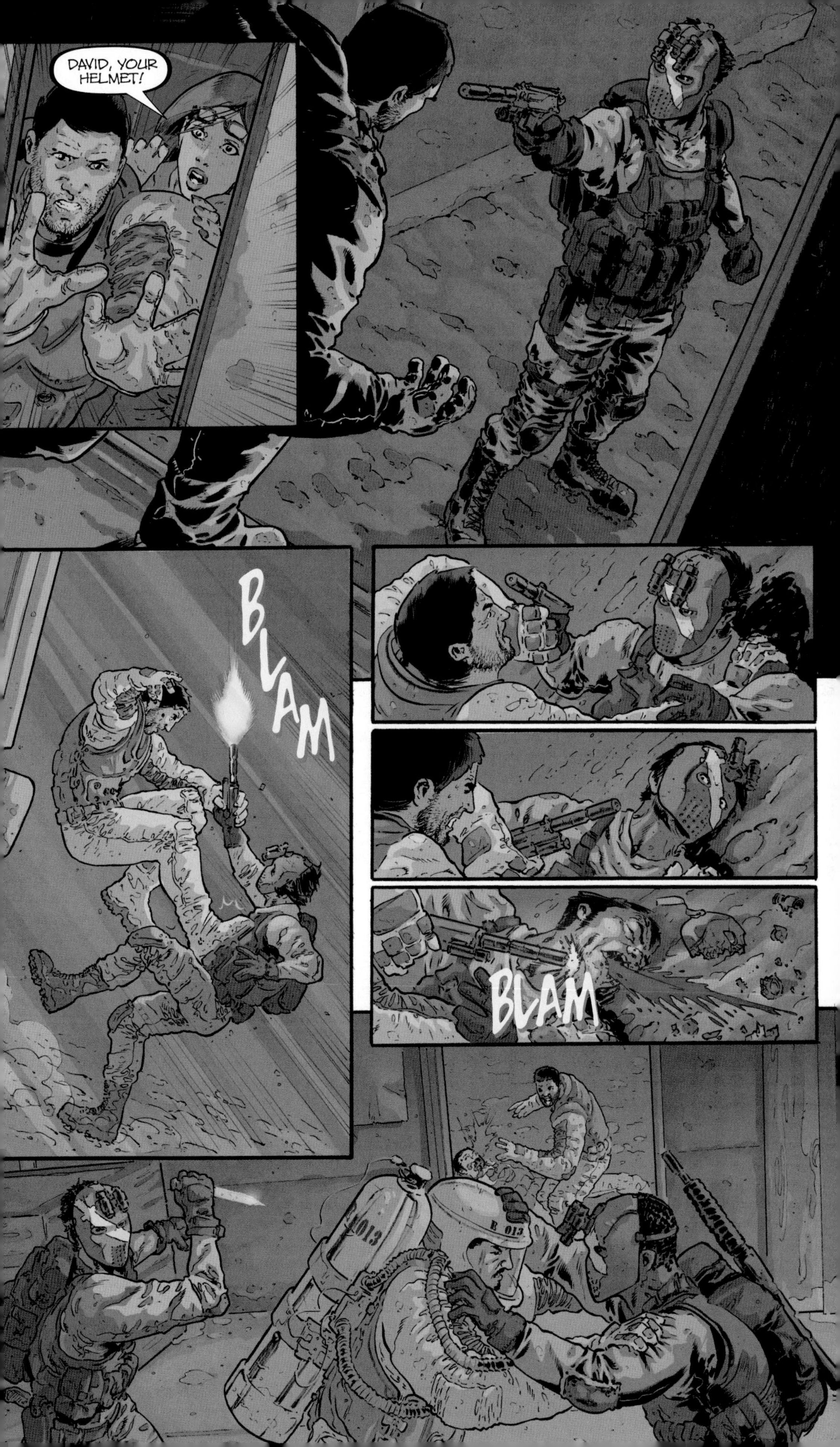

DAVID, YOUR HELMET!
BLAM
B 013
BLAM

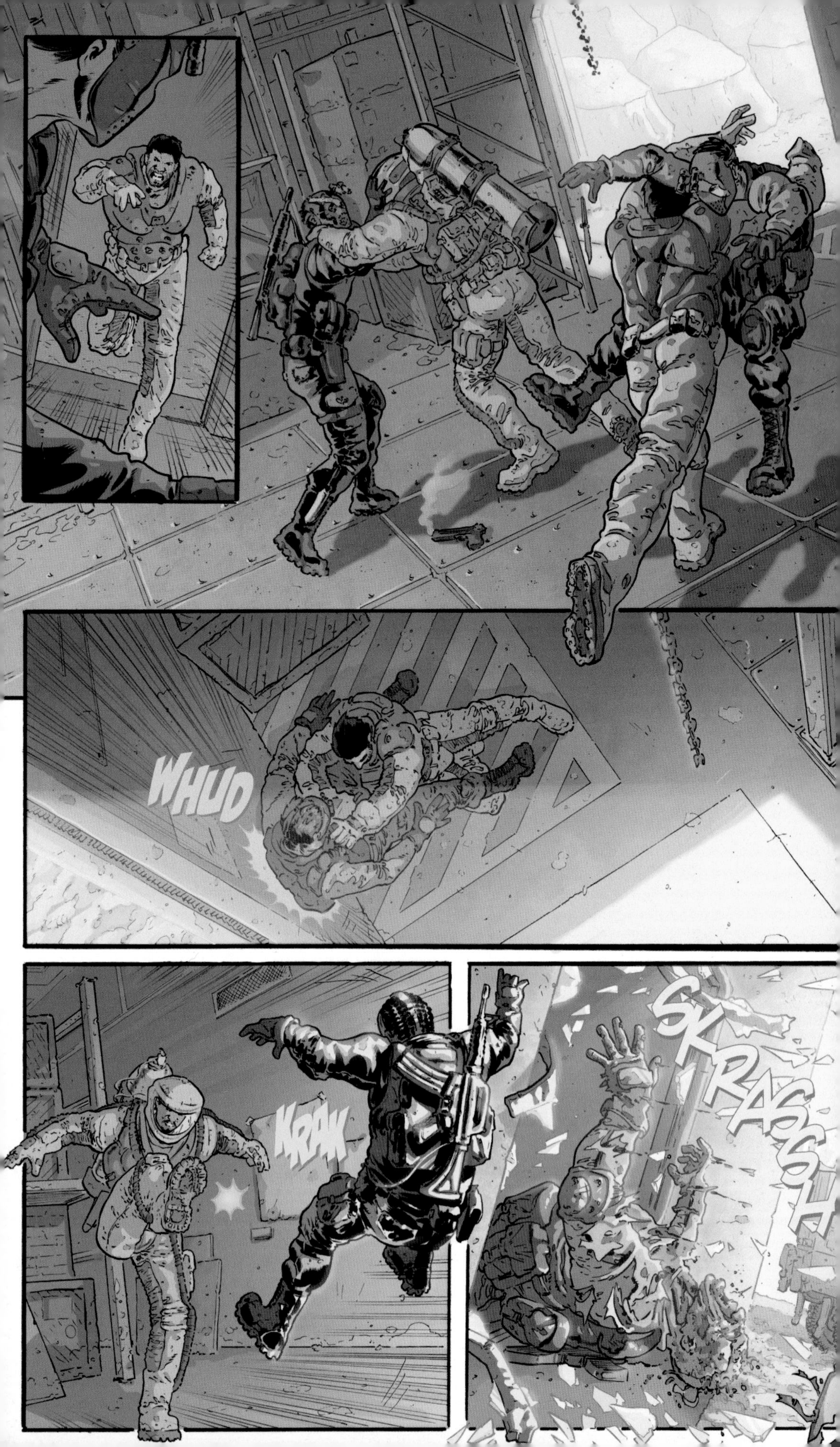
WHUD
KRAK
SKRASSH

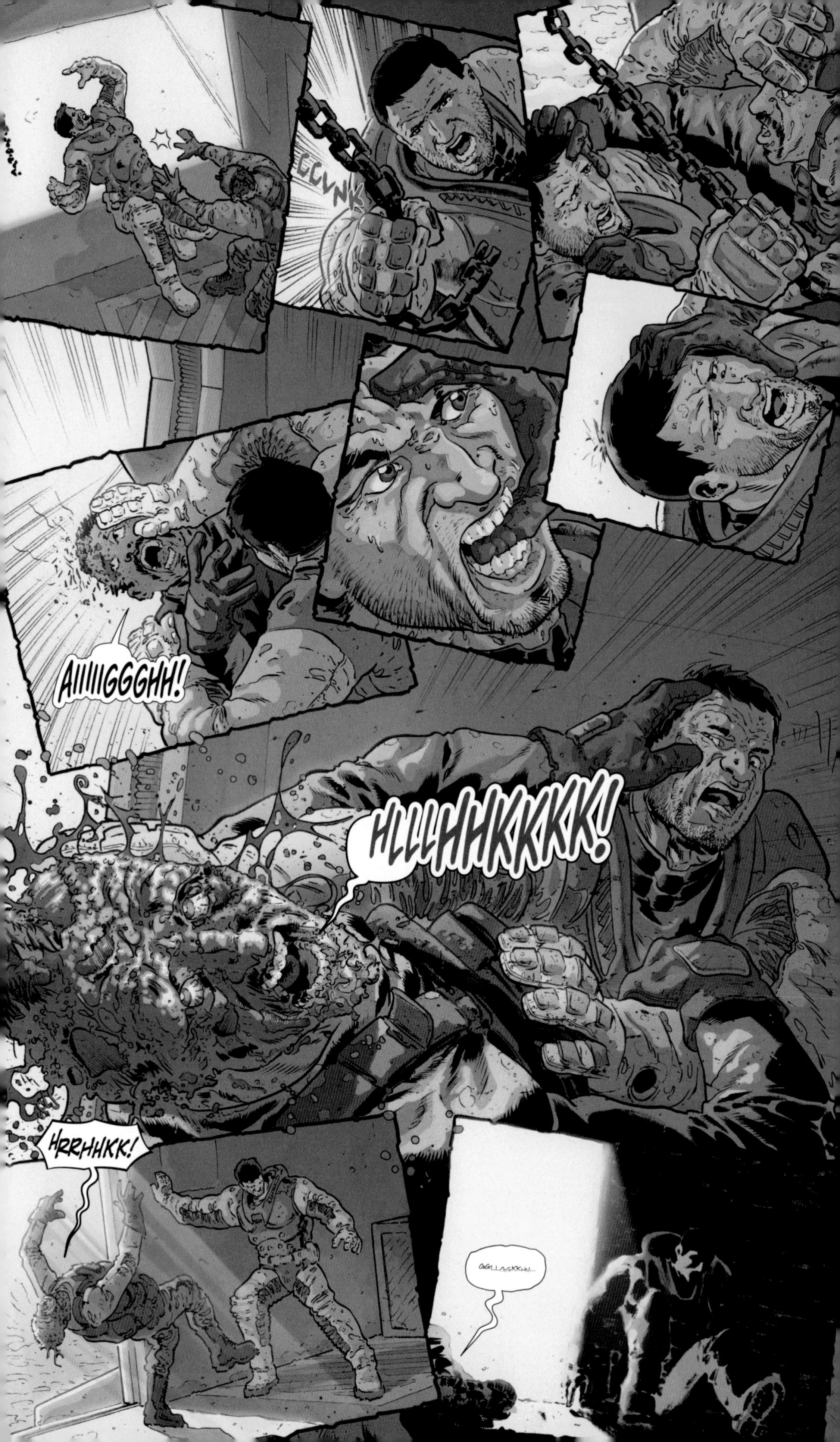
CCUNK
AIIIIIGGGHH!
HLLLHHKKKK!
HRRHHKK!
GGLLGGKKHH...

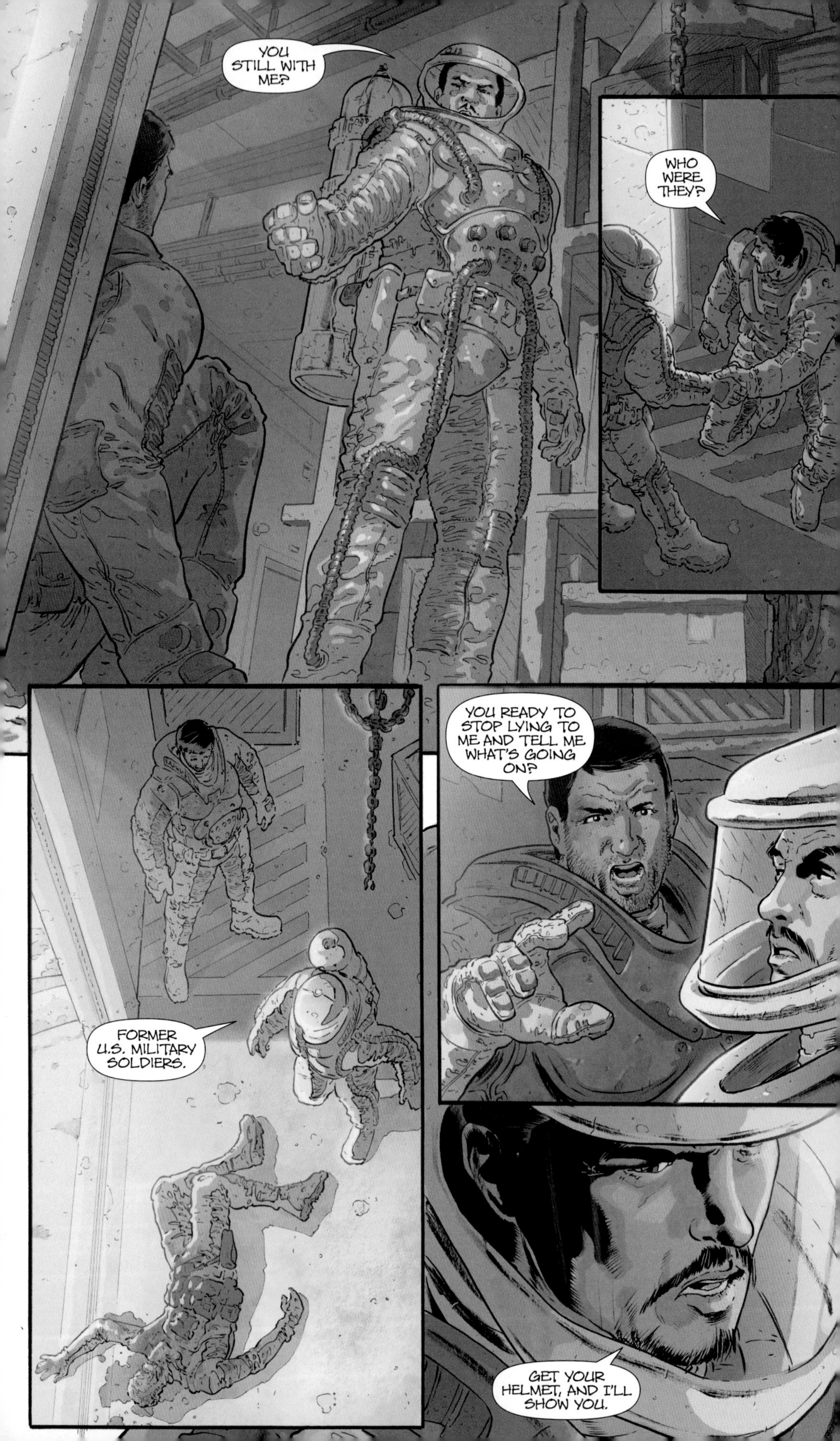
YOU STILL WITH ME?
WHO WERE THEY?
FORMER U.S. MILITARY SOLDIERS.
YOU READY TO STOP LYING TO ME AND TELL ME WHAT'S GOING ON?
GET YOUR HELMET, AND I'LL SHOW YOU.

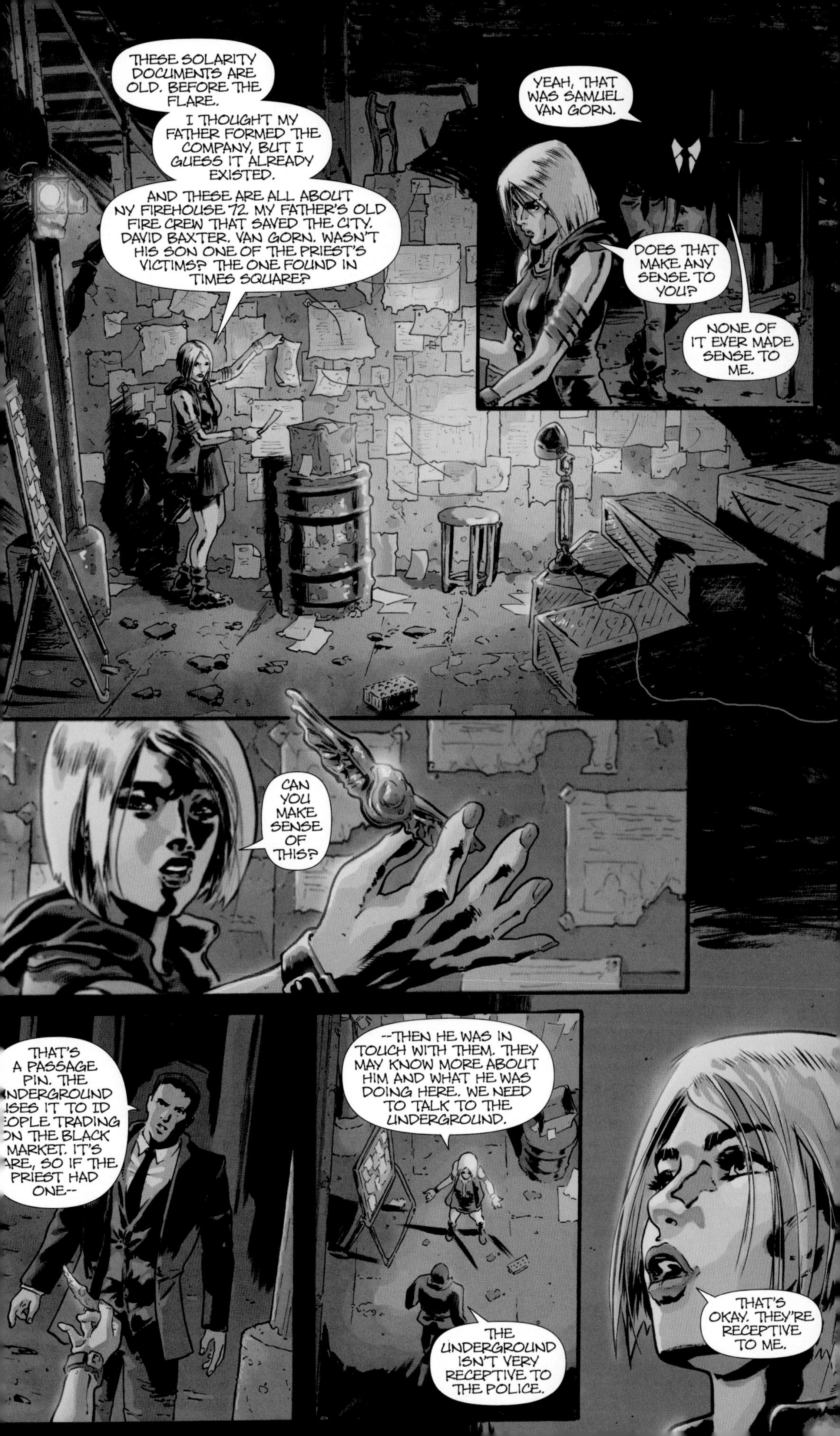

THESE SOLARITY DOCUMENTS ARE OLD. BEFORE THE FLARE.
I THOUGHT MY FATHER FORMED THE COMPANY, BUT I GUESS IT ALREADY EXISTED.
AND THESE ARE ALL ABOUT NY FIREHOUSE 72. MY FATHER'S OLD FIRE CREW THAT SAVED THE CITY. DAVID BAXTER. VAN GORN. WASN'T HIS SON ONE OF THE PRIEST'S VICTIMS? THE ONE FOUND IN TIMES SQUARE?
YEAH, THAT WAS SAMUEL VAN GORN.
DOES THAT MAKE ANY SENSE TO YOU?
NONE OF IT EVER MADE SENSE TO ME.
CAN YOU MAKE SENSE OF THIS?
THAT'S A PASSAGE PIN. THE UNDERGROUND USES IT TO ID PEOPLE TRADING ON THE BLACK MARKET. IT'S RARE, SO IF THE PRIEST HAD ONE--
--THEN HE WAS IN TOUCH WITH THEM. THEY MAY KNOW MORE ABOUT HIM AND WHAT HE WAS DOING HERE. WE NEED TO TALK TO THE UNDERGROUND.
THE UNDERGROUND ISN'T VERY RECEPTIVE TO THE POLICE.
THAT'S OKAY. THEY'RE RECEPTIVE TO ME.

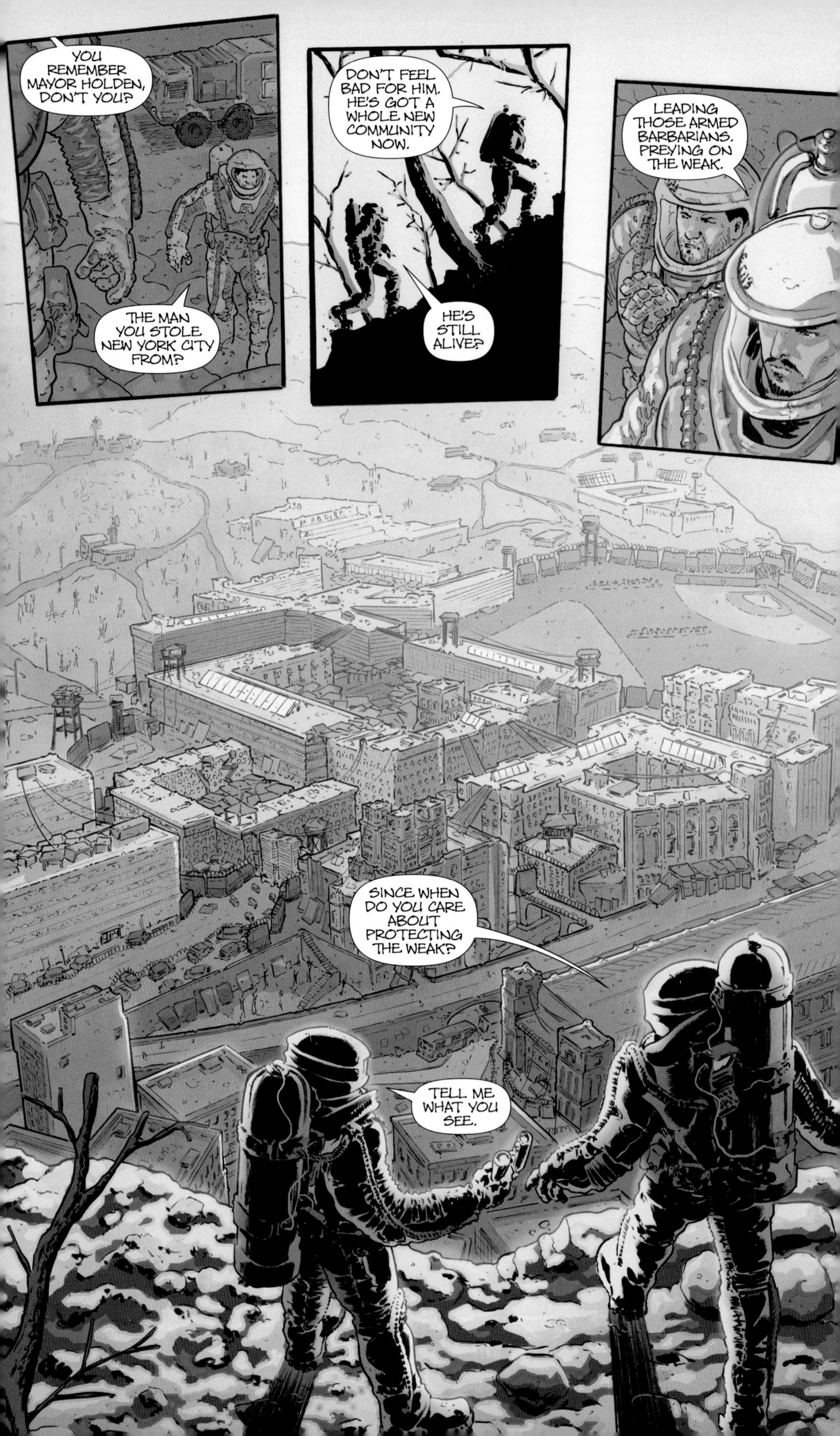
YOU REMEMBER MAYOR HOLDEN, DON'T YOU?
THE MAN YOU STOLE NEW YORK CITY FROM?
DON'T FEEL BAD FOR HIM. HE'S GOT A WHOLE NEW COMMUNITY NOW.
HE'S STILL ALIVE?
LEADING THOSE ARMED BARBARIANS. PREYING ON THE WEAK.
SINCE WHEN DO YOU CARE ABOUT PROTECTING THE WEAK?
TELL ME WHAT YOU SEE.

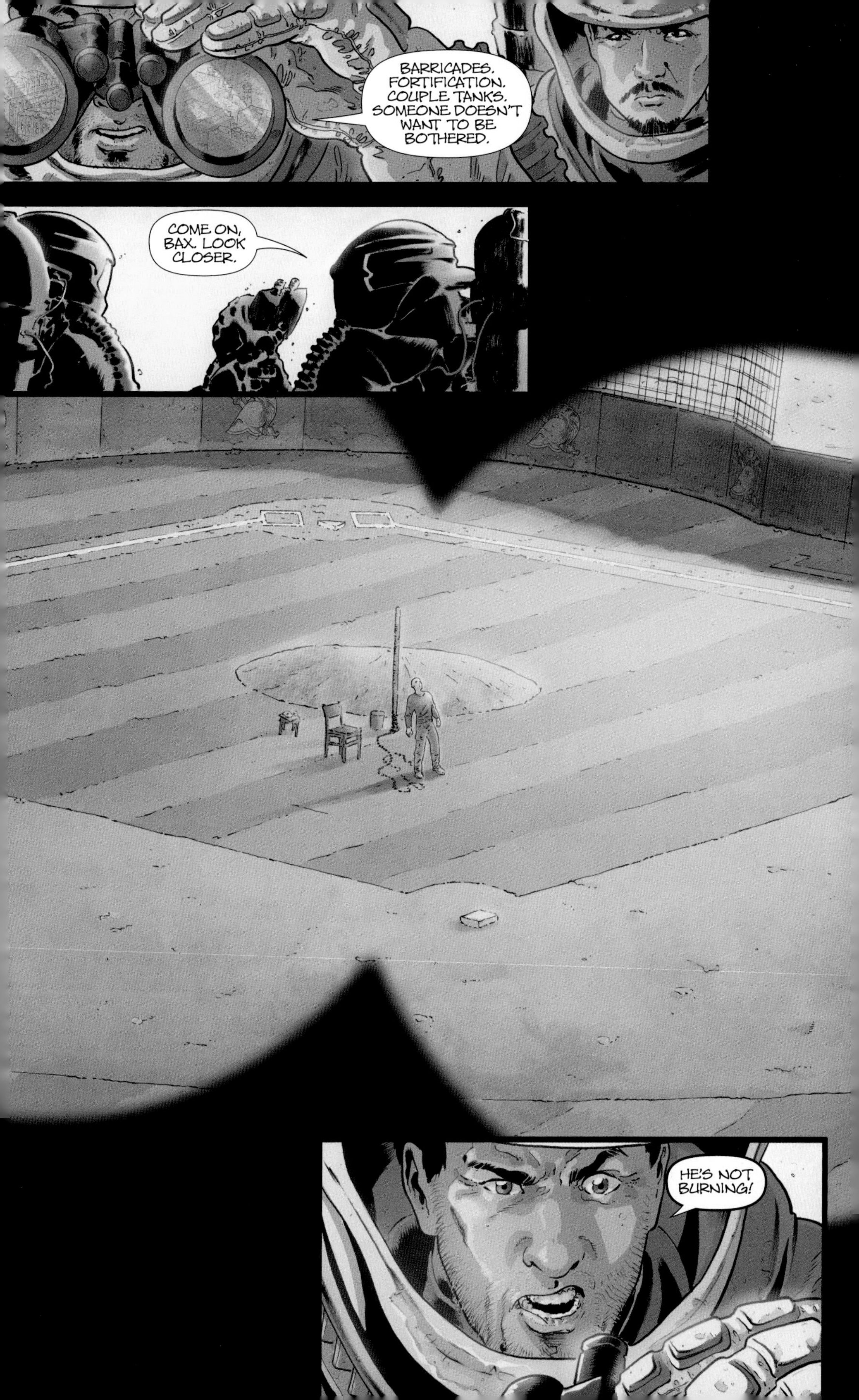
BARRICADES. FORTIFICATION. COUPLE TANKS. SOMEONE DOESN'T WANT TO BE BOTHERED.
COME ON, BAX. LOOK CLOSER.
HE'S NOT BURNING!

CHAPTER SIX

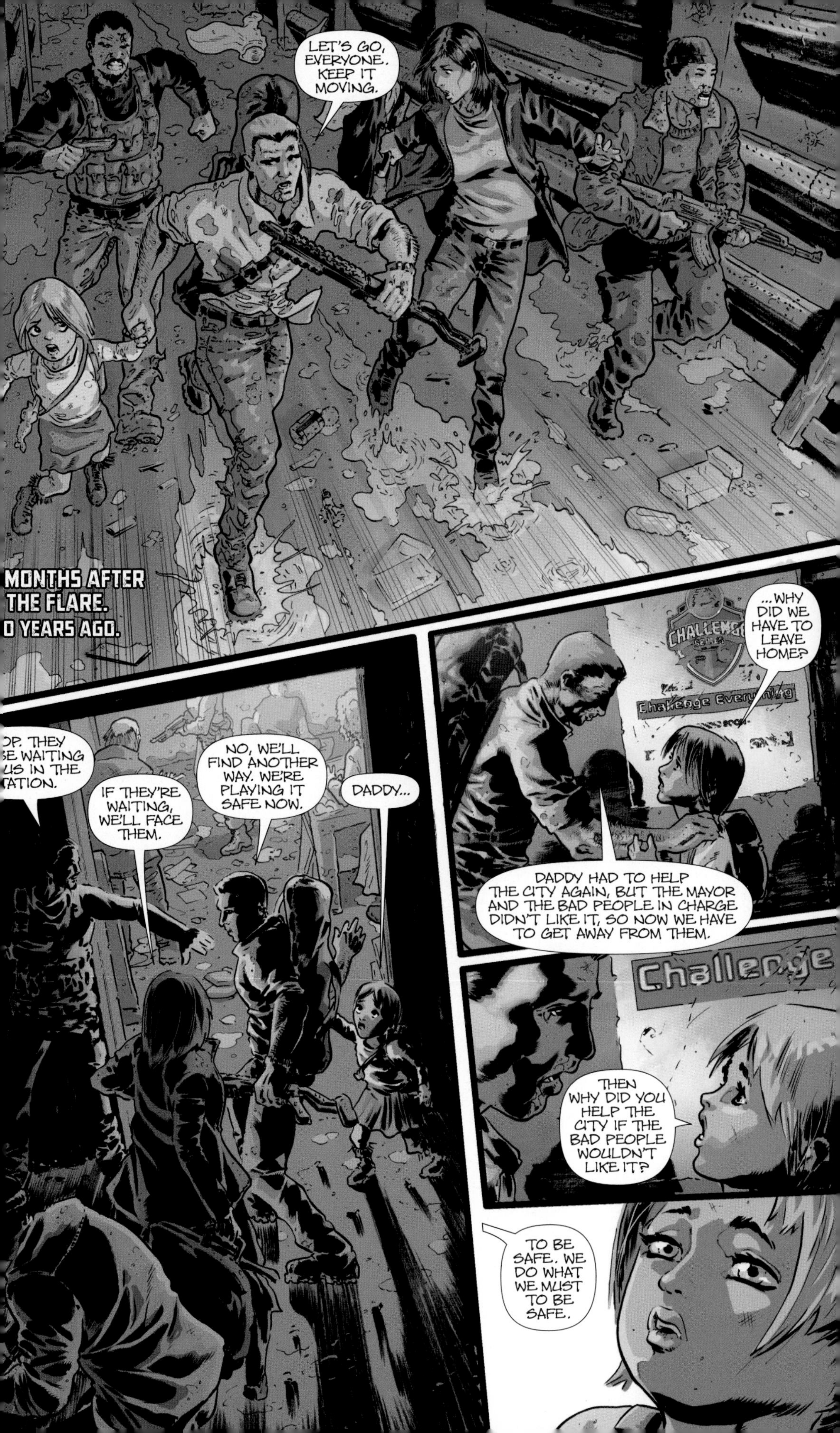
LET'S GO, EVERYONE. KEEP IT MOVING.
MONTHS AFTER THE FLARE.
O YEARS AGO.
OP. THEY E WAITING US IN THE TATION.
IF THEY'RE WAITING, WE'LL FACE THEM.
NO, WE'LL FIND ANOTHER WAY. WE'RE PLAYING IT SAFE NOW.
DADDY...
...WHY DID WE HAVE TO LEAVE HOME?
Challenge Everything
DADDY HAD TO HELP THE CITY AGAIN, BUT THE MAYOR AND THE BAD PEOPLE IN CHARGE DIDN'T LIKE IT, SO NOW WE HAVE TO GET AWAY FROM THEM.
Challenge
THEN WHY DID YOU HELP THE CITY IF THE BAD PEOPLE WOULDN'T LIKE IT?
TO BE SAFE. WE DO WHAT WE MUST TO BE SAFE.

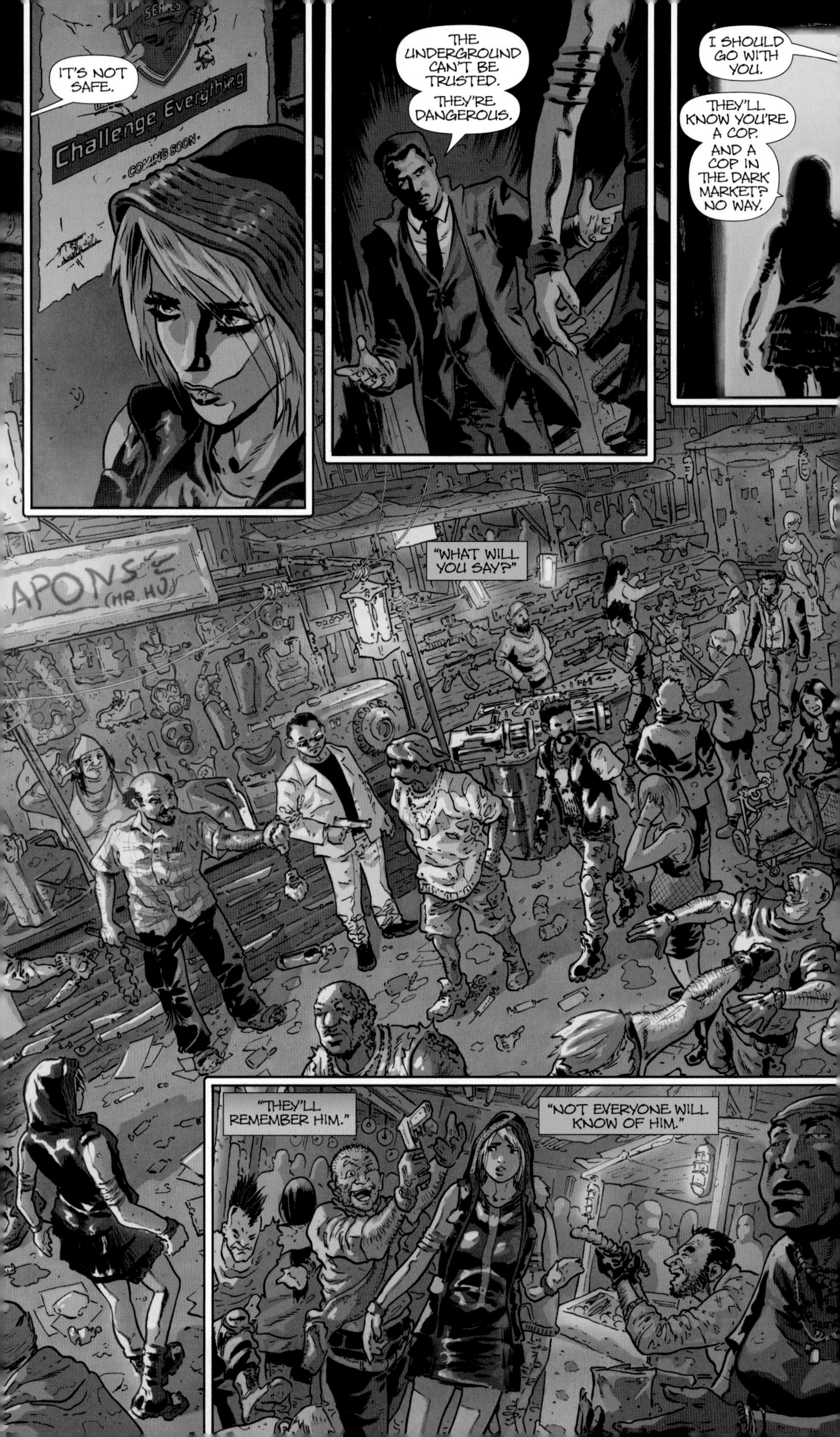
IT'S NOT SAFE.
Challenge Everything
COMING SOON
THE UNDERGROUND CAN'T BE TRUSTED.
THEY'RE DANGEROUS.
I SHOULD GO WITH YOU.
THEY'LL KNOW YOU'RE A COP.
AND A COP IN THE DARK MARKET? NO WAY.
"WHAT WILL YOU SAY?"
APONS (MR. H)
"THEY'LL REMEMBER HIM."
"NOT EVERYONE WILL KNOW OF HIM."

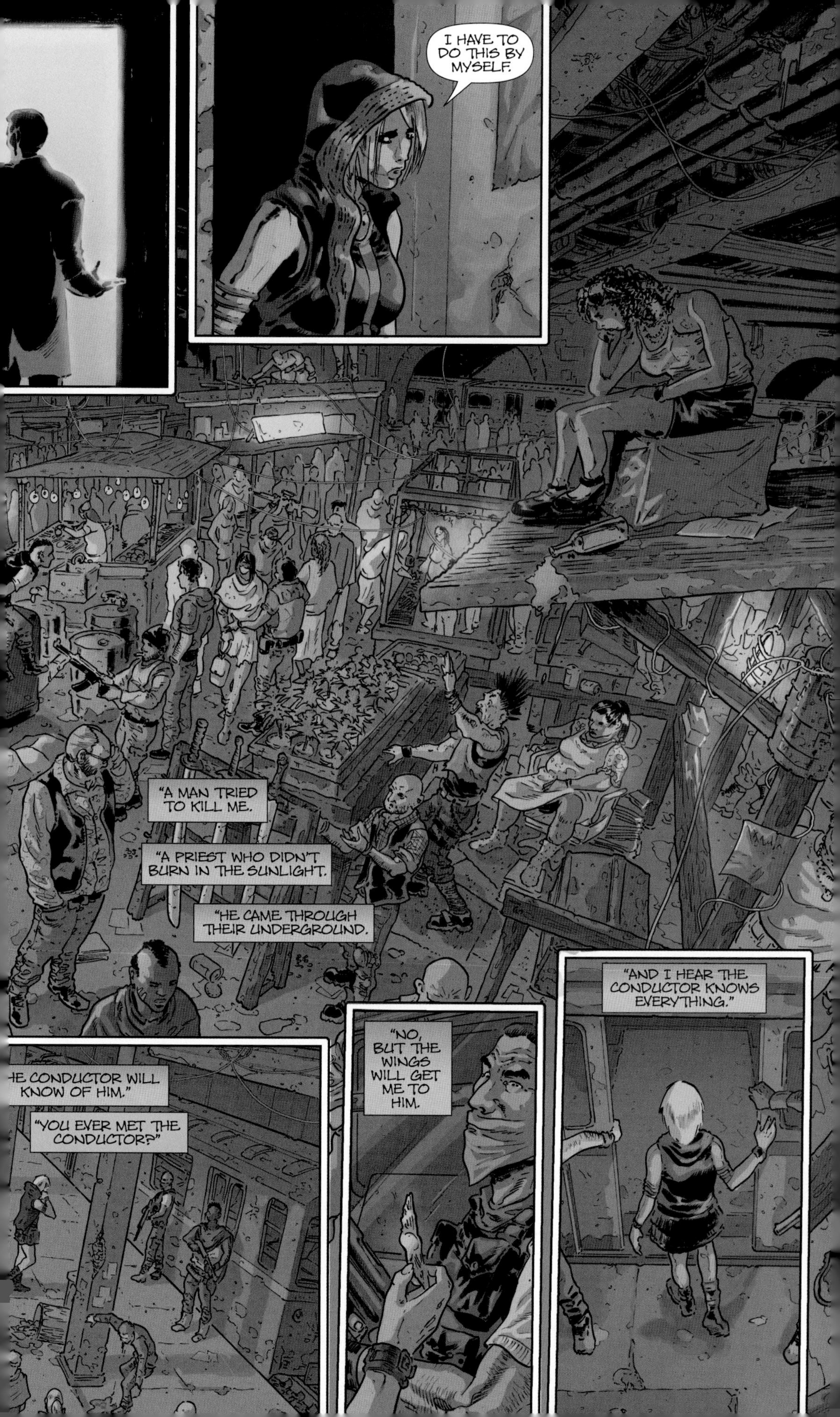
I HAVE TO DO THIS BY MYSELF.
"A MAN TRIED TO KILL ME.
"A PRIEST WHO DIDN'T BURN IN THE SUNLIGHT.
"HE CAME THROUGH THEIR UNDERGROUND.
"AND I HEAR THE CONDUCTOR KNOWS EVERYTHING."
HE CONDUCTOR WILL KNOW OF HIM."
"YOU EVER MET THE CONDUCTOR?"
"NO, BUT THE WINGS WILL GET ME TO HIM.

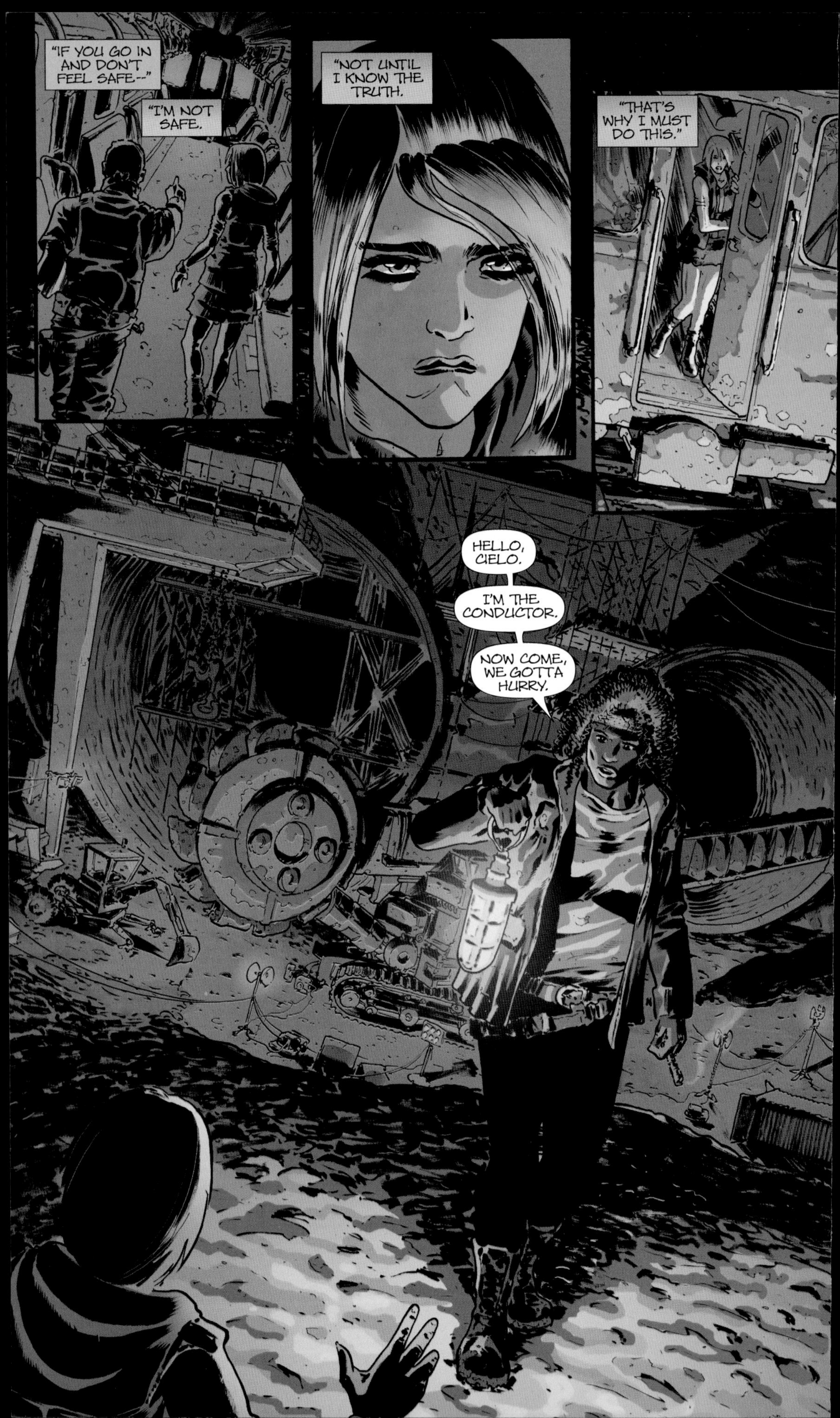
"IF YOU GO IN AND DON'T FEEL SAFE--"
"I'M NOT SAFE.
"NOT UNTIL I KNOW THE TRUTH.
"THAT'S WHY I MUST DO THIS."
HELLO, CIELO.
I'M THE CONDUCTOR.
NOW COME, WE GOTTA HURRY.

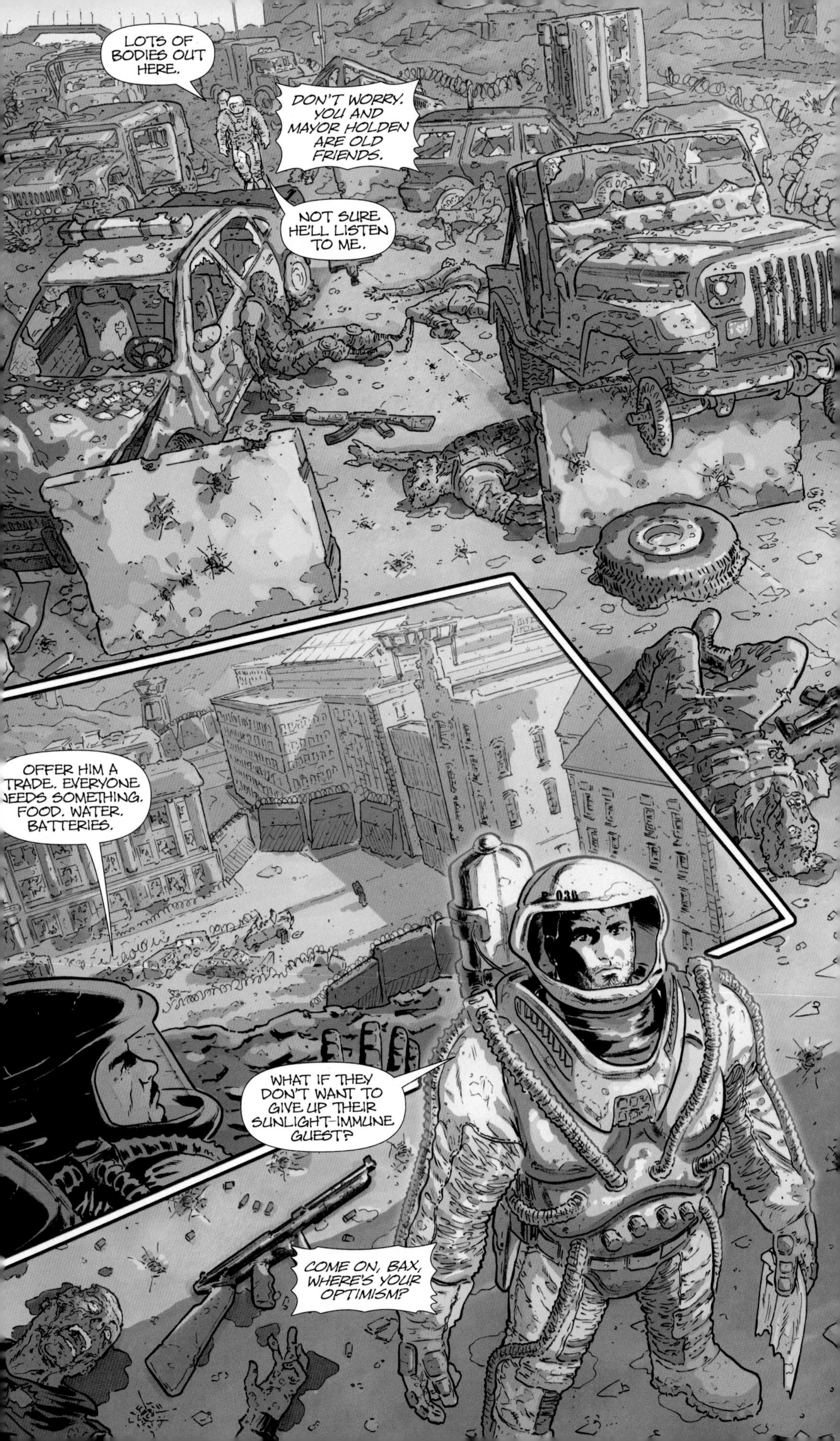
LOTS OF BODIES OUT HERE.
DON'T WORRY. YOU AND MAYOR HOLDEN ARE OLD FRIENDS.
NOT SURE HE'LL LISTEN TO ME.
OFFER HIM A TRADE. EVERYONE NEEDS SOMETHING. FOOD. WATER. BATTERIES.
WHAT IF THEY DON'T WANT TO GIVE UP THEIR SUNLIGHT-IMMUNE GUEST?
COME ON, BAX, WHERE'S YOUR OPTIMISM?

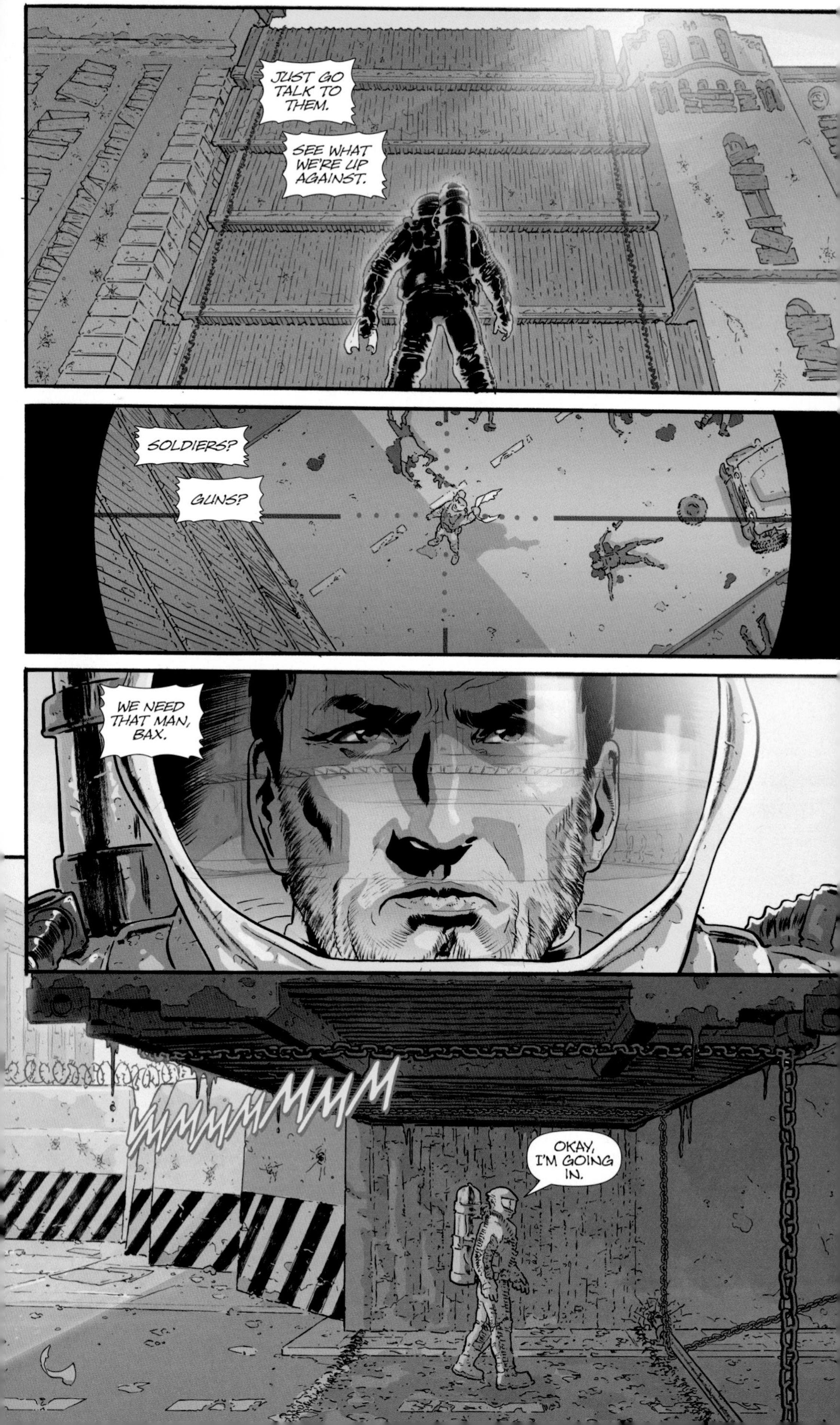
JUST GO TALK TO THEM.
SEE WHAT WE'RE UP AGAINST.
SOLDIERS?
GUNS?
WE NEED THAT MAN, BAX.
VMMMMMMM
OKAY, I'M GOING IN.

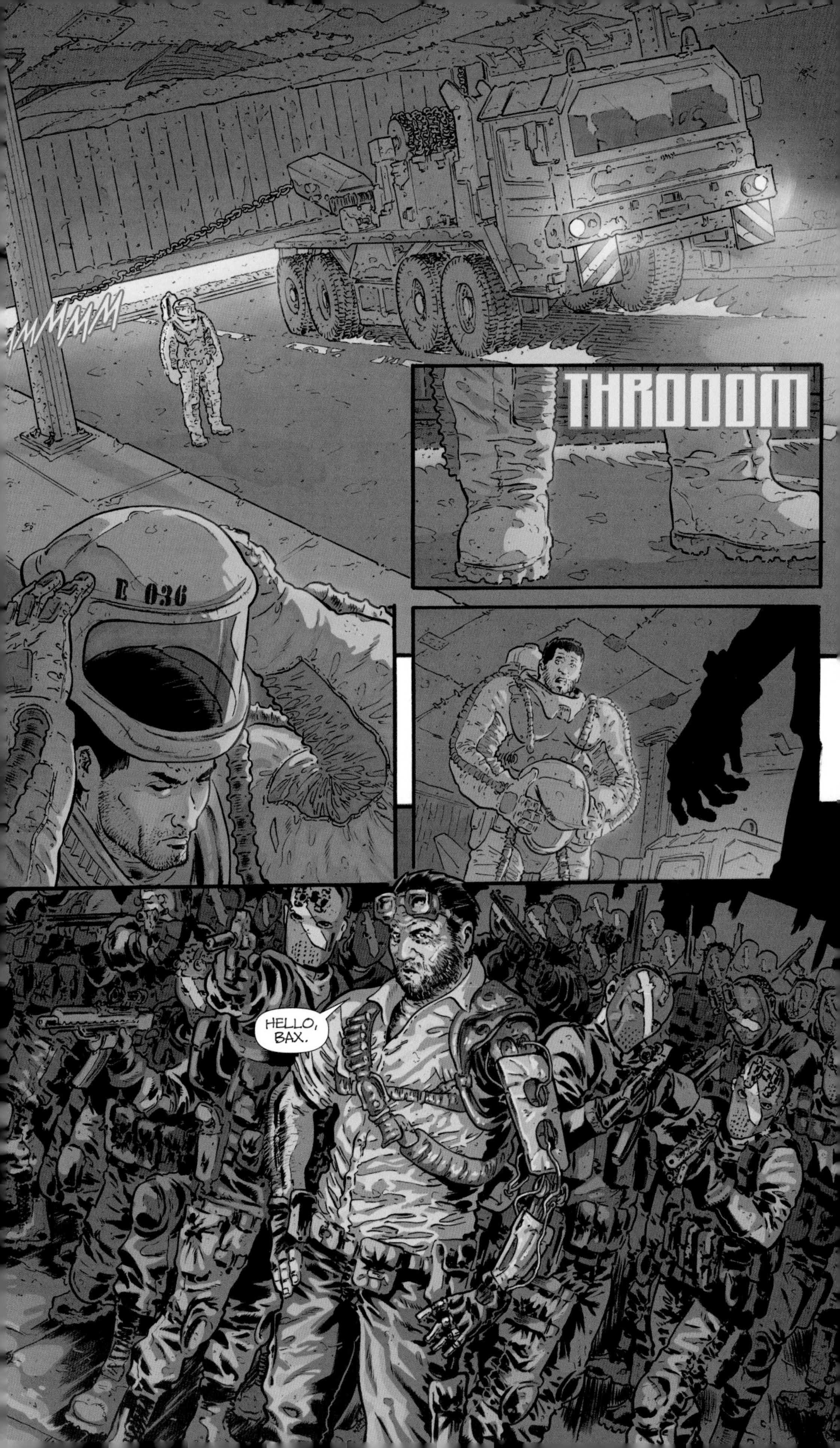
MMMMM
THROOOM
E 036
HELLO, BAX.

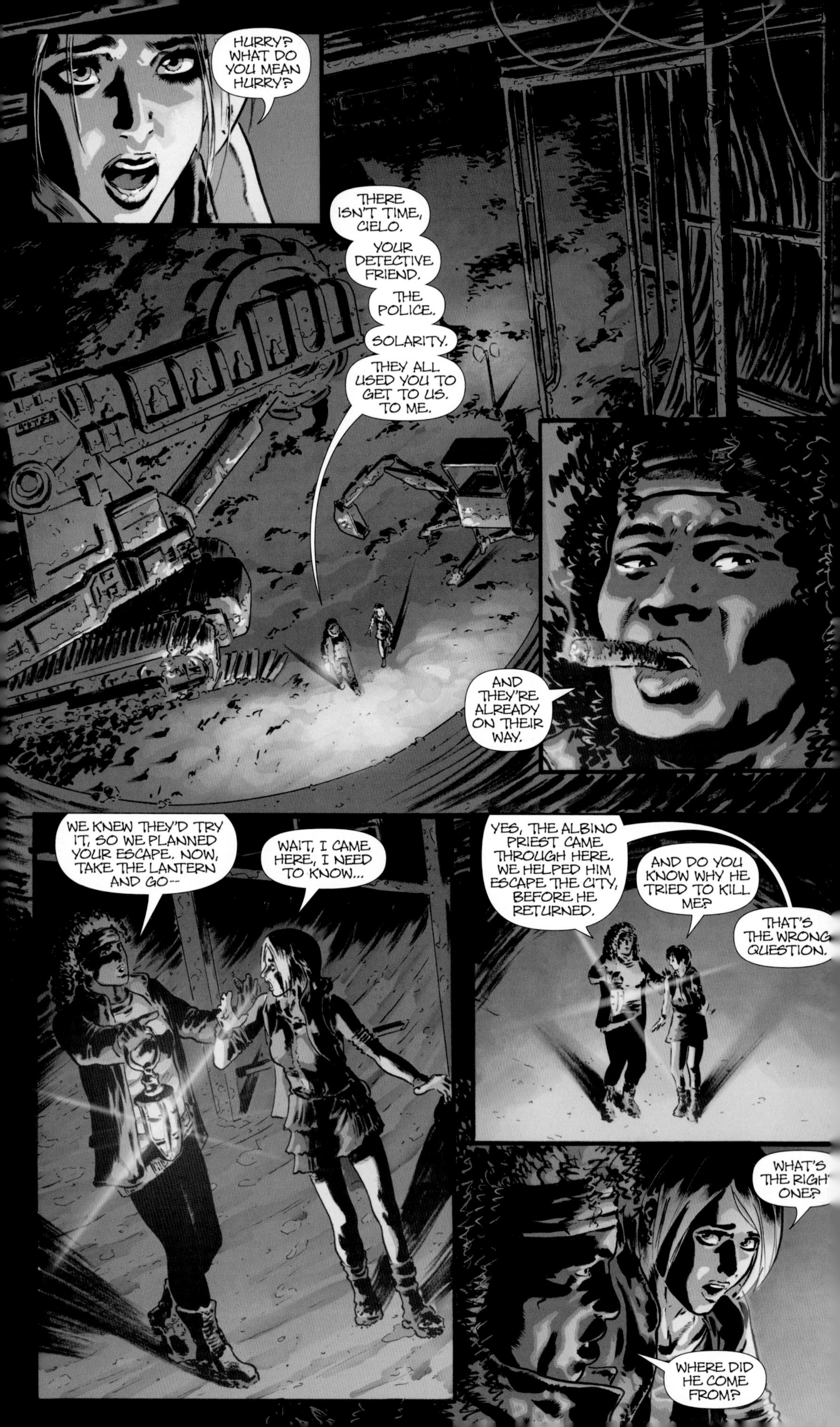
HURRY? WHAT DO YOU MEAN HURRY?
THERE ISN'T TIME, CIELO.
YOUR DETECTIVE FRIEND.
THE POLICE.
SOLARITY.
THEY ALL USED YOU TO GET TO US. TO ME.
AND THEY'RE ALREADY ON THEIR WAY.
WE KNEW THEY'D TRY IT, SO WE PLANNED YOUR ESCAPE. NOW, TAKE THE LANTERN AND GO--
WAIT, I CAME HERE, I NEED TO KNOW...
YES, THE ALBINO PRIEST CAME THROUGH HERE. WE HELPED HIM ESCAPE THE CITY, BEFORE HE RETURNED.
AND DO YOU KNOW WHY HE TRIED TO KILL ME?
THAT'S THE WRONG QUESTION.
WHAT'S THE RIGH ONE?
WHERE DID HE COME FROM?

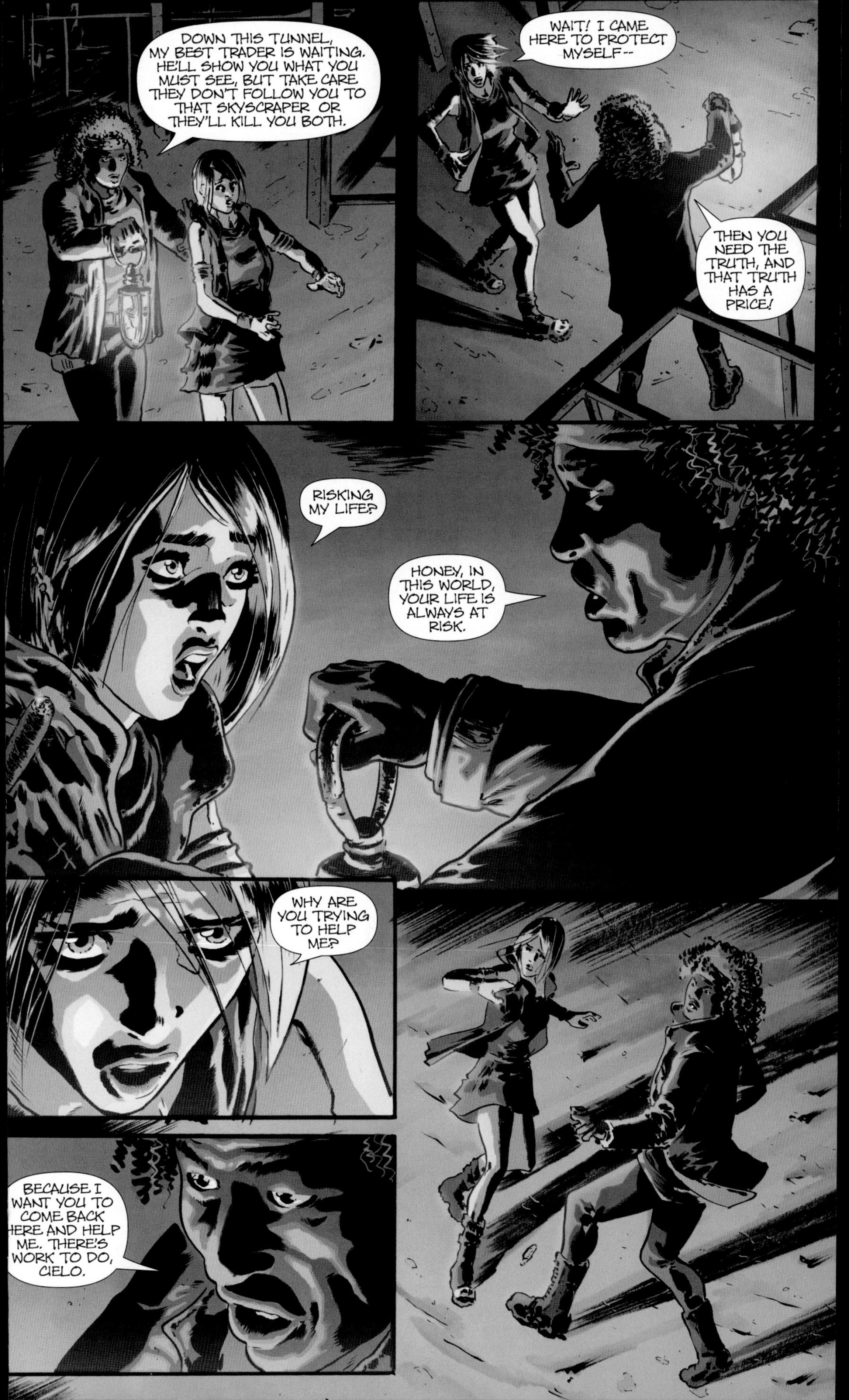
DOWN THIS TUNNEL, MY BEST TRADER IS WAITING. HE'LL SHOW YOU WHAT YOU MUST SEE, BUT TAKE CARE THEY DON'T FOLLOW YOU TO THAT SKYSCRAPER OR THEY'LL KILL YOU BOTH.
WAIT! I CAME HERE TO PROTECT MYSELF--
THEN YOU NEED THE TRUTH, AND THAT TRUTH HAS A PRICE!
RISKING MY LIFE?
HONEY, IN THIS WORLD, YOUR LIFE IS ALWAYS AT RISK.
WHY ARE YOU TRYING TO HELP ME?
BECAUSE I WANT YOU TO COME BACK HERE AND HELP ME. THERE'S WORK TO DO, CIELO.

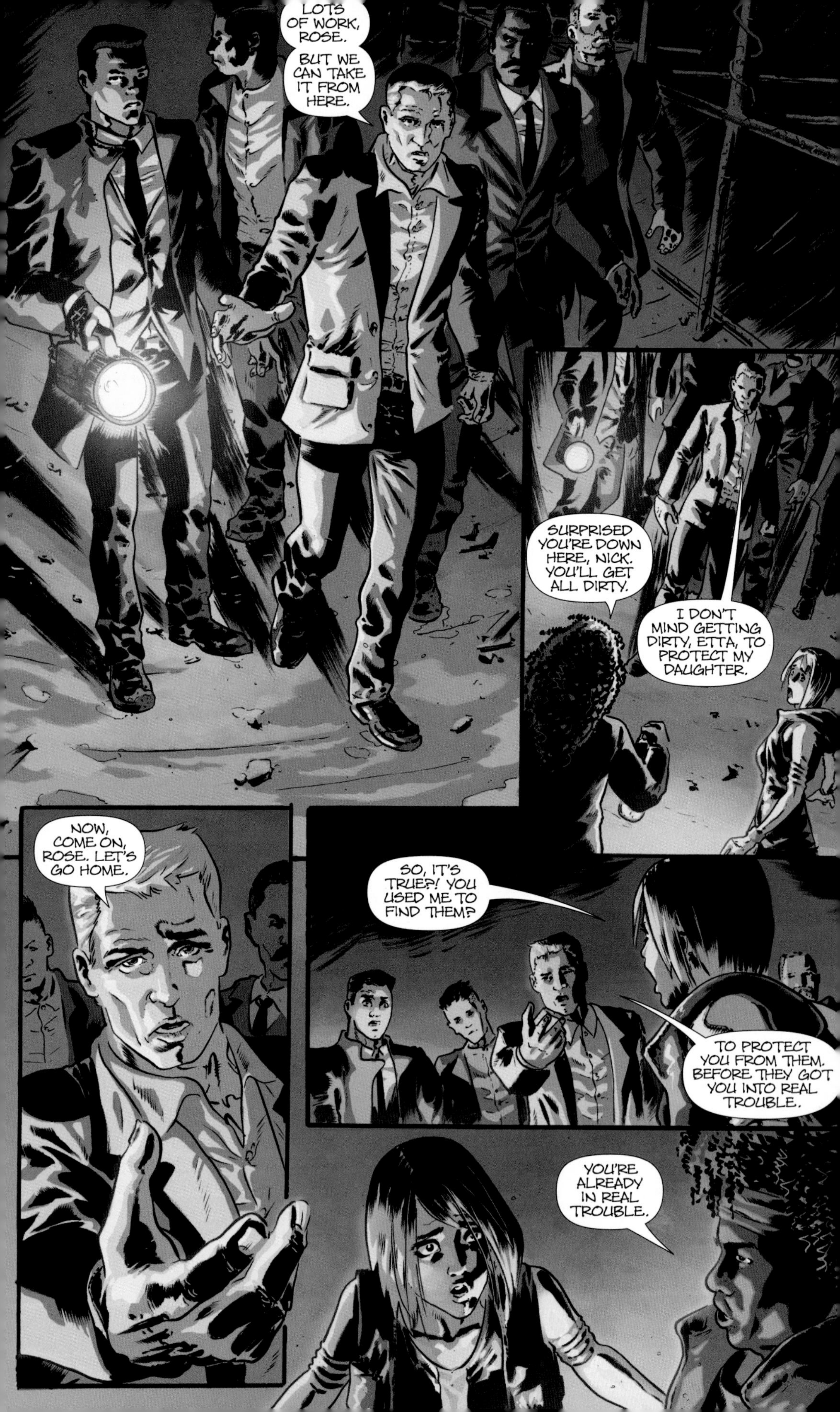
LOTS OF WORK, ROSE.
BUT WE CAN TAKE IT FROM HERE.
SURPRISED YOU'RE DOWN HERE, NICK. YOU'LL GET ALL DIRTY.
I DON'T MIND GETTING DIRTY, ETTA, TO PROTECT MY DAUGHTER.
NOW, COME ON, ROSE. LET'S GO HOME.
SO, IT'S TRUE?! YOU USED ME TO FIND THEM?
TO PROTECT YOU FROM THEM. BEFORE THEY GOT YOU INTO REAL TROUBLE.
YOU'RE ALREADY IN REAL TROUBLE.

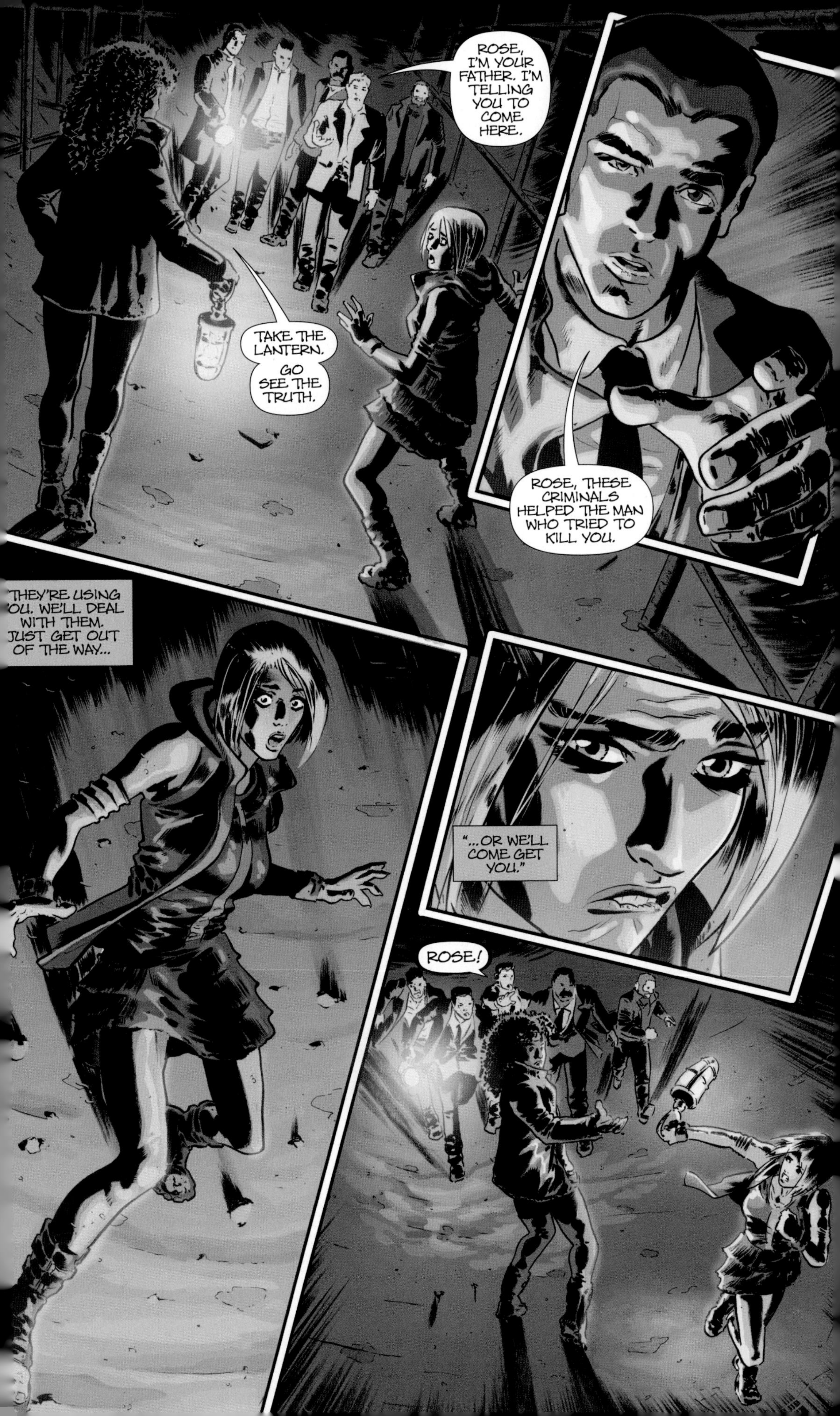
ROSE, I'M YOUR FATHER. I'M TELLING YOU TO COME HERE.
TAKE THE LANTERN. GO SEE THE TRUTH.
ROSE, THESE CRIMINALS HELPED THE MAN WHO TRIED TO KILL YOU.
THEY'RE USING YOU. WE'LL DEAL WITH THEM. JUST GET OUT OF THE WAY...
"...OR WE'LL COME GET YOU."
ROSE!

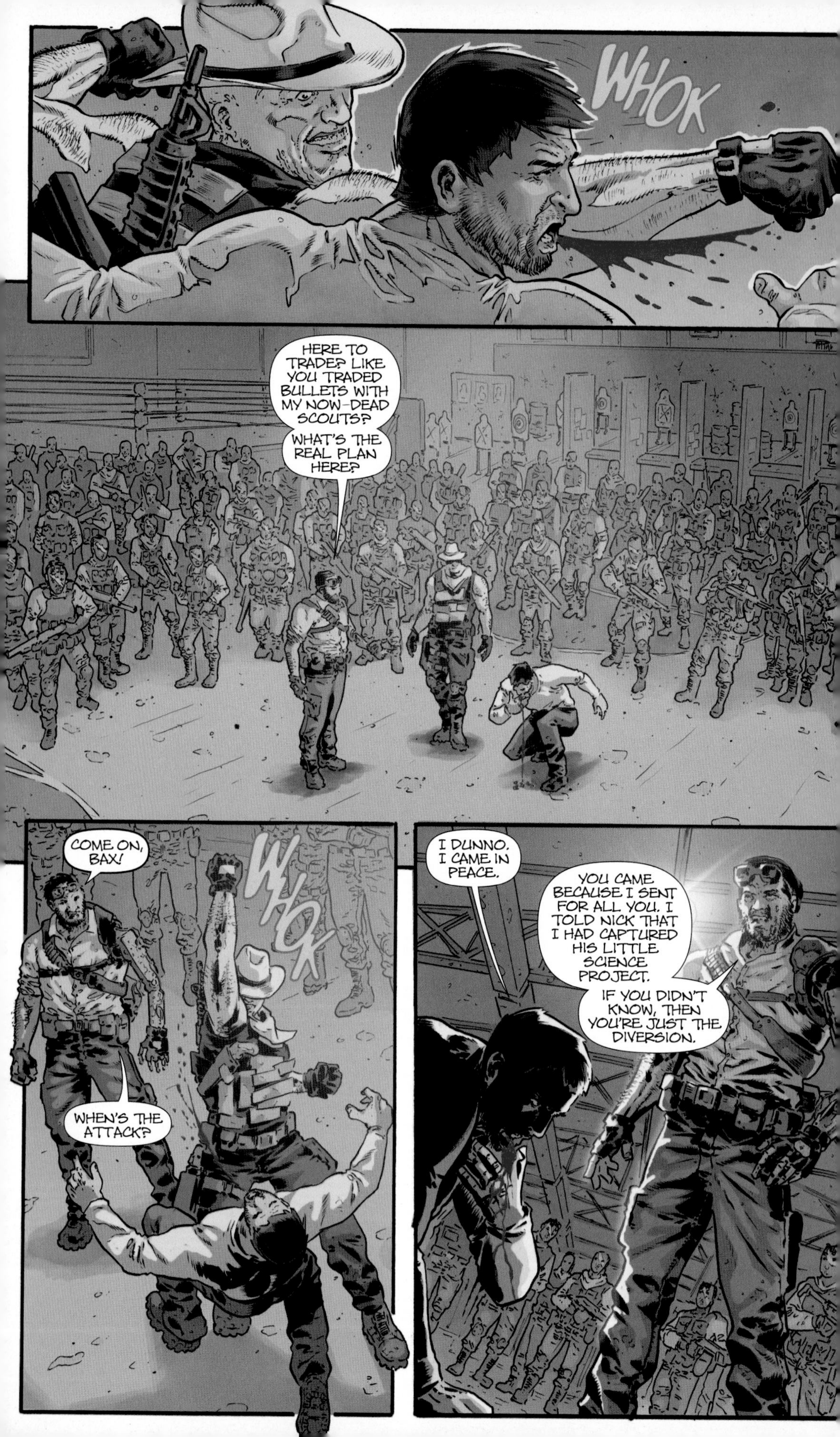
WHOK
HERE TO TRADE? LIKE YOU TRADED BULLETS WITH MY NOW-DEAD SCOUTS?
WHAT'S THE REAL PLAN HERE?
COME ON, BAX!
WHOK
WHEN'S THE ATTACK?
I DUNNO. I CAME IN PEACE.
YOU CAME BECAUSE I SENT FOR ALL YOU. I TOLD NICK THAT I HAD CAPTURED HIS LITTLE SCIENCE PROJECT.
IF YOU DIDN'T KNOW, THEN YOU'RE JUST THE DIVERSION.

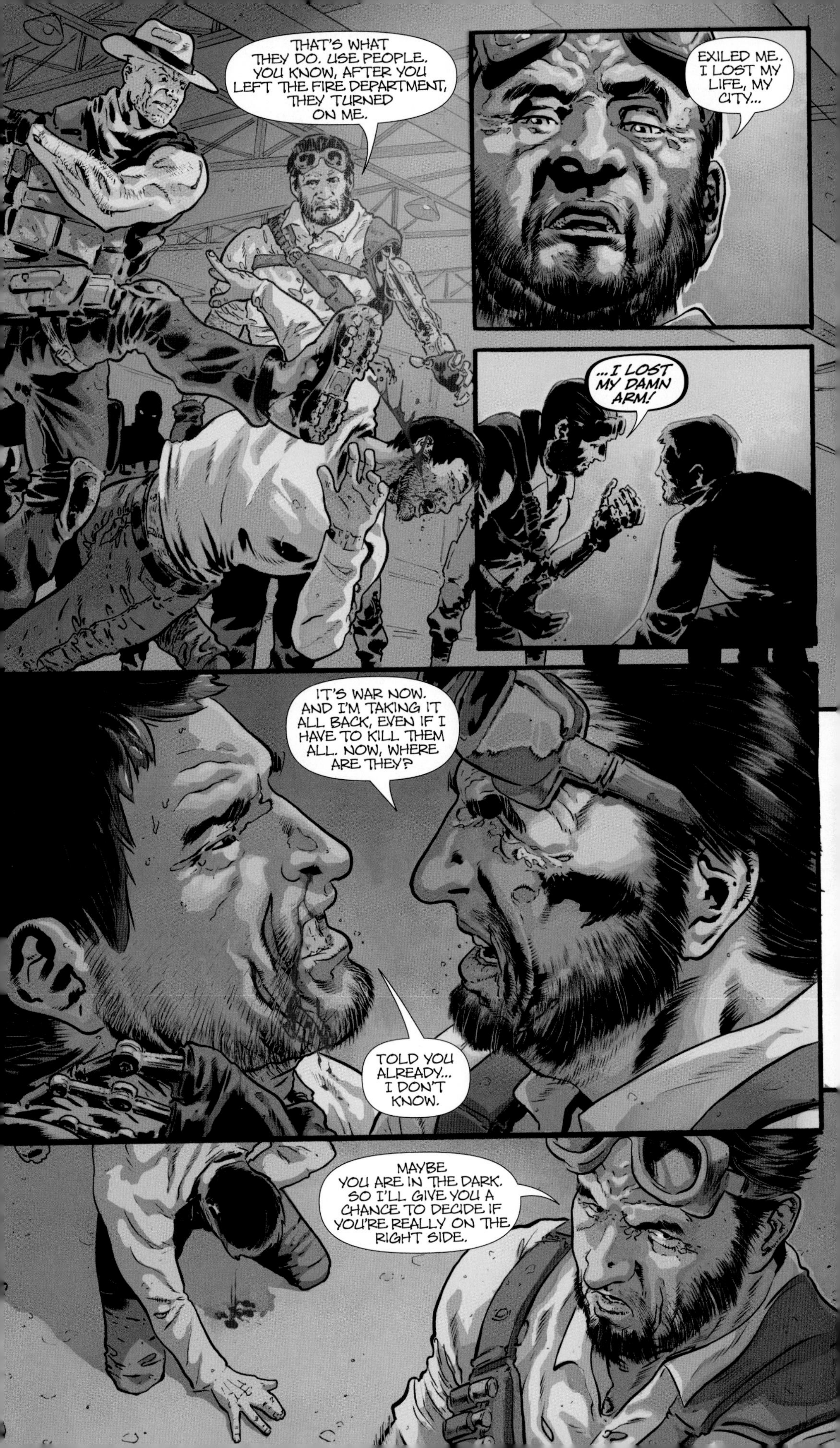
THAT'S WHAT THEY DO. USE PEOPLE. YOU KNOW, AFTER YOU LEFT THE FIRE DEPARTMENT, THEY TURNED ON ME.
EXILED ME. I LOST MY LIFE, MY CITY...
...I LOST MY DAMN ARM!
IT'S WAR NOW. AND I'M TAKING IT ALL BACK, EVEN IF I HAVE TO KILL THEM ALL. NOW, WHERE ARE THEY?
TOLD YOU ALREADY... I DON'T KNOW.
MAYBE YOU ARE IN THE DARK. SO I'LL GIVE YOU A CHANCE TO DECIDE IF YOU'RE REALLY ON THE RIGHT SIDE.

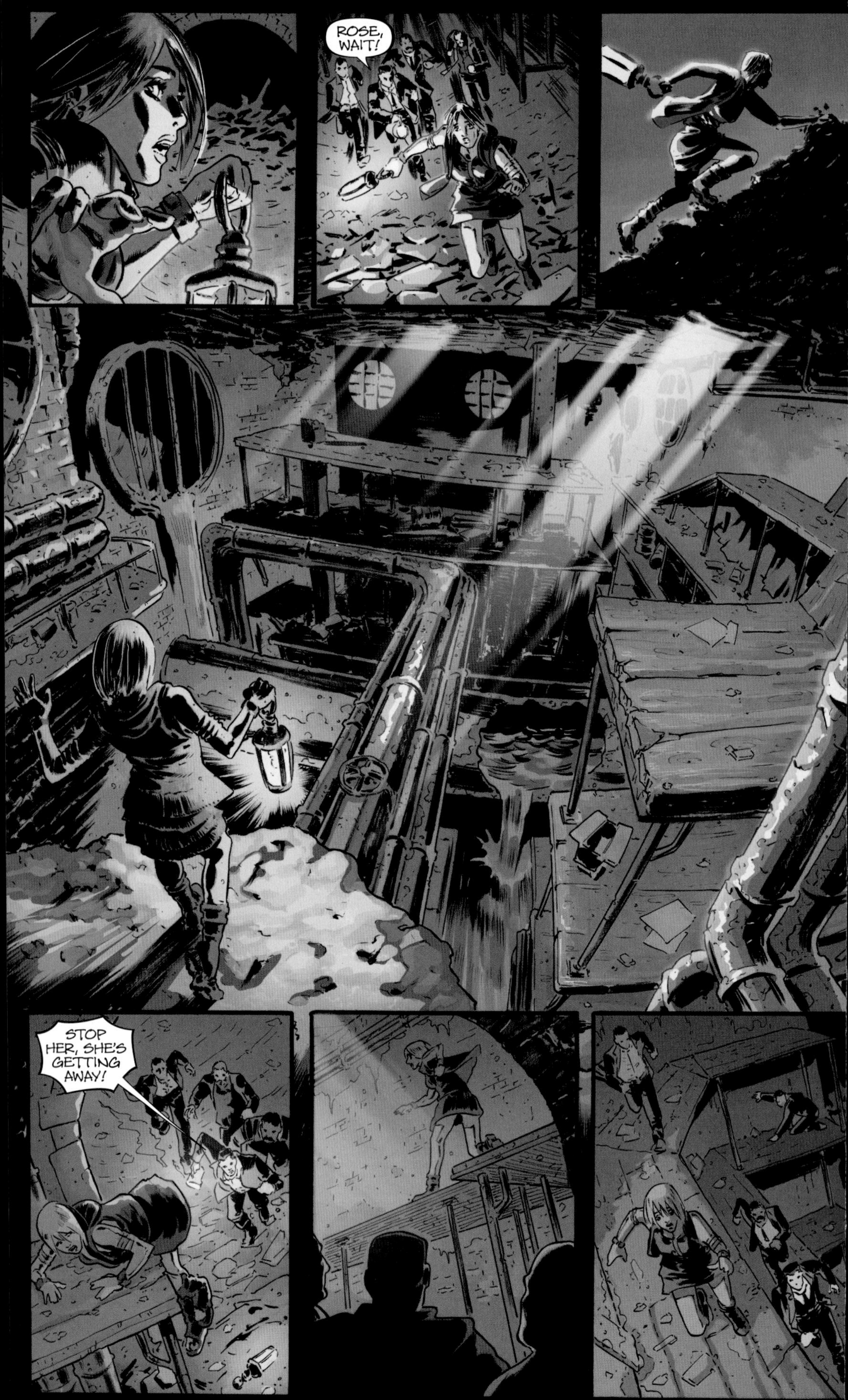
ROSE, WAIT!
STOP HER, SHE'S GETTING AWAY!

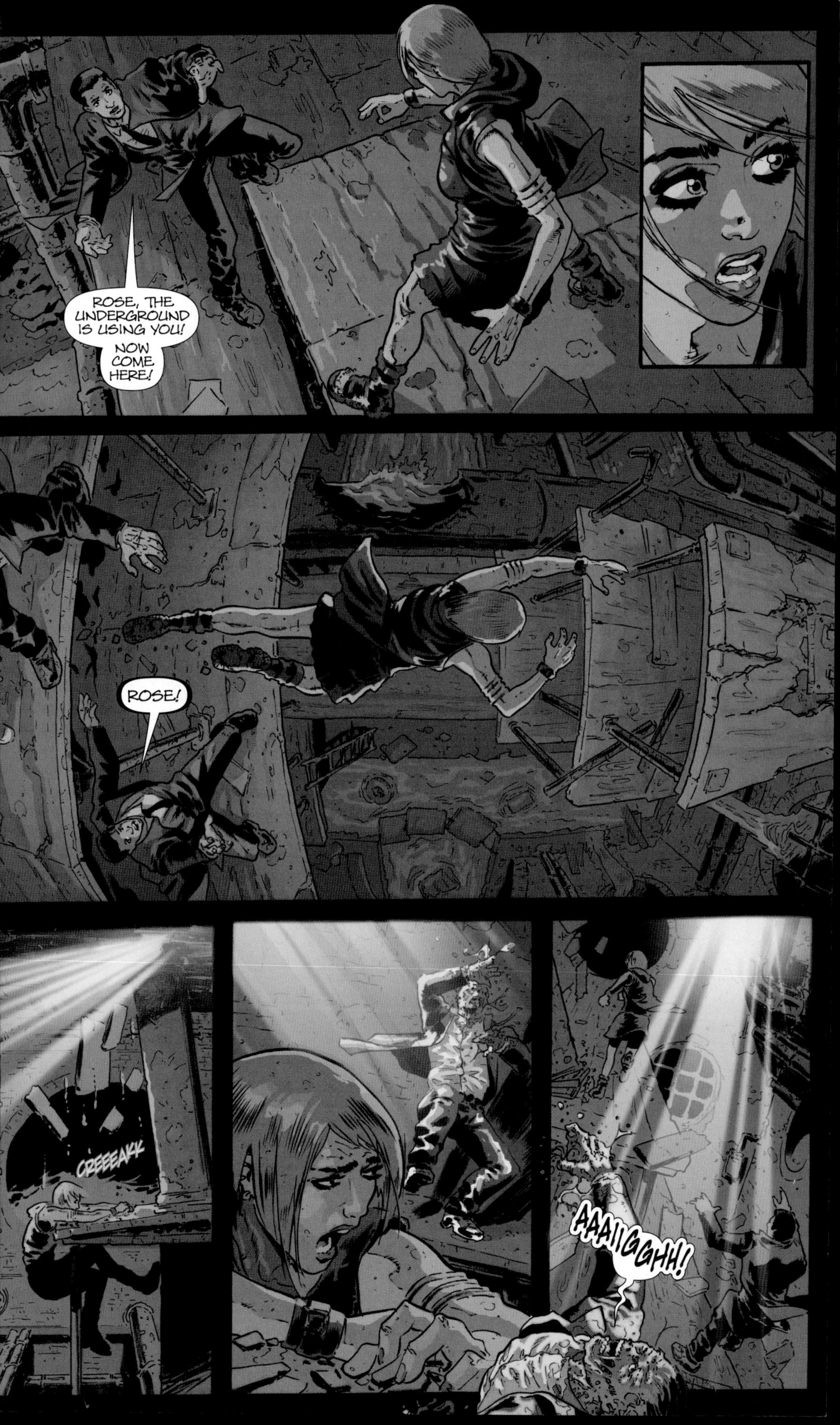
ROSE, THE UNDERGROUND IS USING YOU!
NOW COME HERE!
ROSE!
CREEEAKK
AAAIIGGHH!

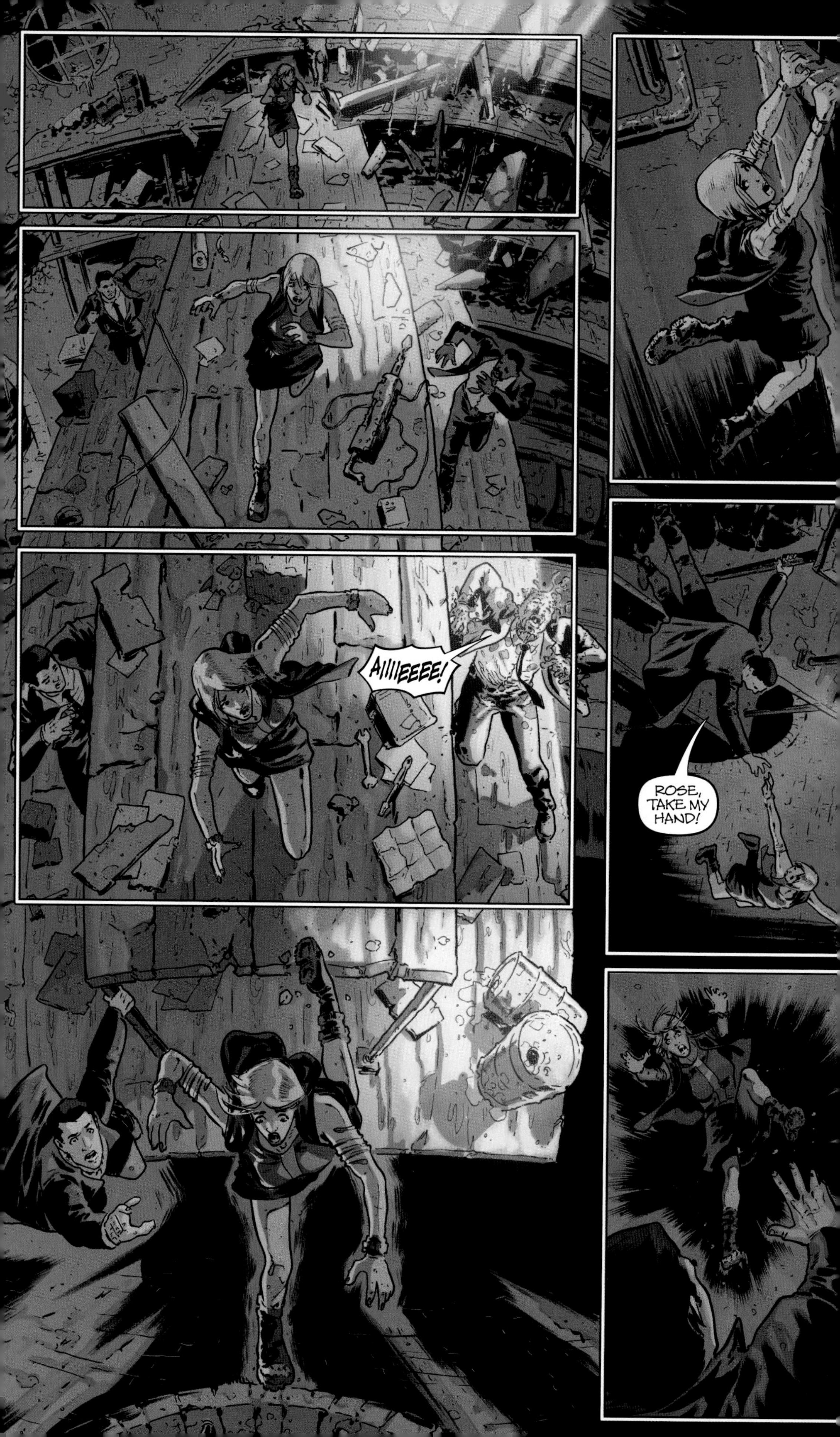
AIIIIEEEE!
ROSE, TAKE MY HAND!

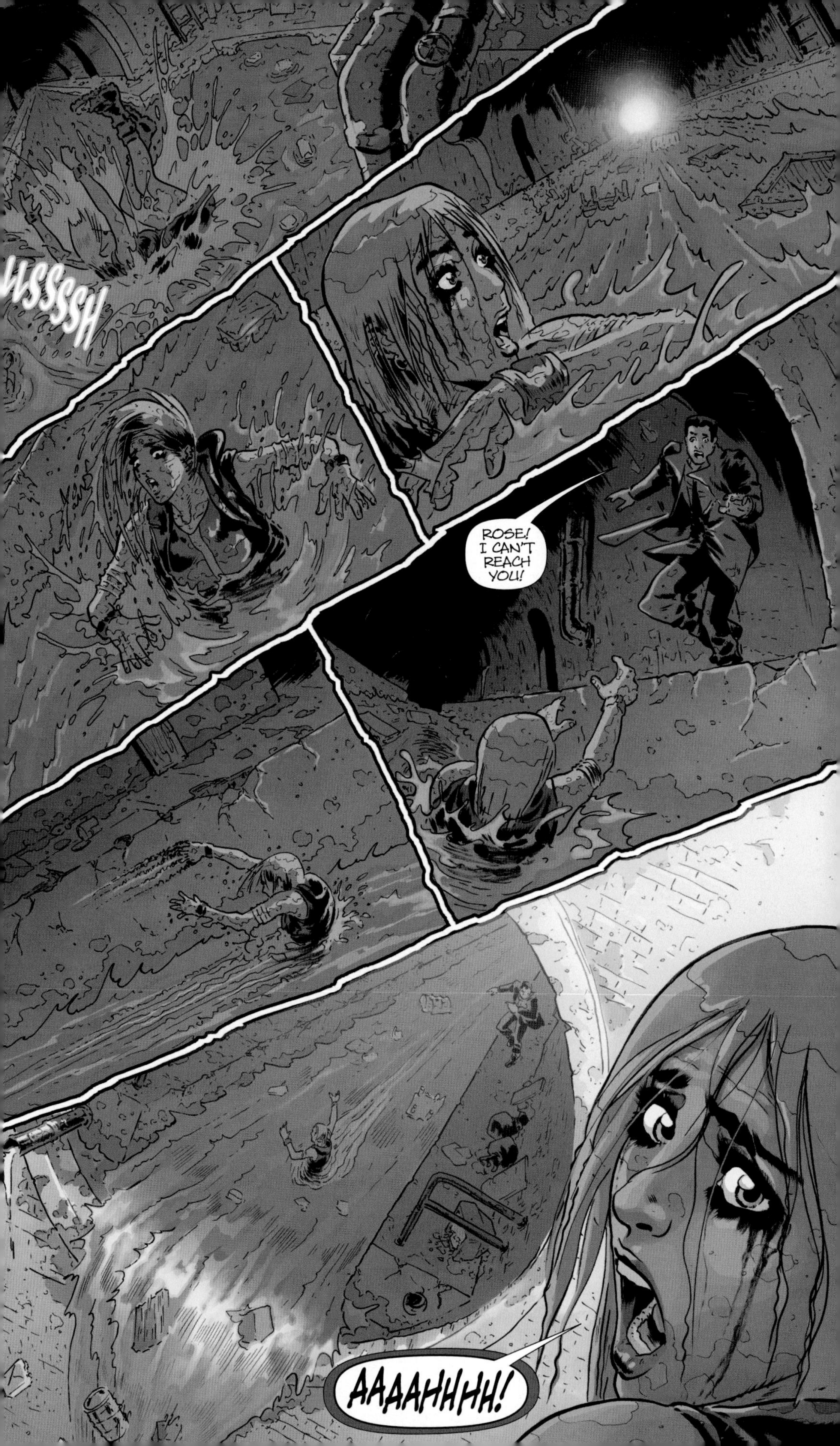
HSSSSH
ROSE! I CAN'T REACH YOU!
AAAAHHHH!

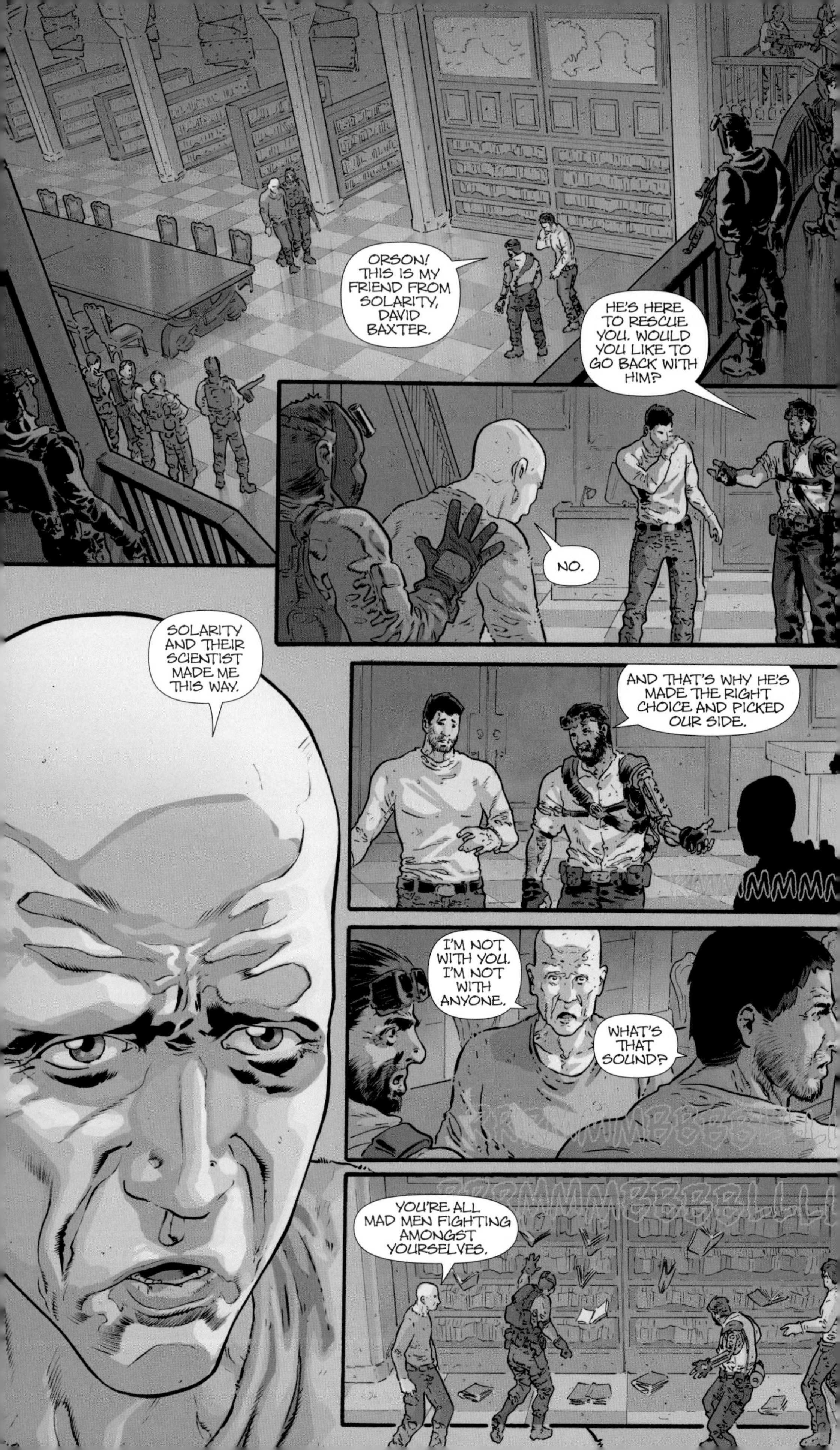
ORSON! THIS IS MY FRIEND FROM SOLARITY, DAVID BAXTER.
HE'S HERE TO RESCUE YOU. WOULD YOU LIKE TO GO BACK WITH HIM?
NO.
SOLARITY AND THEIR SCIENTIST MADE ME THIS WAY.
AND THAT'S WHY HE'S MADE THE RIGHT CHOICE AND PICKED OUR SIDE.
I'M NOT WITH YOU. I'M NOT WITH ANYONE.
WHAT'S THAT SOUND?
YOU'RE ALL MAD MEN FIGHTING AMONGST YOURSELVES.

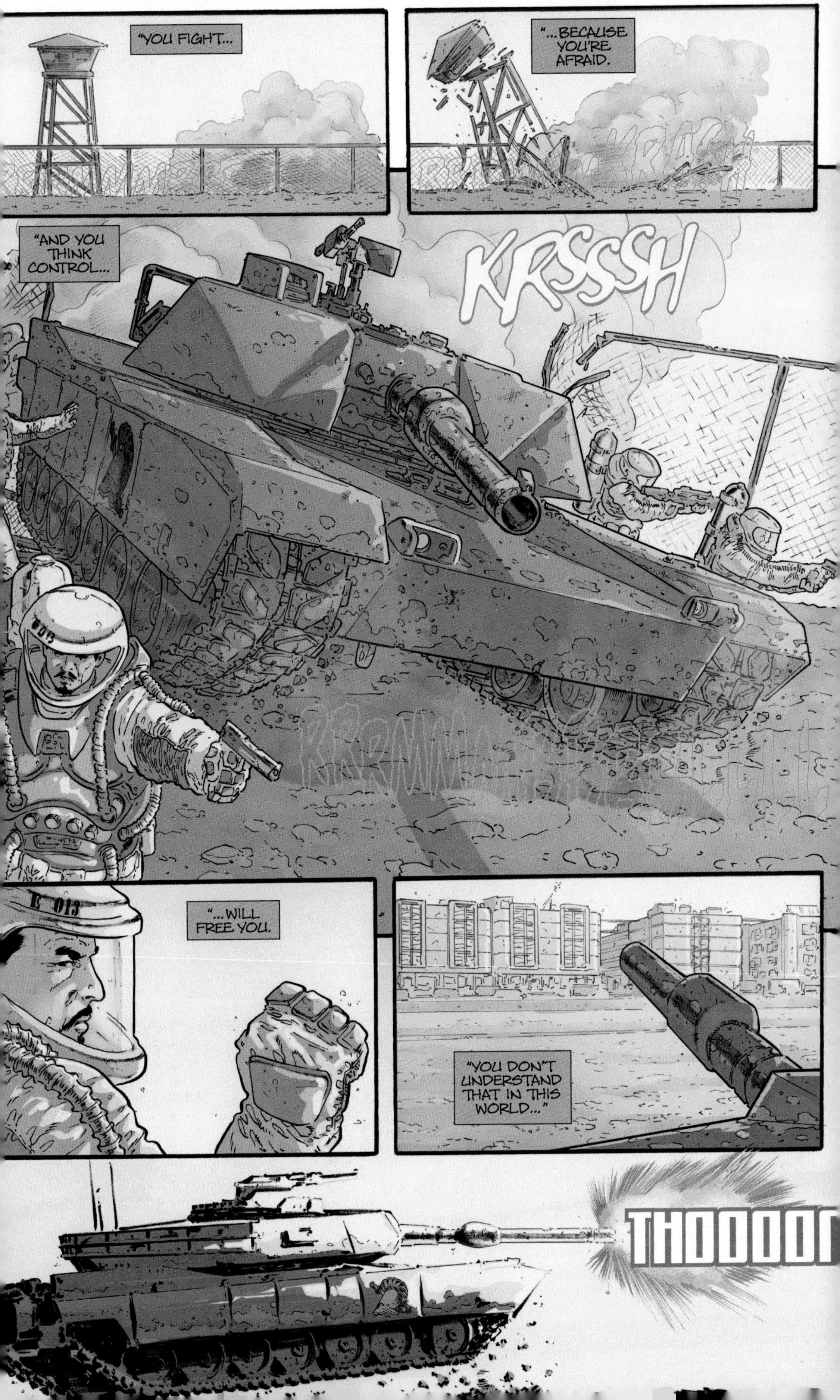
"YOU FIGHT...
"...BECAUSE YOU'RE AFRAID.
"AND YOU THINK CONTROL...
KRSSSH
"...WILL FREE YOU.
"YOU DON'T UNDERSTAND THAT IN THIS WORLD..."
THOOOOM

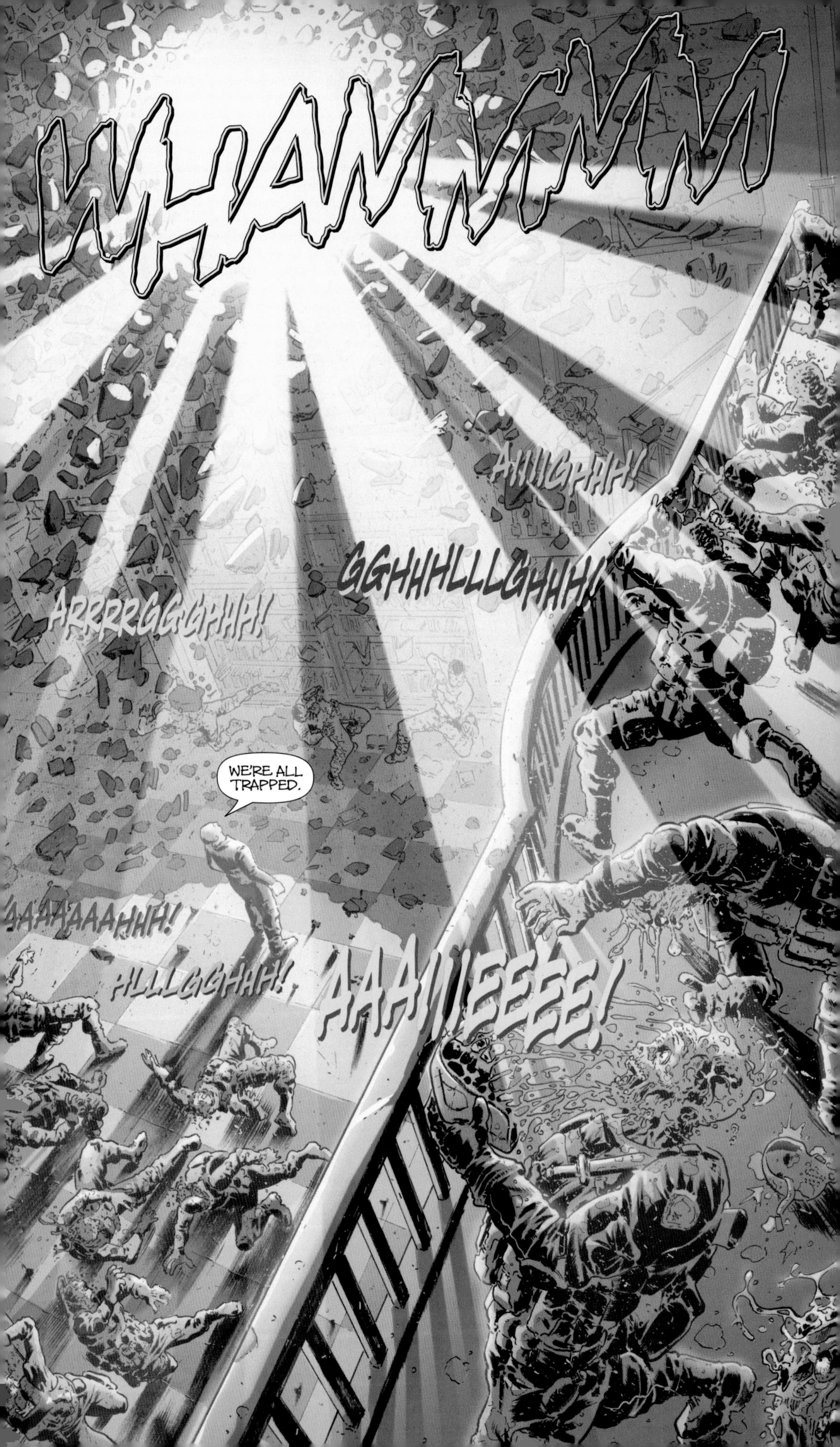
WHAMMMM
AIIIGHHH!
GGHHHLLLGHHH!
ARRRRGGGHHH!
WE'RE ALL TRAPPED.
AAAAAAAHHH!
HLLLGGHHH!
AAAIIEEEE!

CHAPTER SEVEN

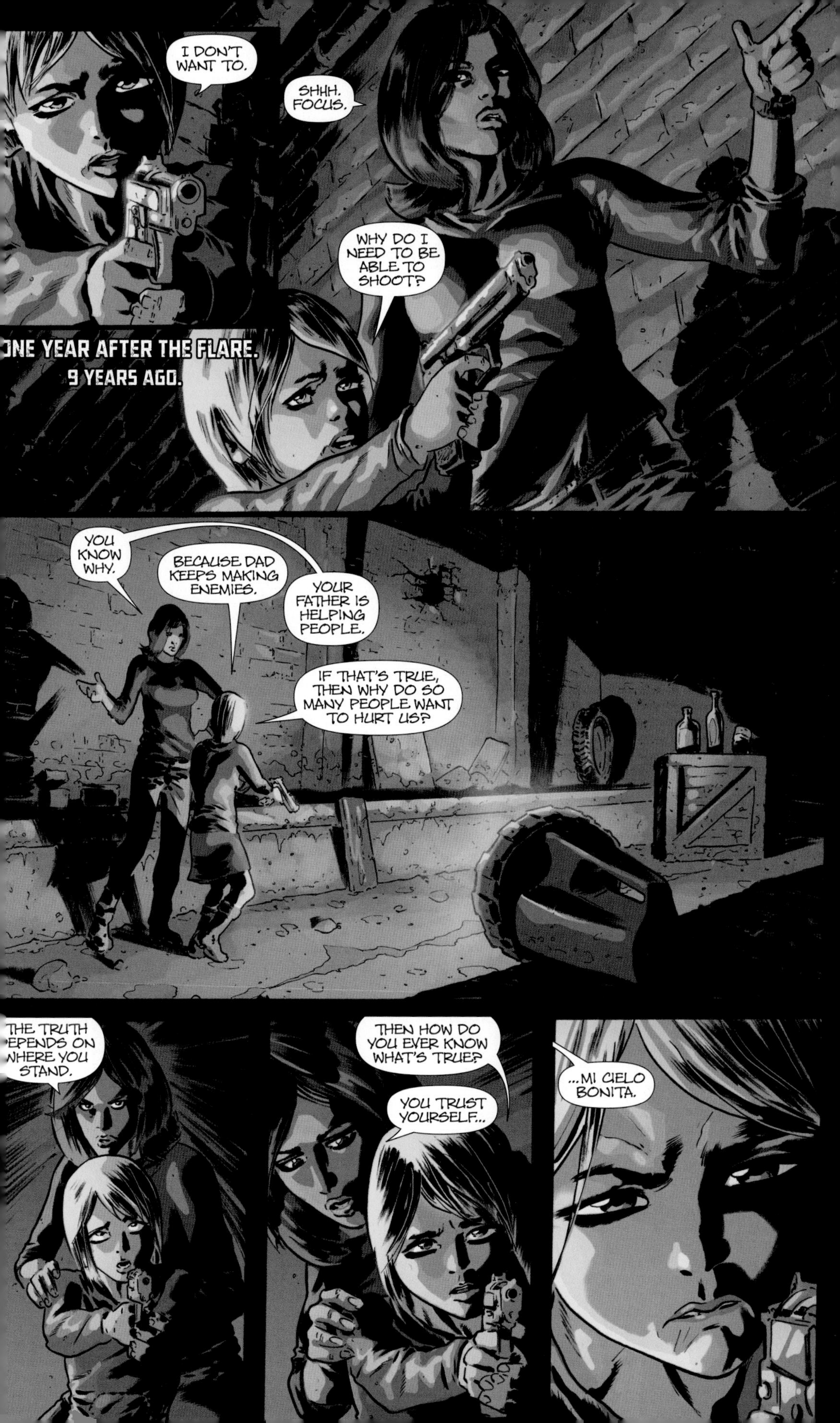
I DON'T WANT TO.
SHHH. FOCUS.
WHY DO I NEED TO BE ABLE TO SHOOT?
ONE YEAR AFTER THE FLARE.
9 YEARS AGO.
YOU KNOW WHY.
BECAUSE DAD KEEPS MAKING ENEMIES.
YOUR FATHER IS HELPING PEOPLE.
IF THAT'S TRUE, THEN WHY DO SO MANY PEOPLE WANT TO HURT US?
THE TRUTH DEPENDS ON WHERE YOU STAND.
THEN HOW DO YOU EVER KNOW WHAT'S TRUE?
YOU TRUST YOURSELF...
...MI CIELO BONITA.

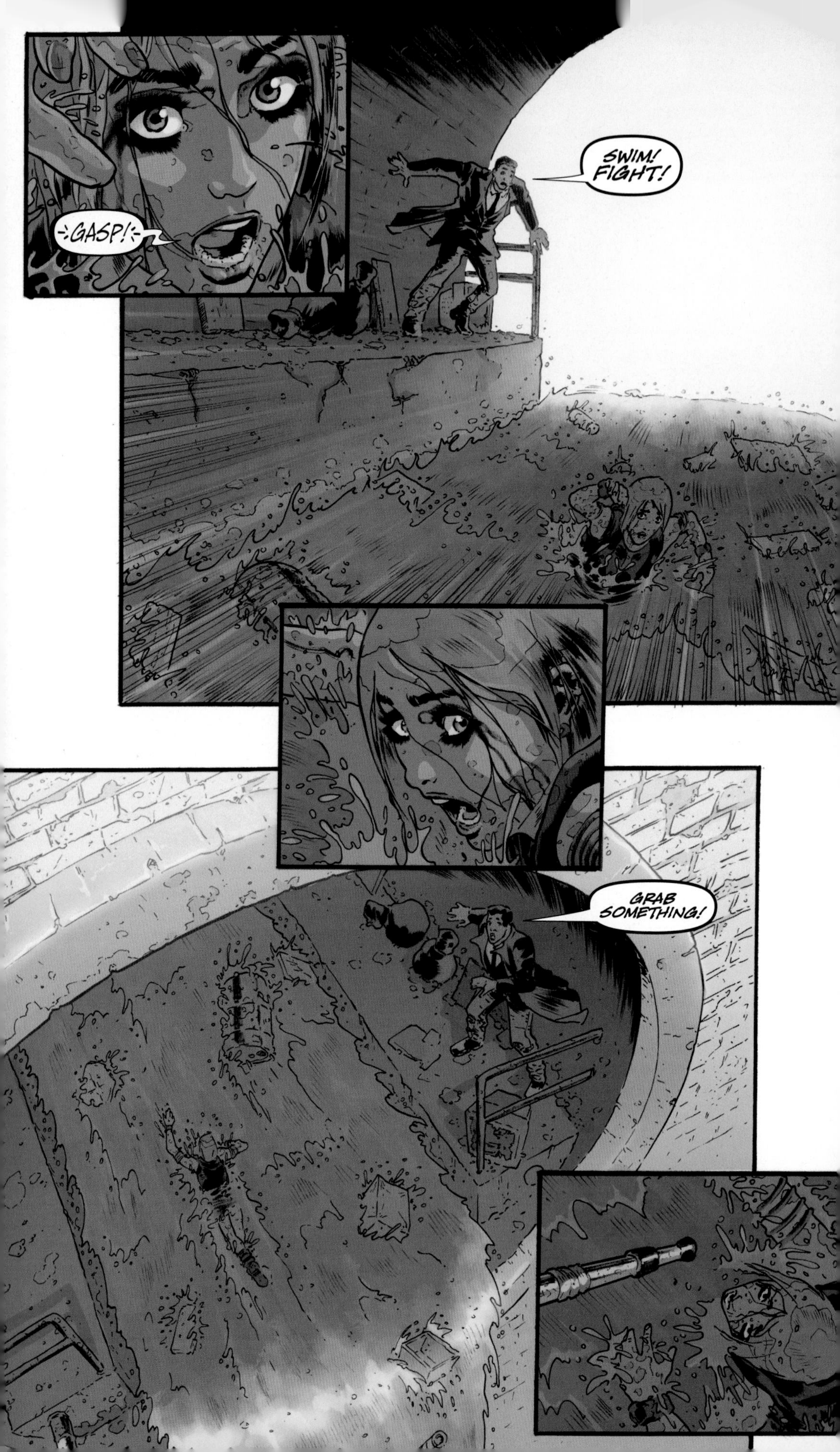
GASP!
SWIM! FIGHT!
GRAB SOMETHING!

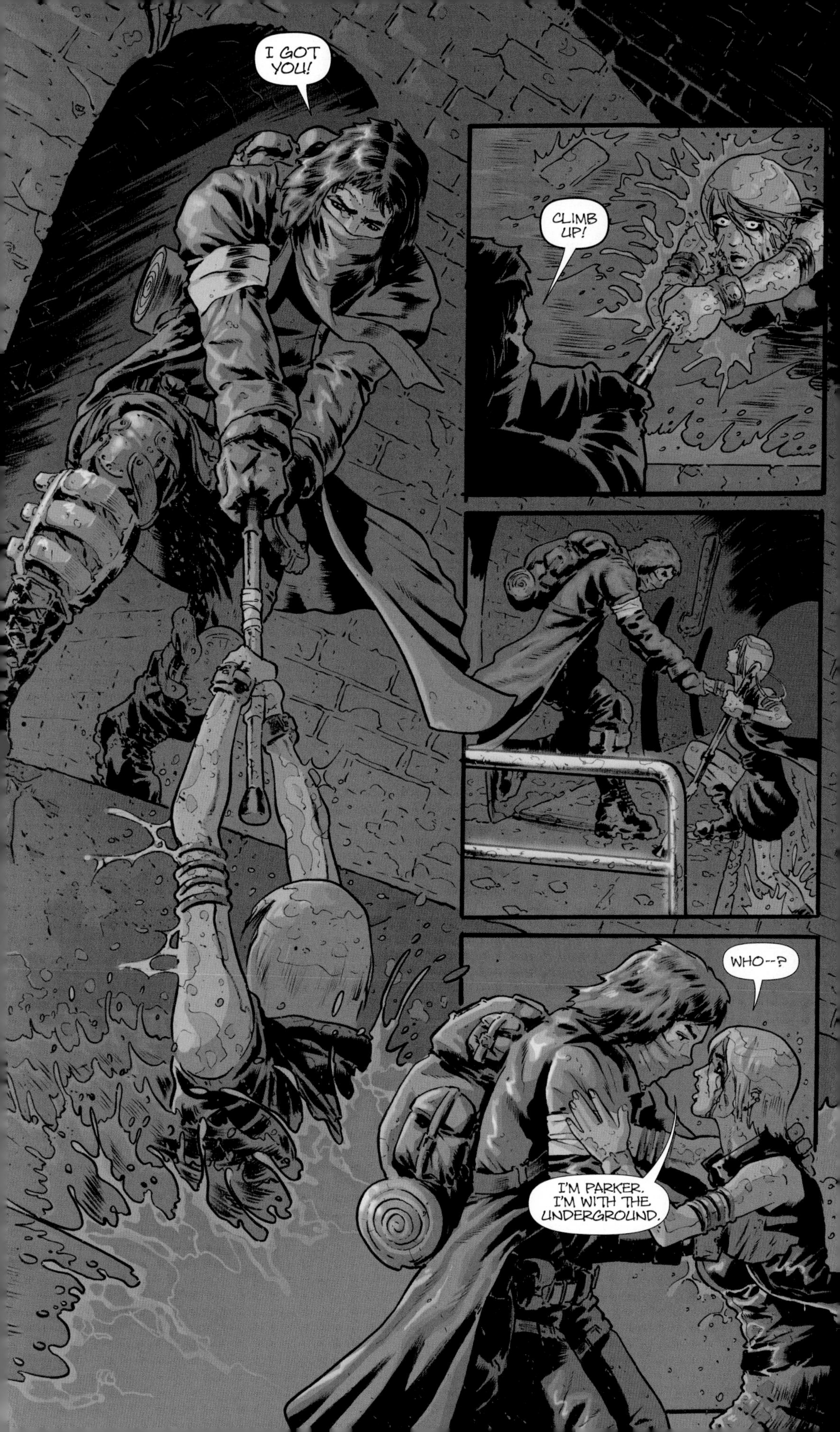
I GOT YOU!
CLIMB UP!
WHO--?
I'M PARKER. I'M WITH THE UNDERGROUND.

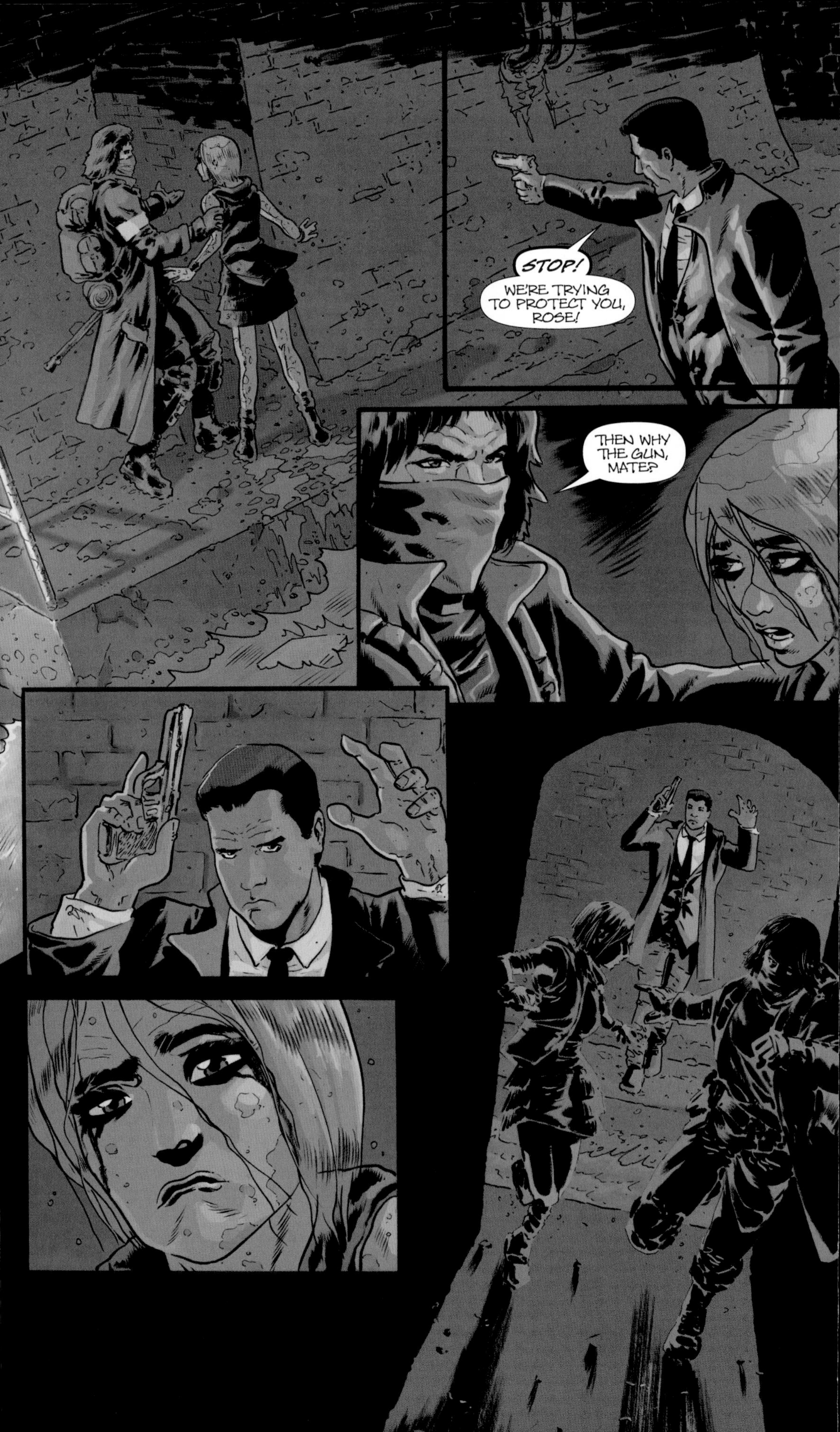
STOP!
WE'RE TRYING TO PROTECT YOU, ROSE!
THEN WHY THE GUN, MATE?

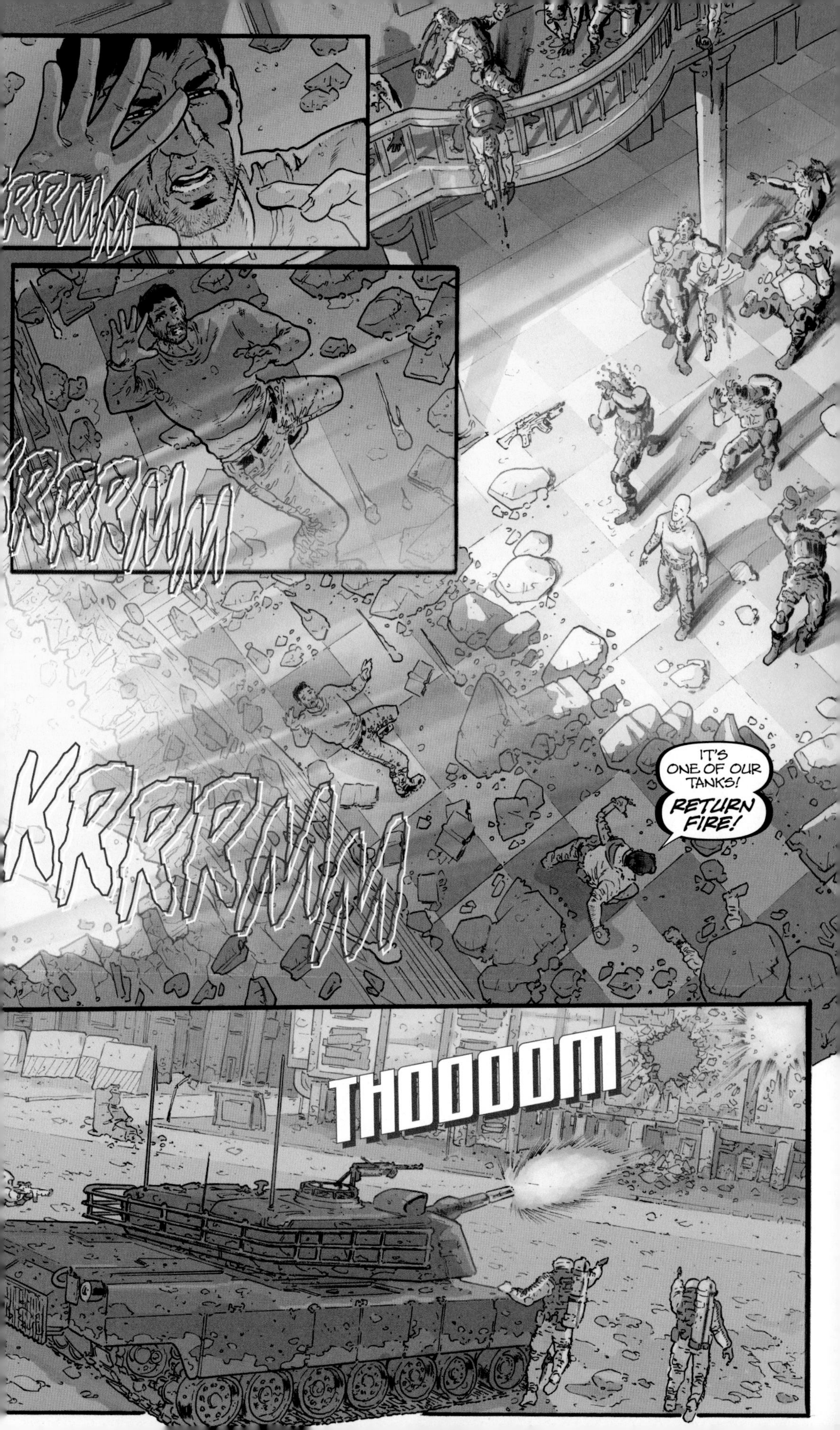
KRRMM
KRRRMM
KRRRMM
IT'S ONE OF OUR TANKS!
RETURN FIRE!
THOOOOM

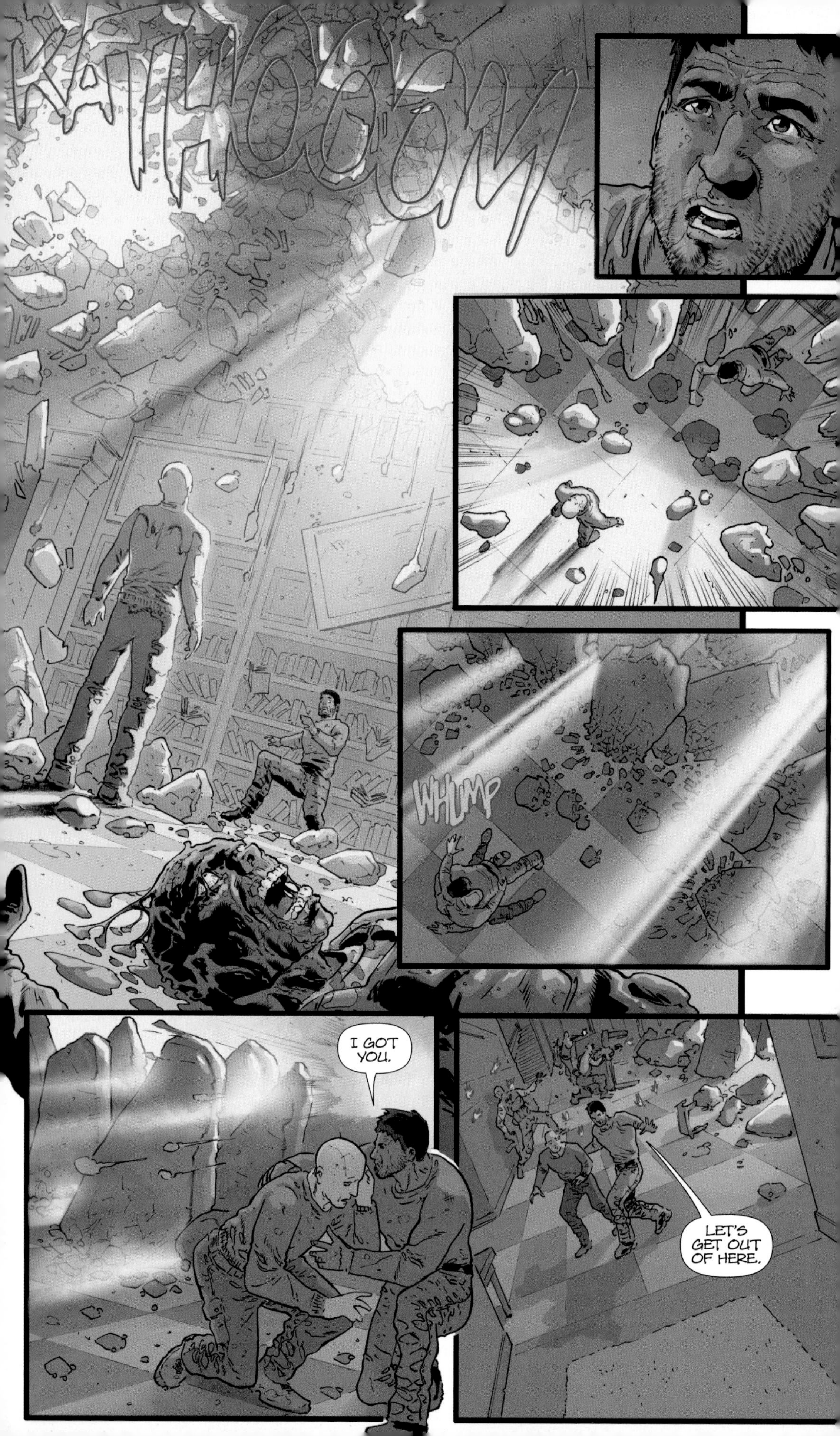
KATHOOOOM
WHUMP
I GOT YOU.
LET'S GET OUT OF HERE.

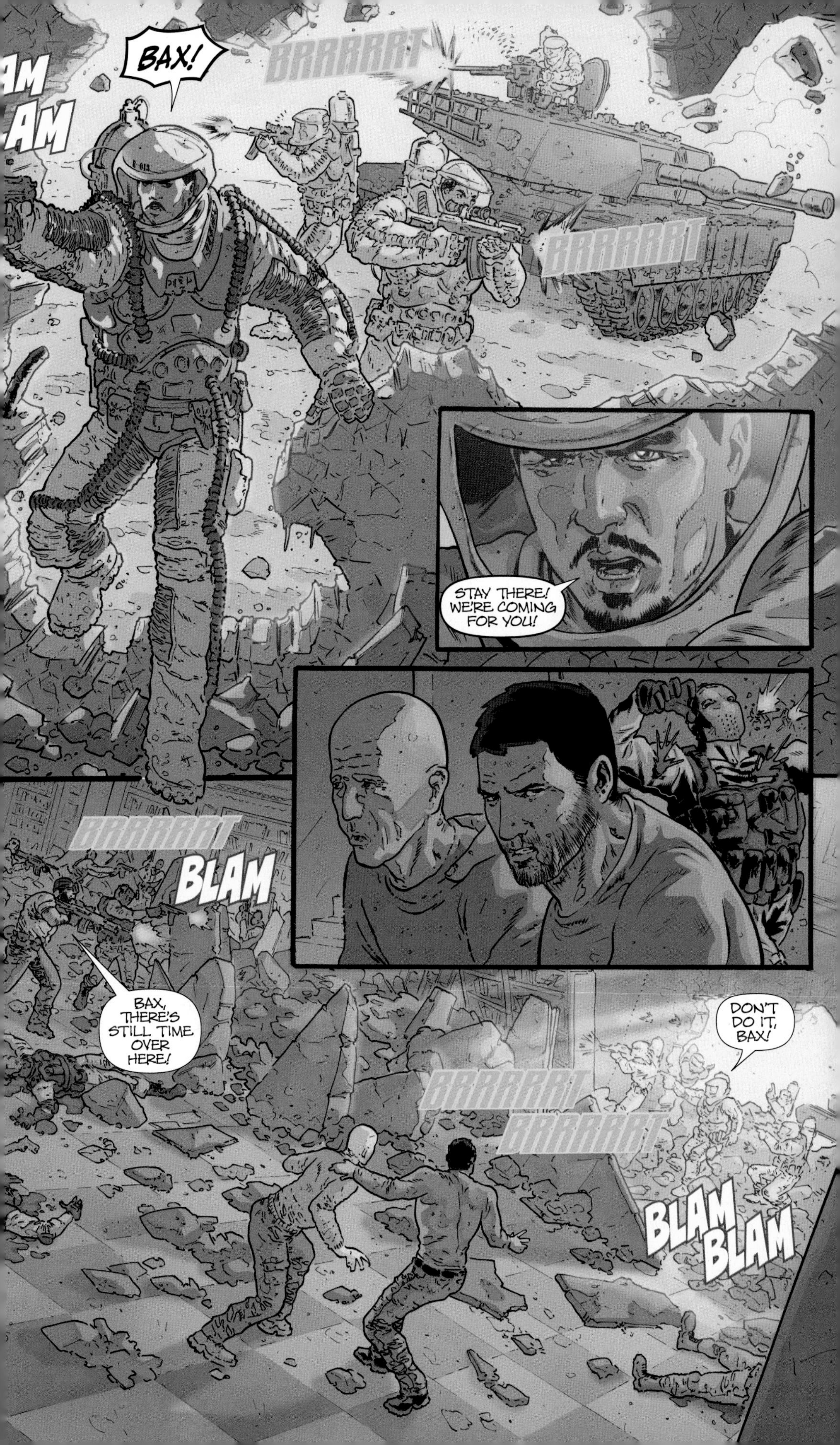
AM
AM
BAX!
BRRRRRT
BRRRRRT
STAY THERE! WE'RE COMING FOR YOU!
BRRRRRT
BLAM
BAX, THERE'S STILL TIME OVER HERE!
DON'T DO IT, BAX!
BRRRRRT
BRRRRRT
BLAM
BLAM

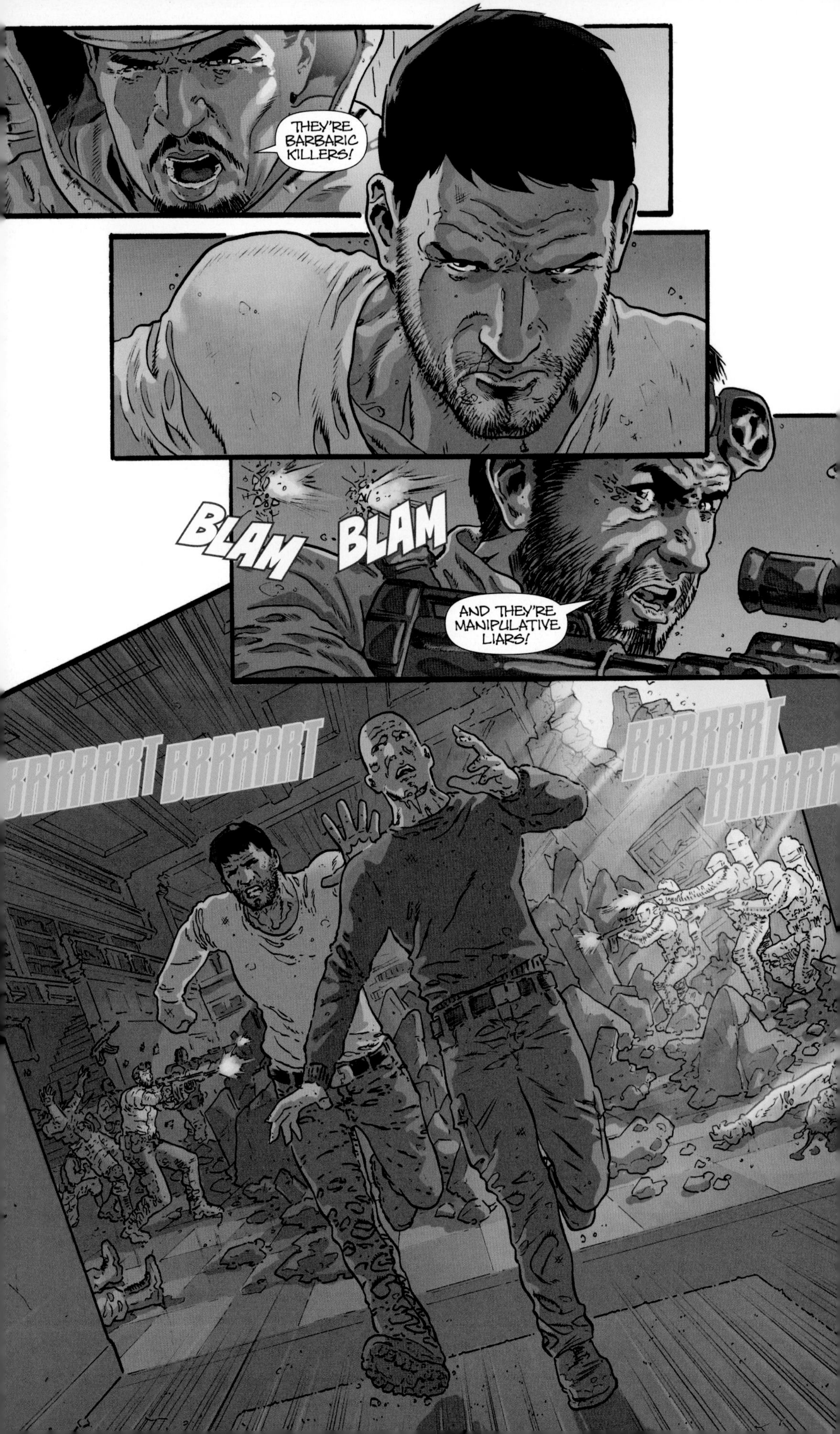
THEY'RE BARBARIC KILLERS!
BLAM
BLAM
AND THEY'RE MANIPULATIVE LIARS!
BRRRRRT BRRRRRT
BRRRRRT

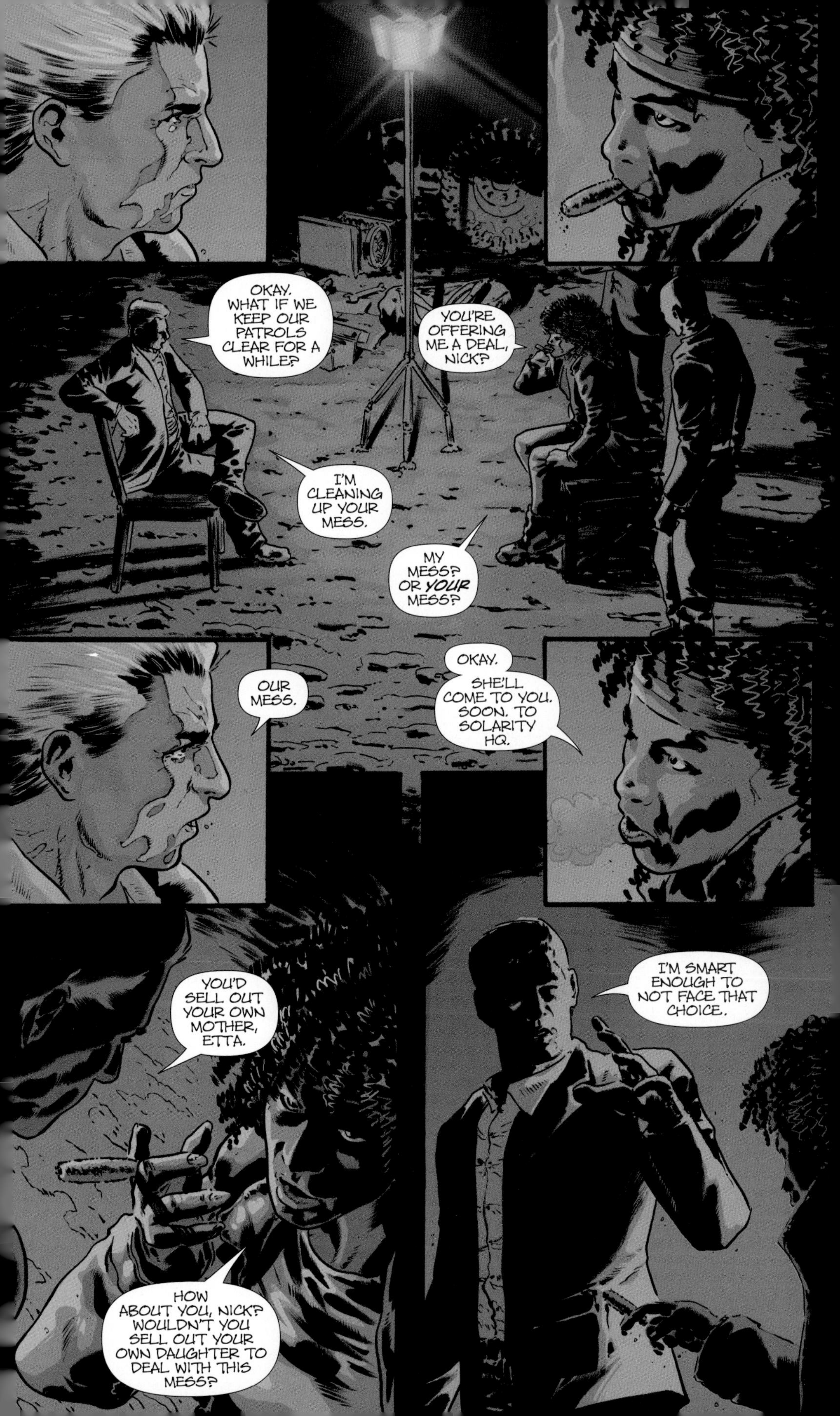
OKAY. WHAT IF WE KEEP OUR PATROLS CLEAR FOR A WHILE?
YOU'RE OFFERING ME A DEAL, NICK?
I'M CLEANING UP YOUR MESS.
MY MESS? OR *YOUR* MESS?
OUR MESS.
OKAY.
SHE'LL COME TO YOU. SOON. TO SOLARITY HQ.
YOU'D SELL OUT YOUR OWN MOTHER, ETTA.
HOW ABOUT YOU, NICK? WOULDN'T YOU SELL OUT YOUR OWN DAUGHTER TO DEAL WITH THIS MESS?
I'M SMART ENOUGH TO NOT FACE THAT CHOICE.

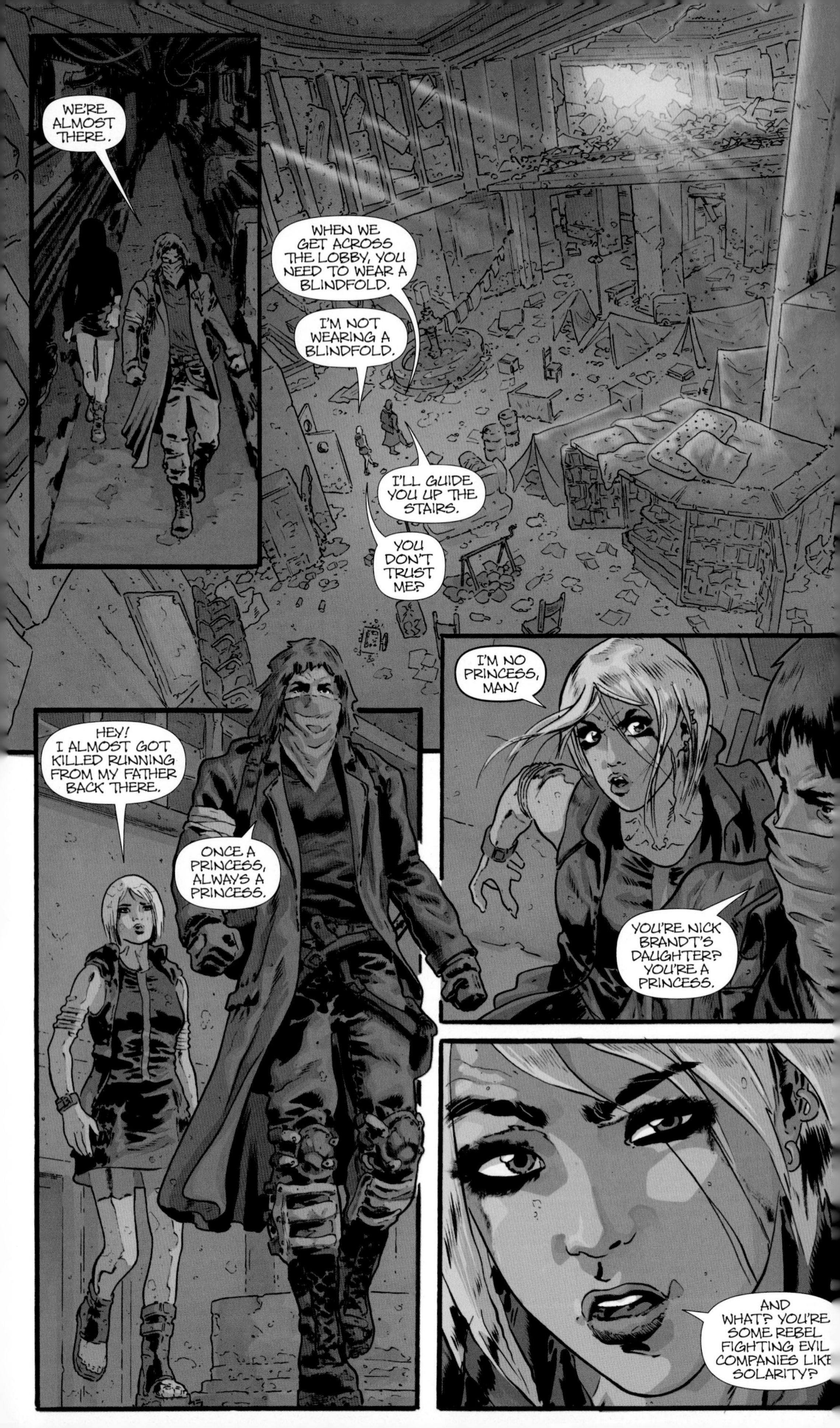
WE'RE ALMOST THERE.
WHEN WE GET ACROSS THE LOBBY, YOU NEED TO WEAR A BLINDFOLD.
I'M NOT WEARING A BLINDFOLD.
I'LL GUIDE YOU UP THE STAIRS.
YOU DON'T TRUST ME?
HEY! I ALMOST GOT KILLED RUNNING FROM MY FATHER BACK THERE.
ONCE A PRINCESS, ALWAYS A PRINCESS.
I'M NO PRINCESS, MAN!
YOU'RE NICK BRANDT'S DAUGHTER? YOU'RE A PRINCESS.
AND WHAT? YOU'RE SOME REBEL FIGHTING EVIL COMPANIES LIKE SOLARITY?

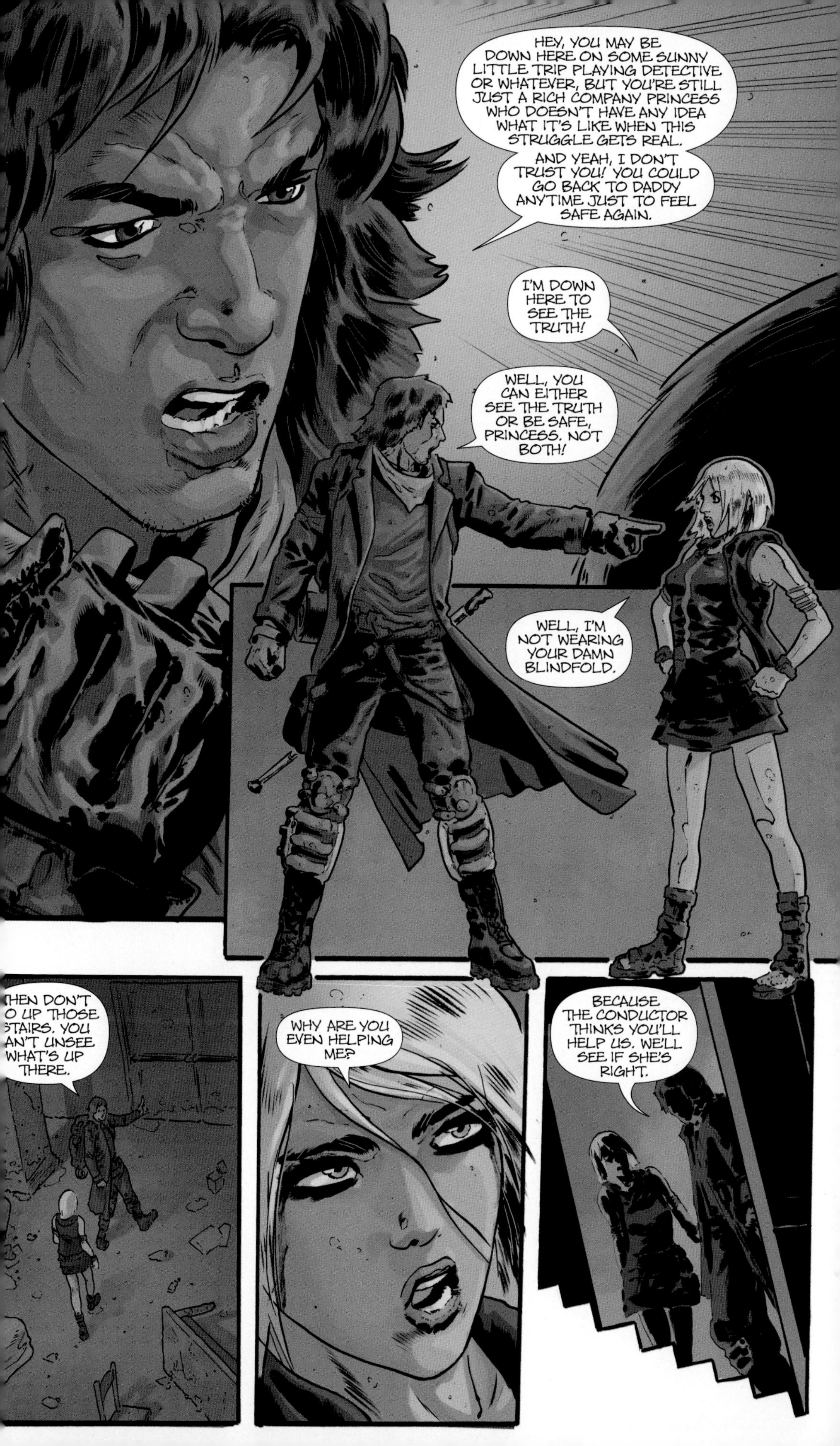
HEY, YOU MAY BE DOWN HERE ON SOME SUNNY LITTLE TRIP PLAYING DETECTIVE OR WHATEVER, BUT YOU'RE STILL JUST A RICH COMPANY PRINCESS WHO DOESN'T HAVE ANY IDEA WHAT IT'S LIKE WHEN THIS STRUGGLE GETS REAL.
AND YEAH, I DON'T TRUST YOU! YOU COULD GO BACK TO DADDY ANYTIME JUST TO FEEL SAFE AGAIN.
I'M DOWN HERE TO SEE THE TRUTH!
WELL, YOU CAN EITHER SEE THE TRUTH OR BE SAFE, PRINCESS. NOT BOTH!
WELL, I'M NOT WEARING YOUR DAMN BLINDFOLD.
HEN DON'T O UP THOSE STAIRS. YOU AN'T UNSEE WHAT'S UP THERE.
WHY ARE YOU EVEN HELPING ME?
BECAUSE THE CONDUCTOR THINKS YOU'LL HELP US. WE'LL SEE IF SHE'S RIGHT.

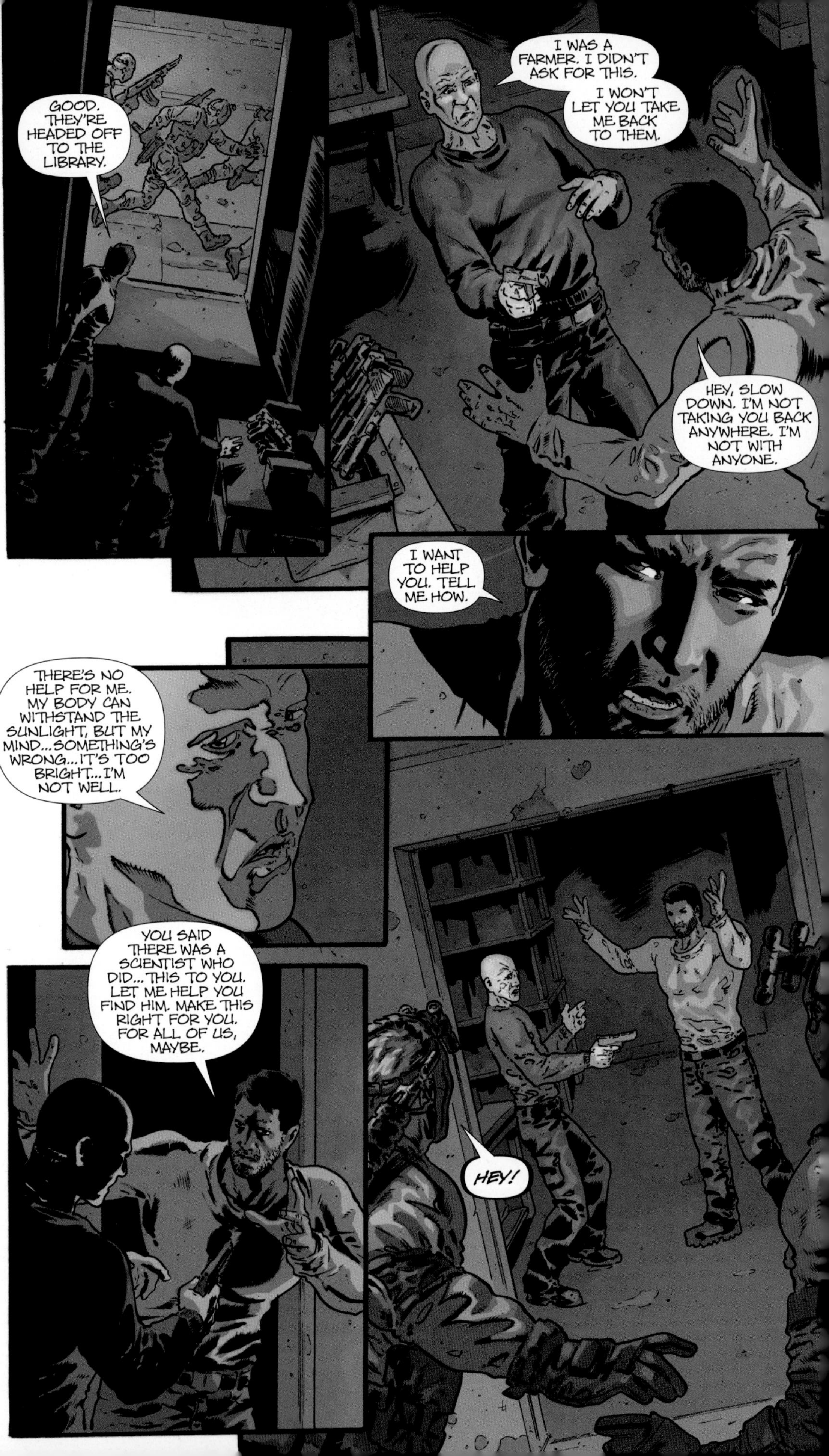
GOOD. THEY'RE HEADED OFF TO THE LIBRARY.
I WAS A FARMER. I DIDN'T ASK FOR THIS.
I WON'T LET YOU TAKE ME BACK TO THEM.
HEY, SLOW DOWN. I'M NOT TAKING YOU BACK ANYWHERE. I'M NOT WITH ANYONE.
I WANT TO HELP YOU. TELL ME HOW.
THERE'S NO HELP FOR ME. MY BODY CAN WITHSTAND THE SUNLIGHT, BUT MY MIND...SOMETHING'S WRONG...IT'S TOO BRIGHT...I'M NOT WELL.
YOU SAID THERE WAS A SCIENTIST WHO DID...THIS TO YOU. LET ME HELP YOU FIND HIM. MAKE THIS RIGHT FOR YOU. FOR ALL OF US, MAYBE.
HEY!

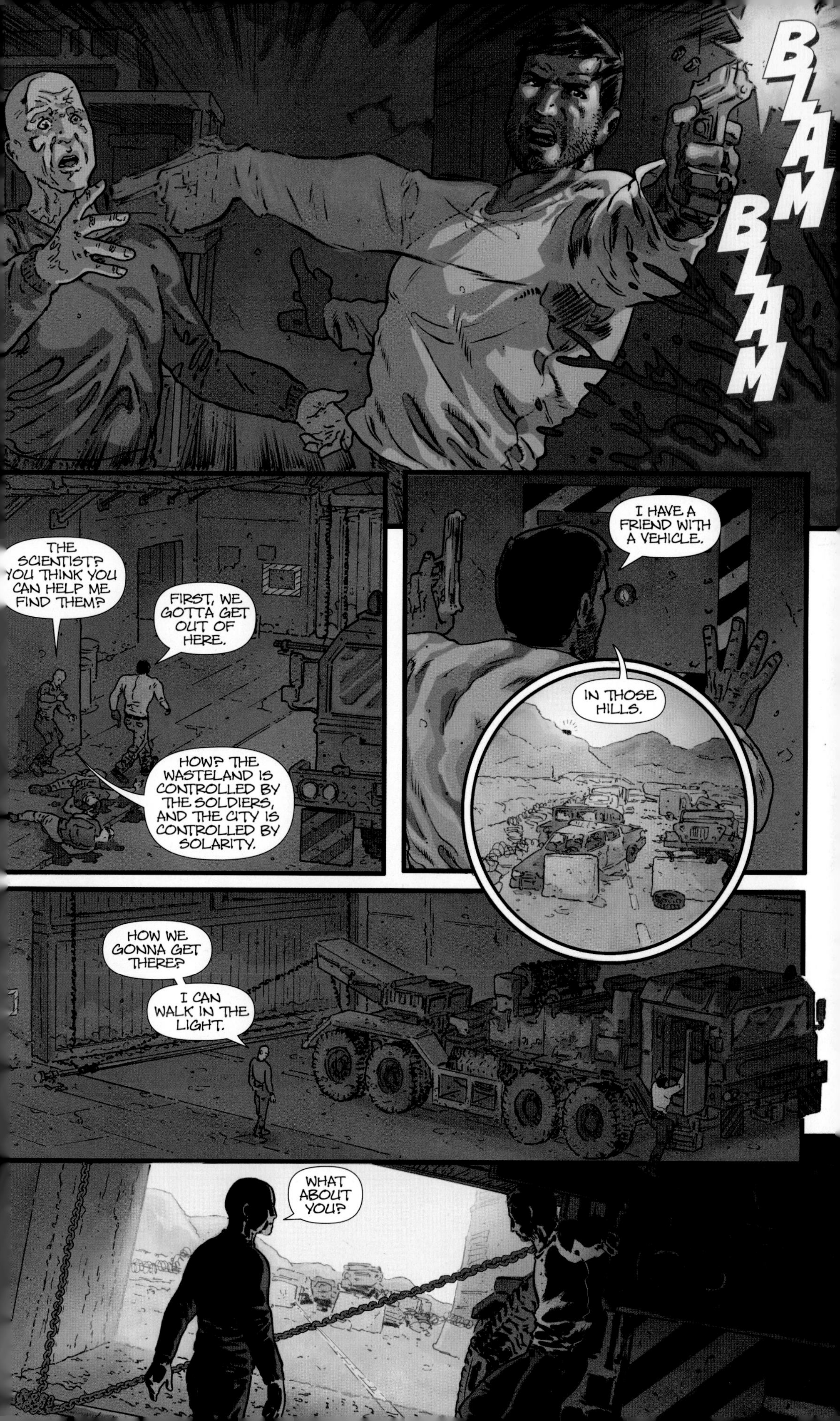
BLAM
BLAM
THE SCIENTIST? YOU THINK YOU CAN HELP ME FIND THEM?
FIRST, WE GOTTA GET OUT OF HERE.
HOW? THE WASTELAND IS CONTROLLED BY THE SOLDIERS, AND THE CITY IS CONTROLLED BY SOLARITY.
I HAVE A FRIEND WITH A VEHICLE.
IN THOSE HILLS.
HOW WE GONNA GET THERE?
I CAN WALK IN THE LIGHT.
WHAT ABOUT YOU?

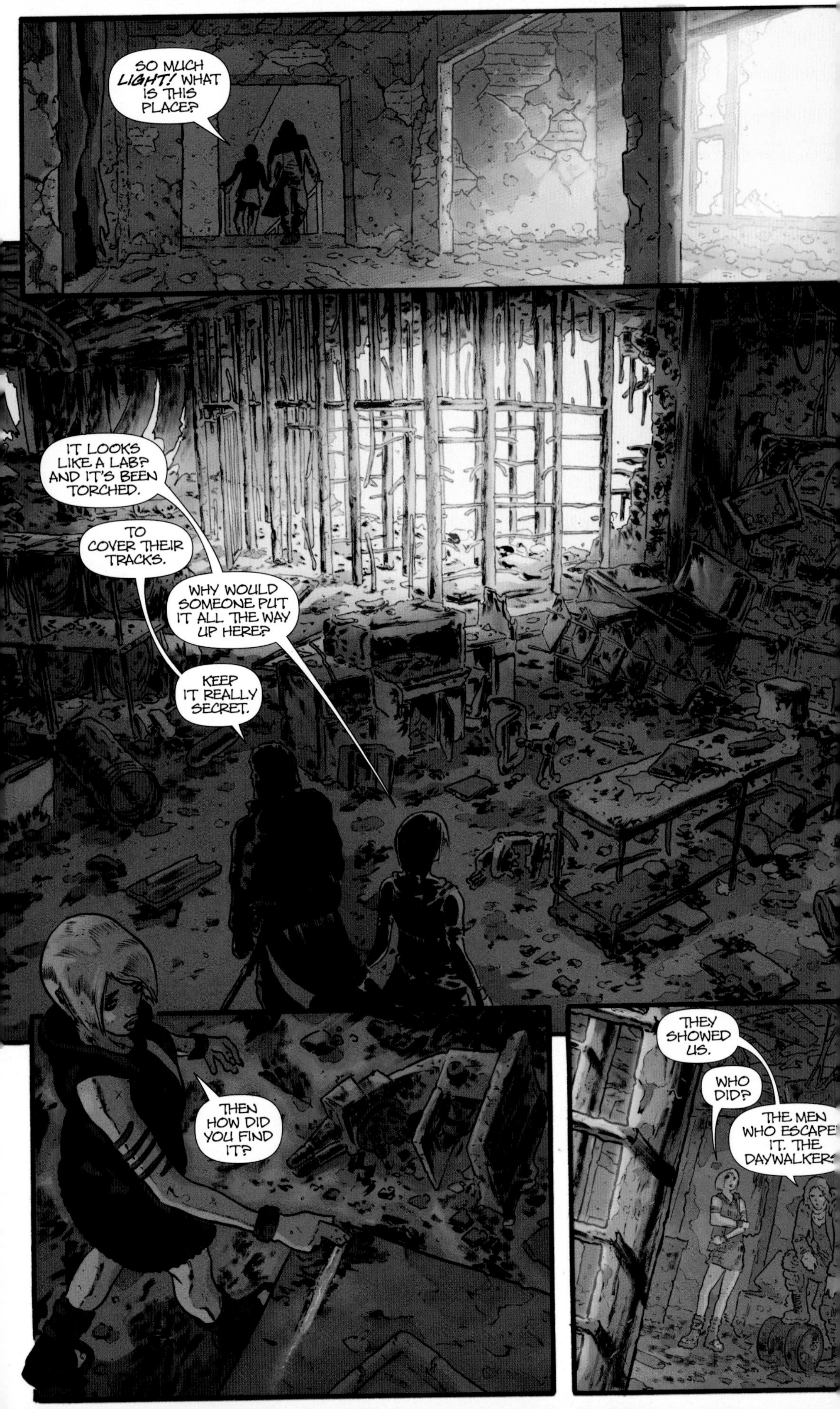
SO MUCH *LIGHT!* WHAT IS THIS PLACE?
IT LOOKS LIKE A LAB? AND IT'S BEEN TORCHED.
TO COVER THEIR TRACKS.
WHY WOULD SOMEONE PUT IT ALL THE WAY UP HERE?
KEEP IT REALLY SECRET.
THEN HOW DID YOU FIND IT?
THEY SHOWED US.
WHO DID?
THE MEN WHO ESCAPE IT. THE DAYWALKER

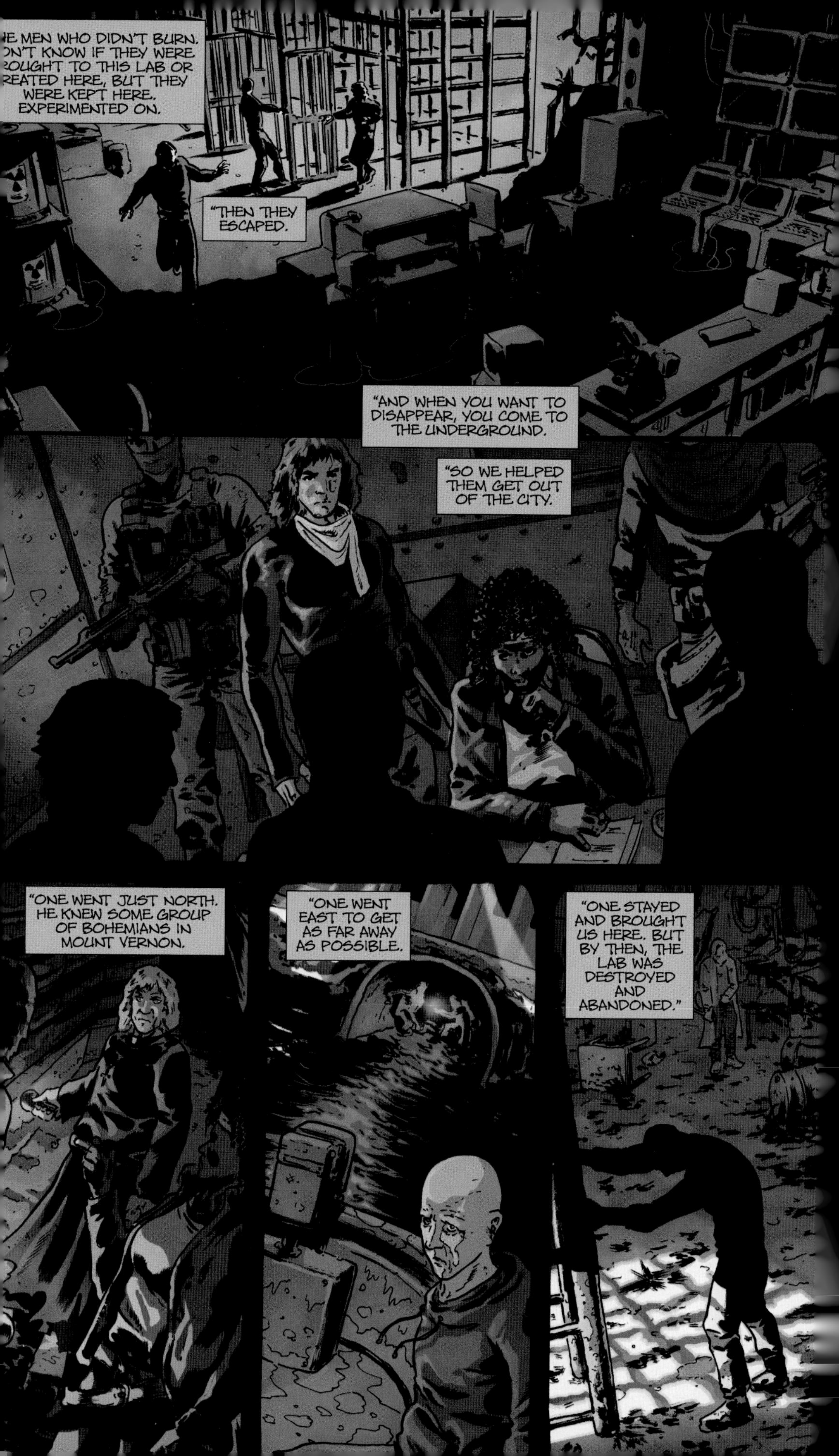
HE MEN WHO DIDN'T BURN. ON'T KNOW IF THEY WERE ROUGHT TO THIS LAB OR REATED HERE, BUT THEY WERE KEPT HERE. EXPERIMENTED ON.
"THEN THEY ESCAPED.
"AND WHEN YOU WANT TO DISAPPEAR, YOU COME TO THE UNDERGROUND.
"SO WE HELPED THEM GET OUT OF THE CITY.
"ONE WENT JUST NORTH. HE KNEW SOME GROUP OF BOHEMIANS IN MOUNT VERNON.
"ONE WENT EAST TO GET AS FAR AWAY AS POSSIBLE.
"ONE STAYED AND BROUGHT US HERE. BUT BY THEN, THE LAB WAS DESTROYED AND ABANDONED."

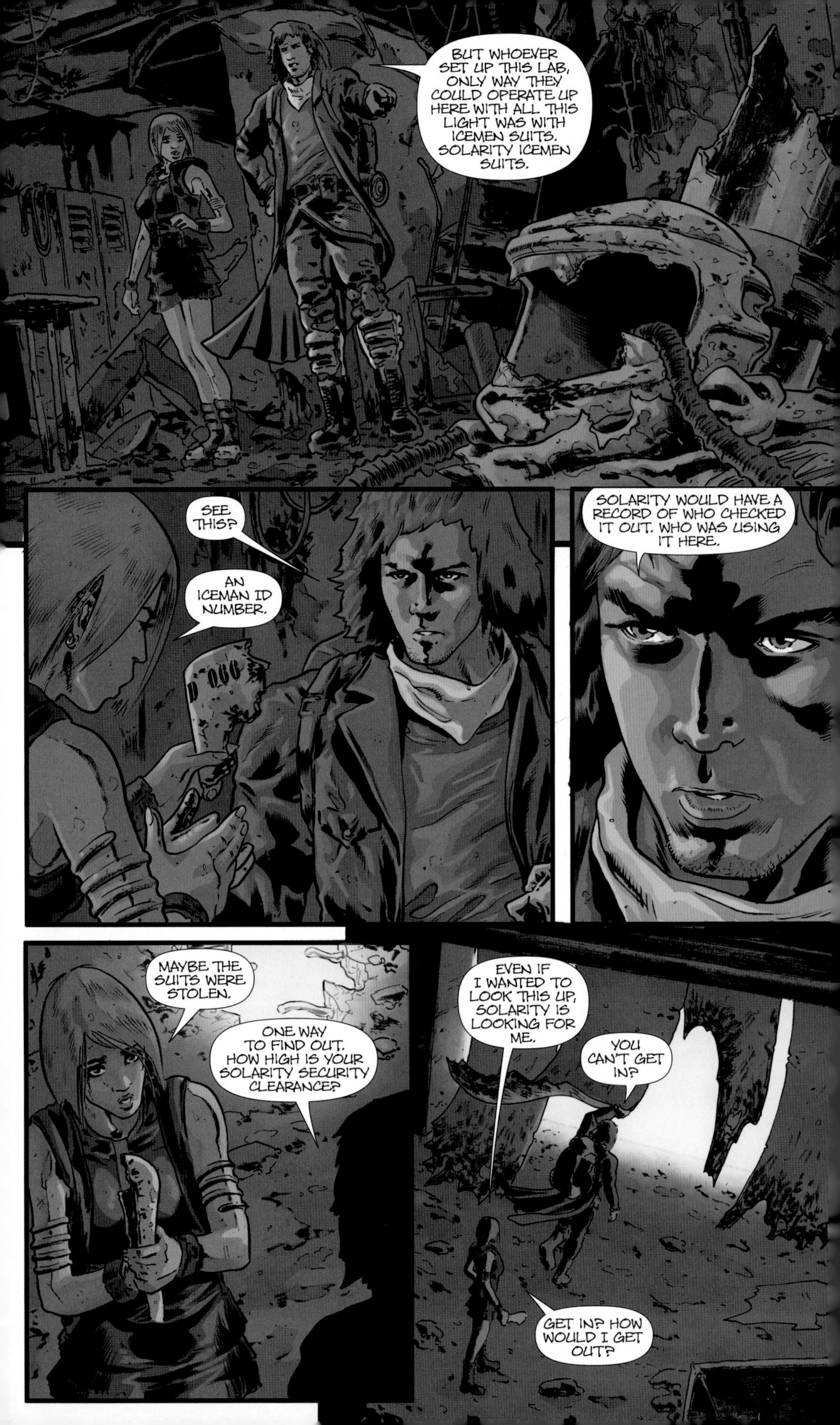
BUT WHOEVER SET UP THIS LAB, ONLY WAY THEY COULD OPERATE UP HERE WITH ALL THIS LIGHT WAS WITH ICEMEN SUITS. SOLARITY ICEMEN SUITS.
SEE THIS?
AN ICEMAN ID NUMBER.
D 060
SOLARITY WOULD HAVE A RECORD OF WHO CHECKED IT OUT. WHO WAS USING IT HERE.
MAYBE THE SUITS WERE STOLEN.
ONE WAY TO FIND OUT. HOW HIGH IS YOUR SOLARITY SECURITY CLEARANCE?
EVEN IF I WANTED TO LOOK THIS UP, SOLARITY IS LOOKING FOR ME.
YOU CAN'T GET IN?
GET IN? HOW WOULD I GET OUT?

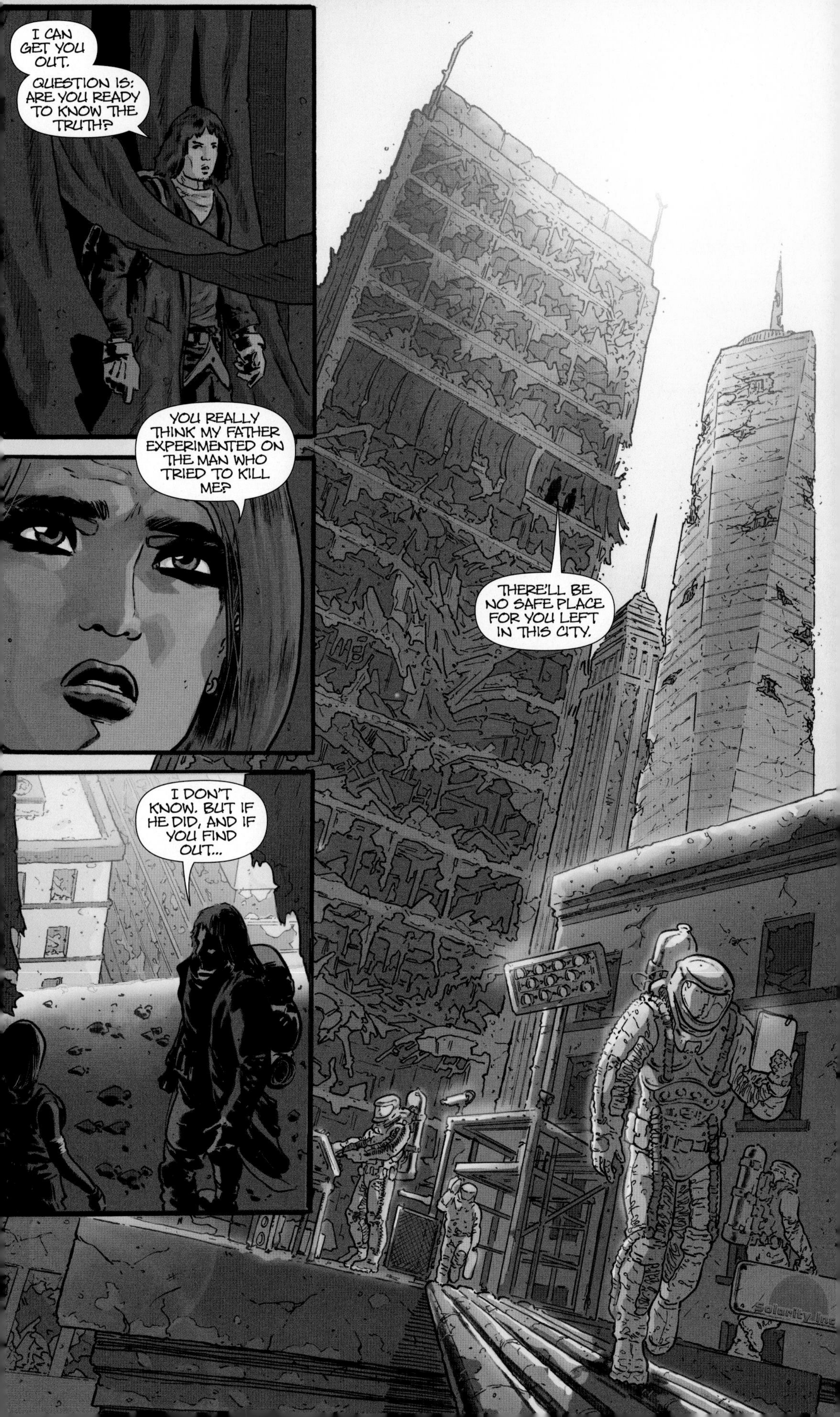
I CAN GET YOU OUT.
QUESTION IS: ARE YOU READY TO KNOW THE TRUTH?
YOU REALLY THINK MY FATHER EXPERIMENTED ON THE MAN WHO TRIED TO KILL ME?
I DON'T KNOW. BUT IF HE DID, AND IF YOU FIND OUT...
THERE'LL BE NO SAFE PLACE FOR YOU LEFT IN THIS CITY.
Solarity Inc

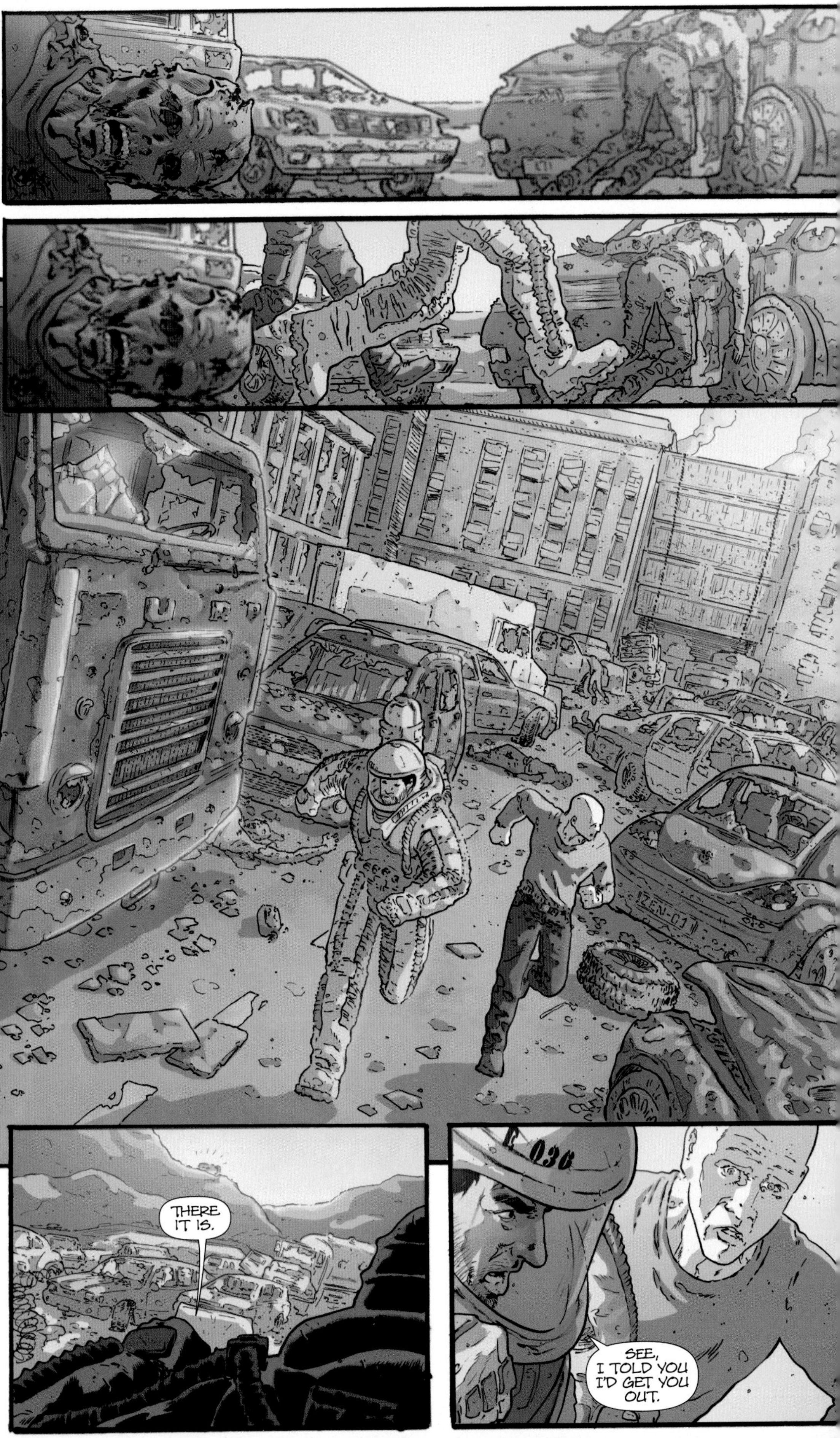
ZEN-01
THERE IT IS.
SEE, I TOLD YOU I'D GET YOU OUT.

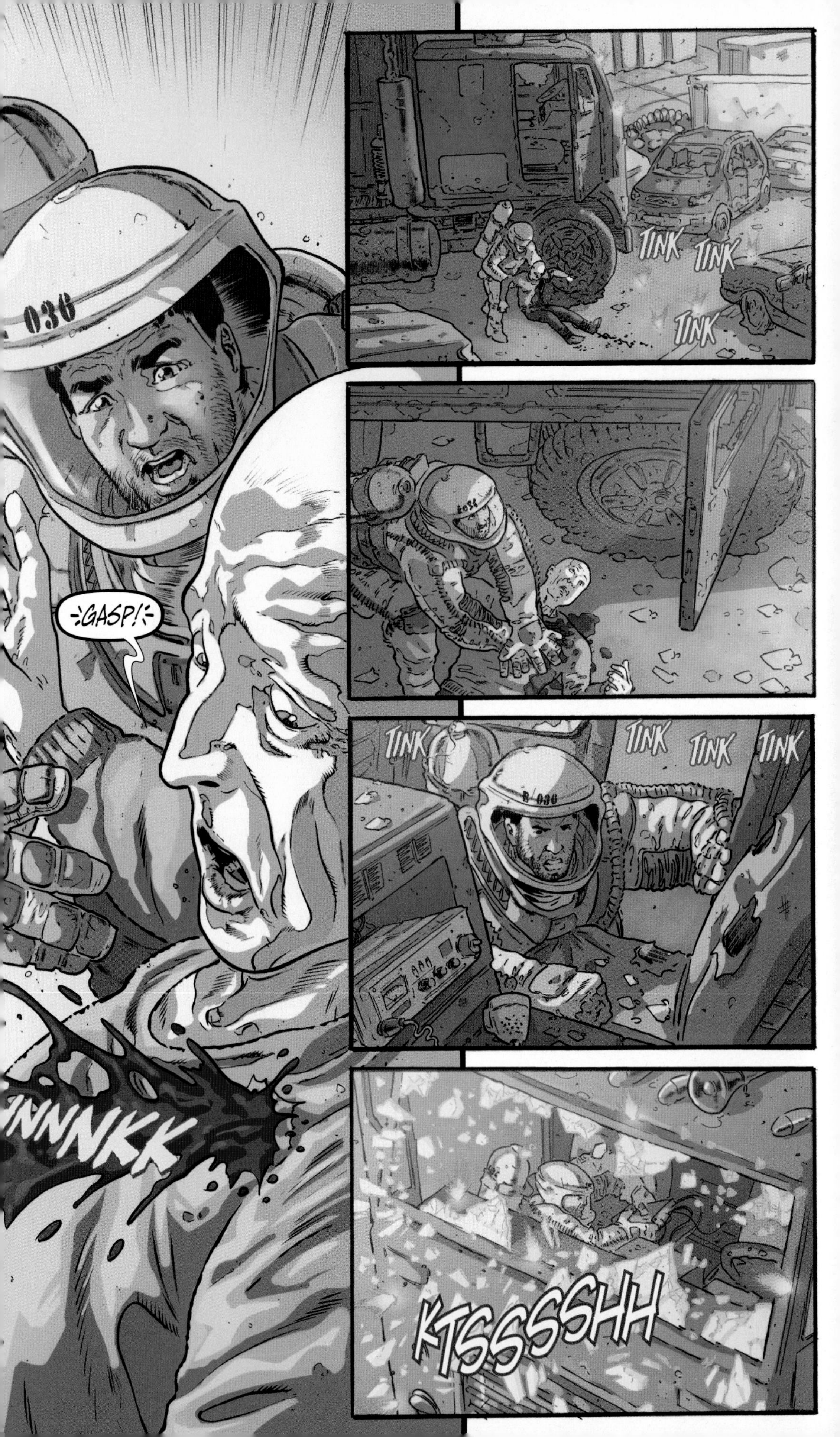
030
GASP!
NNNKK
TINK
TINK
TINK
B 030
TINK
TINK
TINK
TINK
KTSSSSHH

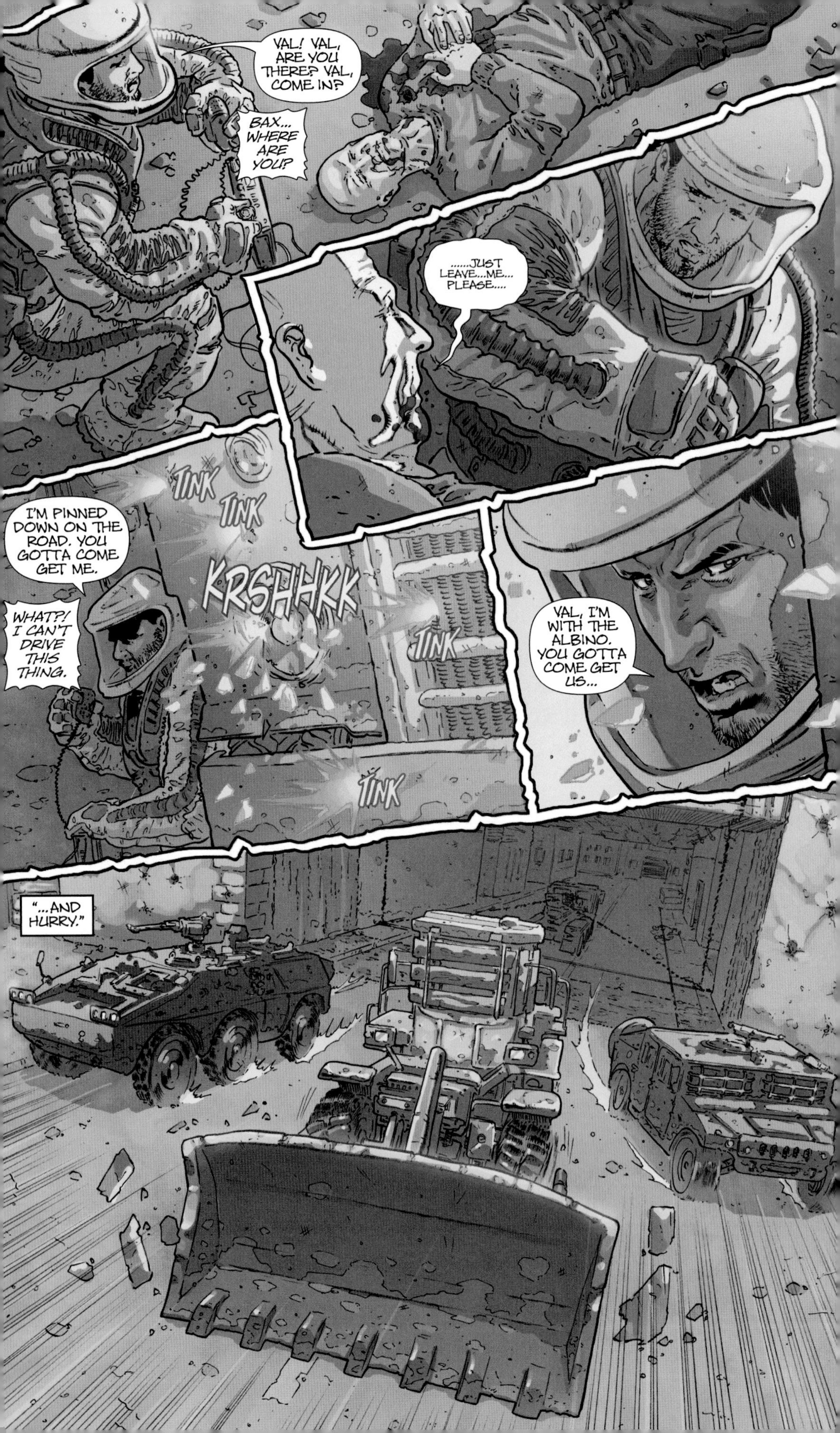
VAL! VAL, ARE YOU THERE? VAL, COME IN?
BAX... WHERE ARE YOU!?
......JUST LEAVE...ME... PLEASE....
I'M PINNED DOWN ON THE ROAD. YOU GOTTA COME GET ME.
WHAT?! I CAN'T DRIVE THIS THING.
TINK
TINK
KRSHHKK
TINK
TINK
VAL, I'M WITH THE ALBINO. YOU GOTTA COME GET US...
"...AND HURRY."

CHAPTER EIGHT

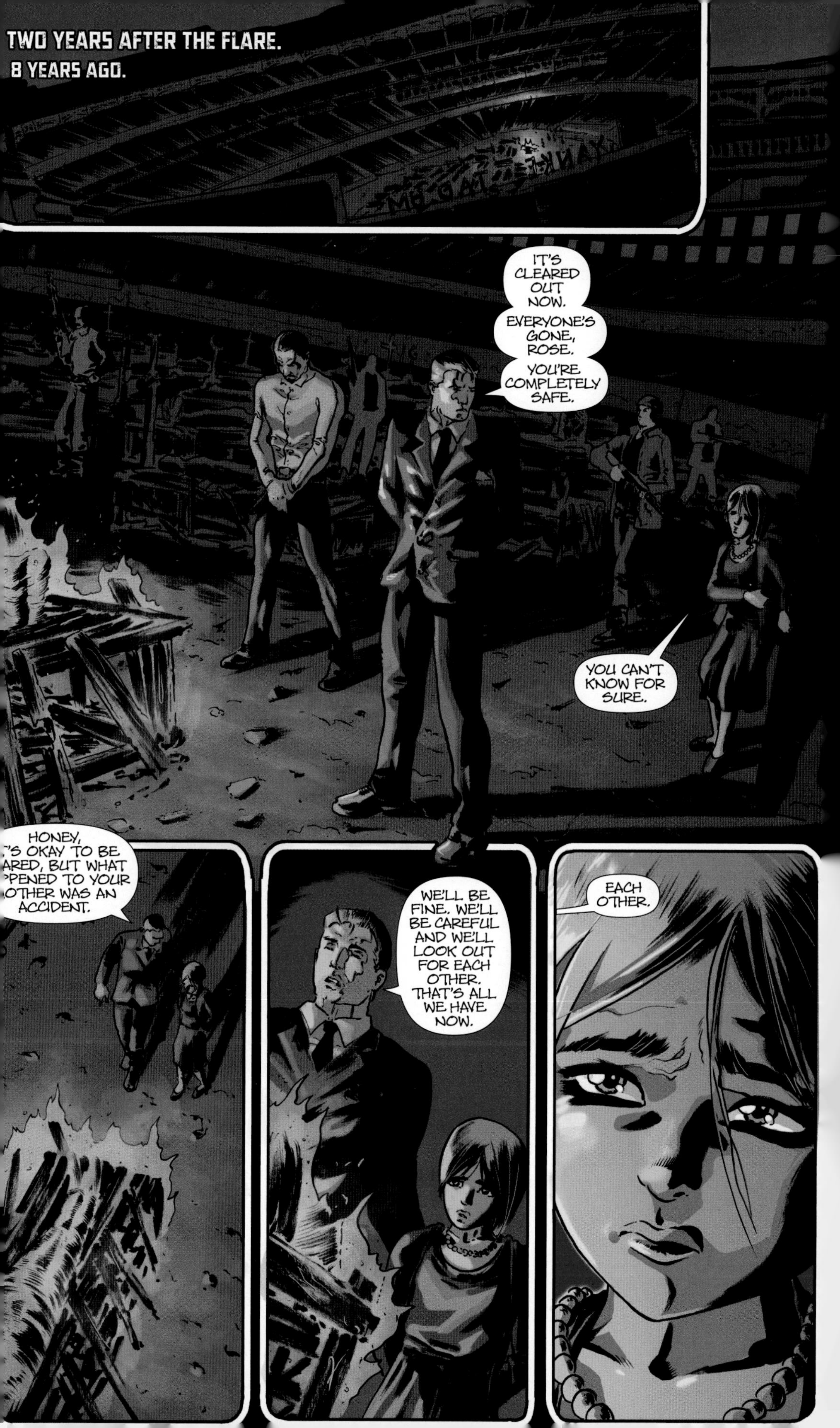
TWO YEARS AFTER THE FLARE.
8 YEARS AGO.
IT'S CLEARED OUT NOW.
EVERYONE'S GONE, ROSE.
YOU'RE COMPLETELY SAFE.
YOU CAN'T KNOW FOR SURE.
HONEY, 'S OKAY TO BE ARED, BUT WHAT PENED TO YOUR OTHER WAS AN ACCIDENT.
WE'LL BE FINE. WE'LL BE CAREFUL AND WE'LL LOOK OUT FOR EACH OTHER. THAT'S ALL WE HAVE NOW.
EACH OTHER.

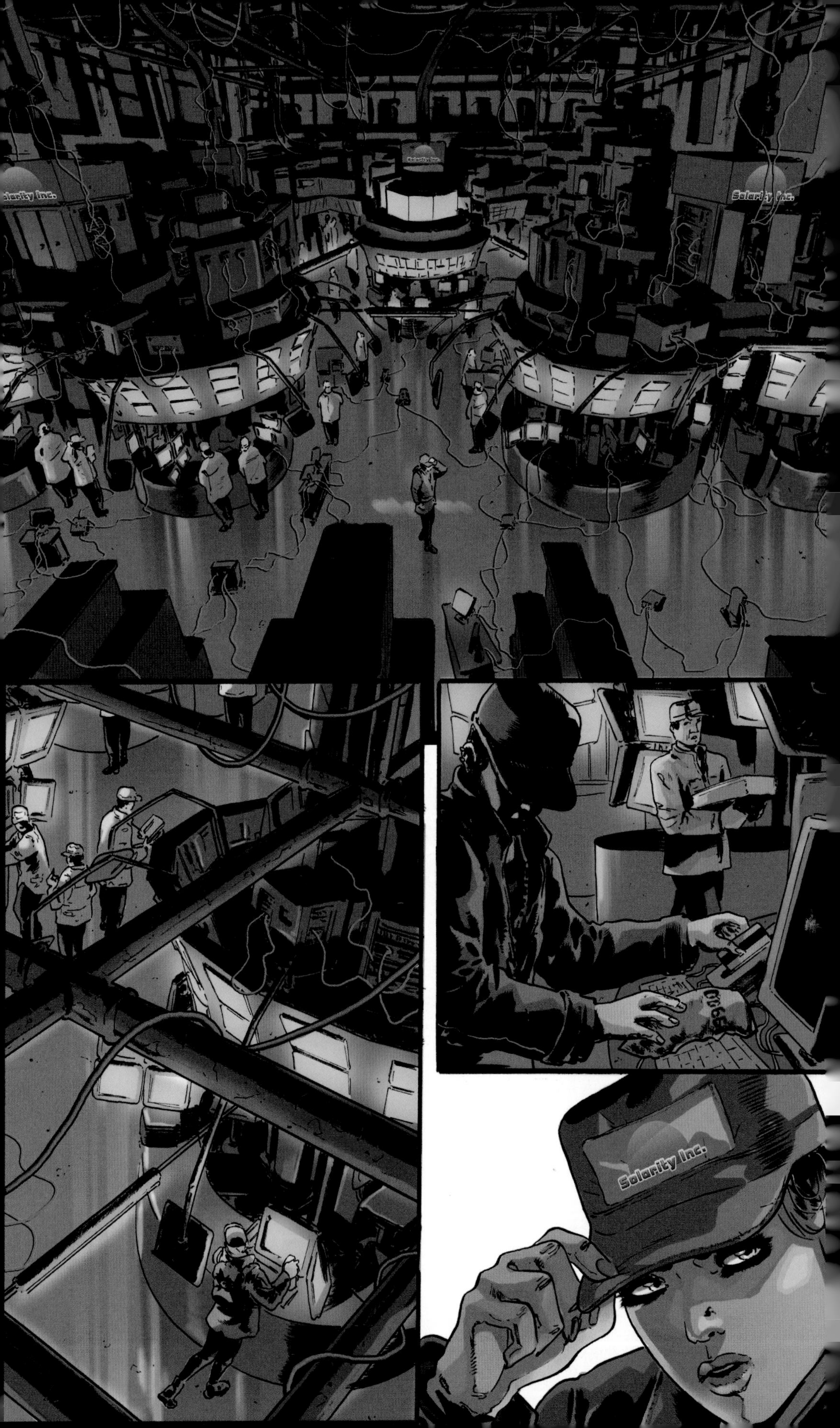
Solarity Inc.
Solarity Inc.

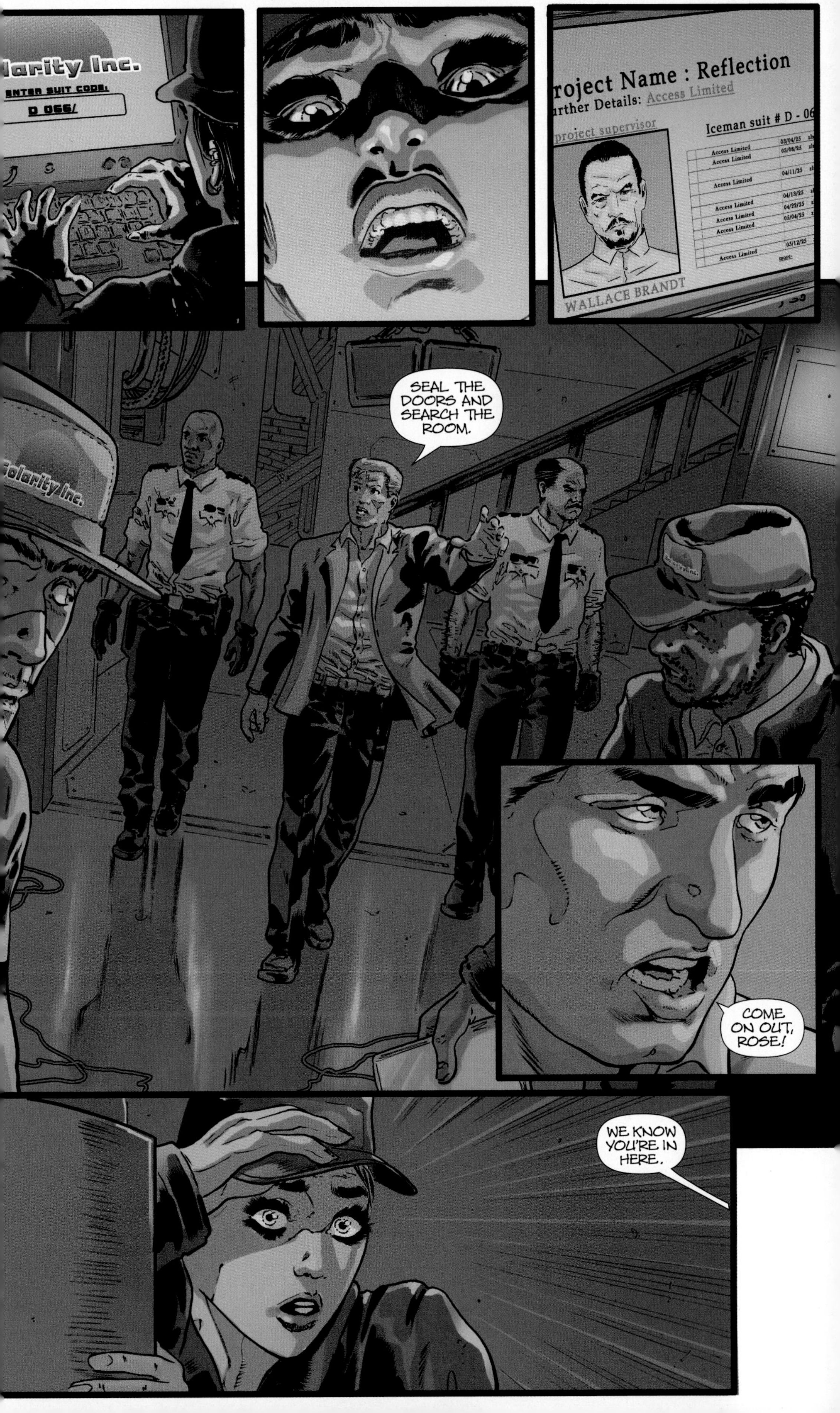

larity Inc.
ENTER SUIT CODE:
D 066/
roject Name : Reflection
urther Details: Access Limited
project supervisor
Iceman suit # D - 06
WALLACE BRANDT
Colarity Inc.
SEAL THE DOORS AND SEARCH THE ROOM.
COME ON OUT, ROSE!
WE KNOW YOU'RE IN HERE.

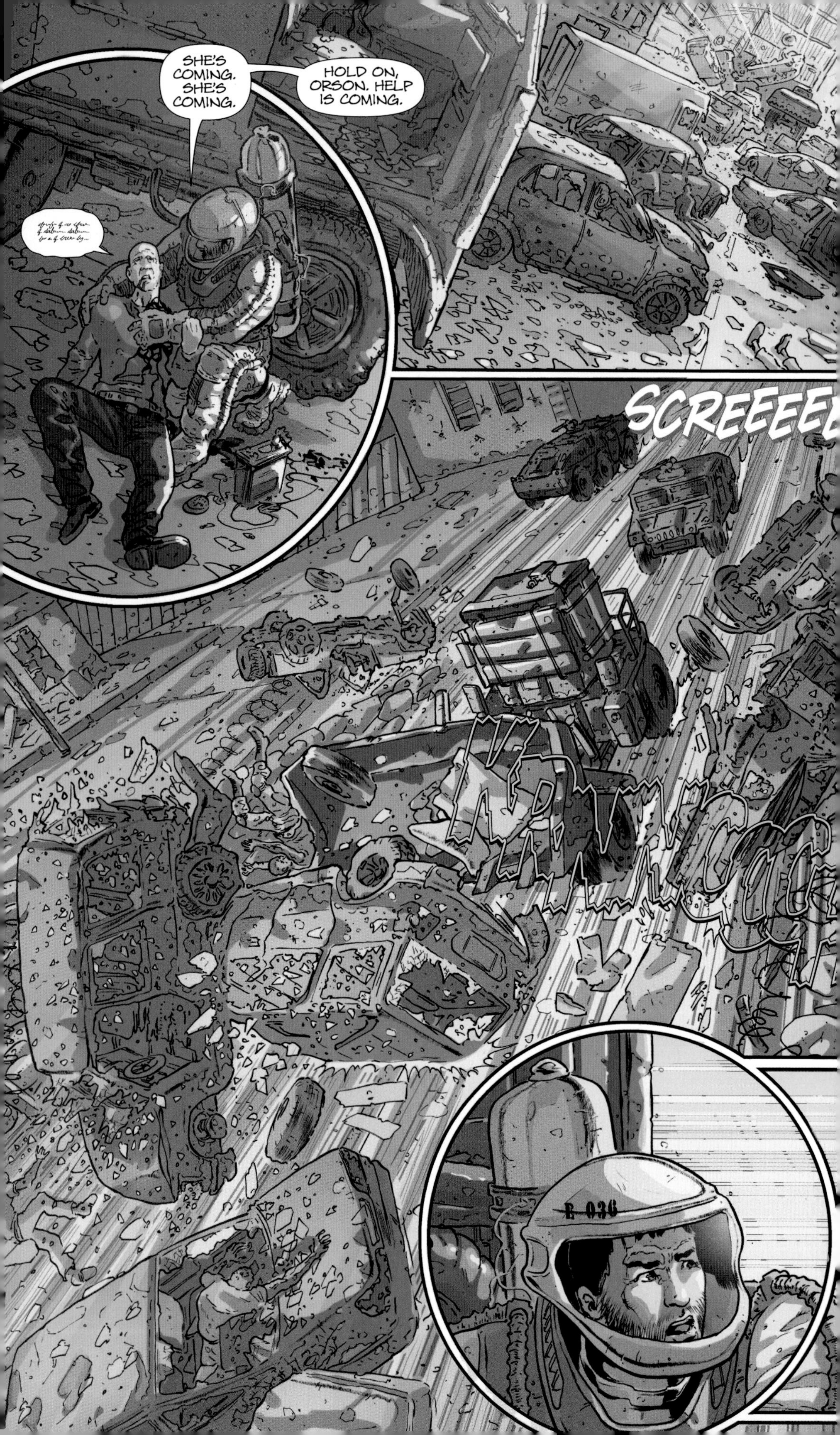
SHE'S COMING. SHE'S COMING.
HOLD ON, ORSON. HELP IS COMING.
SCREEEEE

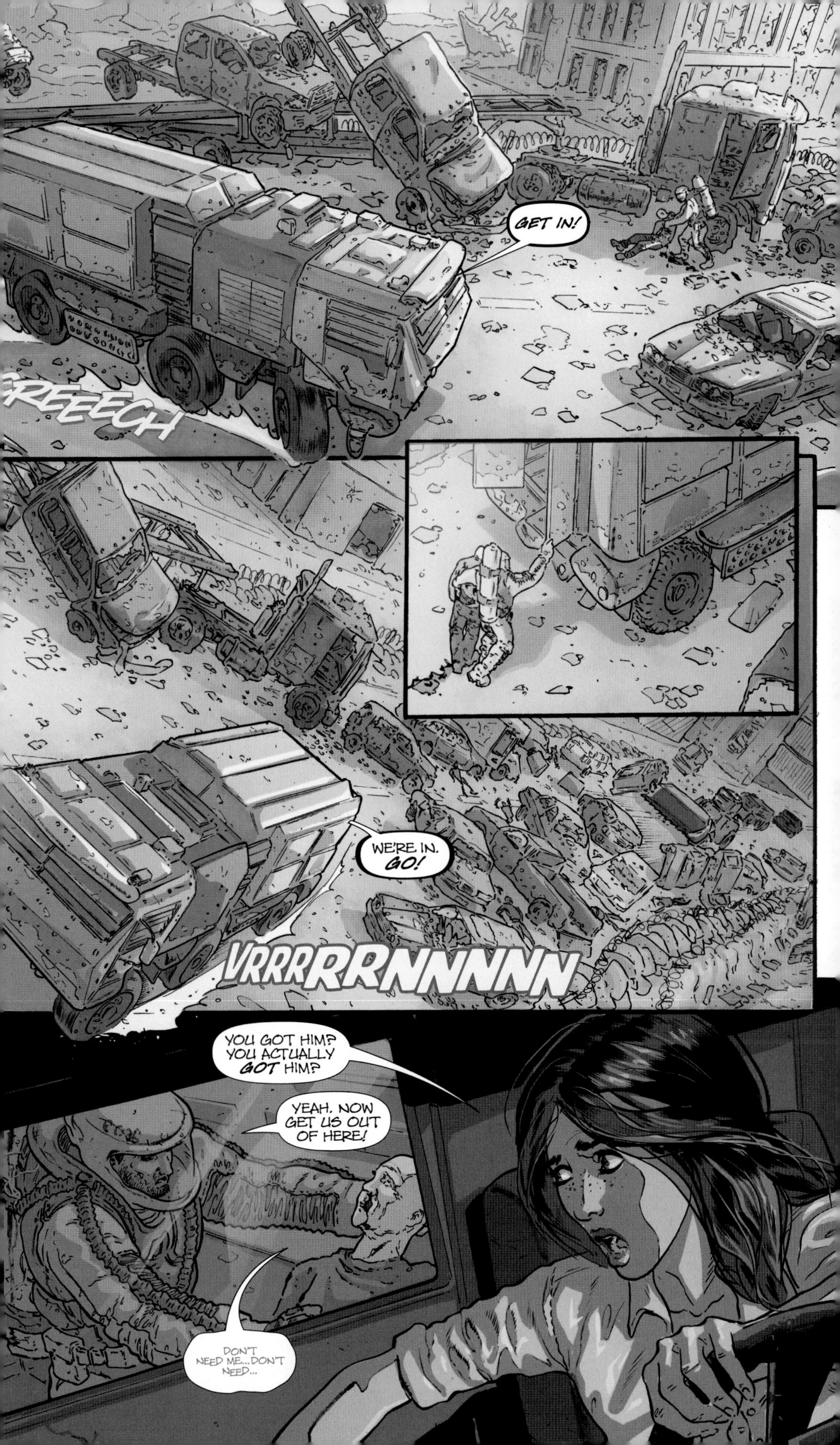
GET IN!
GREEECH
WE'RE IN. GO!
VRRRRRNNNNNN
YOU GOT HIM? YOU ACTUALLY GOT HIM?
YEAH. NOW GET US OUT OF HERE!
DON'T NEED ME...DON'T NEED...

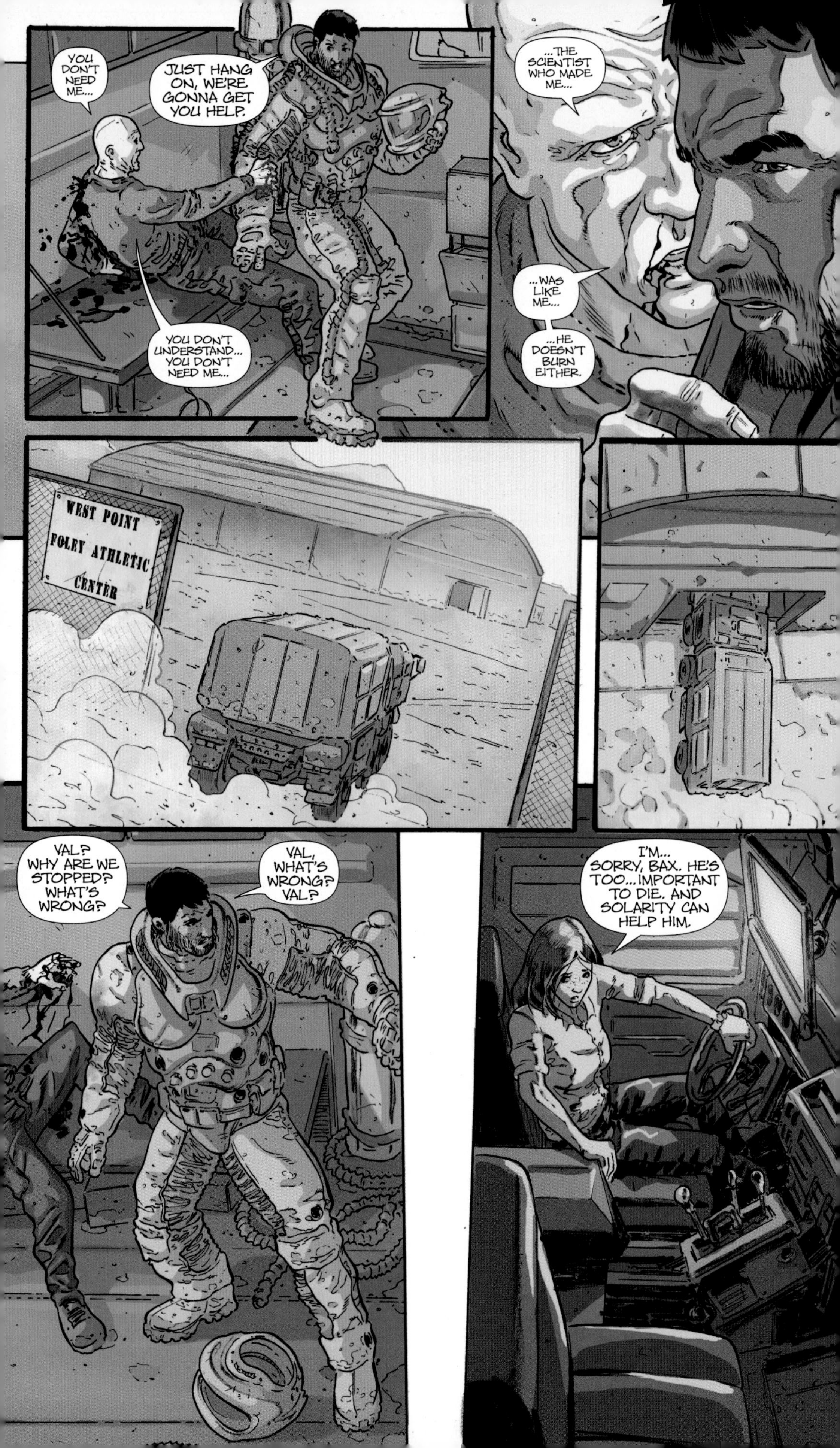
YOU DON'T NEED ME...
JUST HANG ON, WE'RE GONNA GET YOU HELP.
YOU DON'T UNDERSTAND... YOU DON'T NEED ME...
...THE SCIENTIST WHO MADE ME...
...WAS LIKE ME...
...HE DOESN'T BURN EITHER.
WEST POINT
FOLEY ATHLETIC CENTER
VAL? WHY ARE WE STOPPED? WHAT'S WRONG?
VAL, WHAT'S WRONG? VAL?
I'M... SORRY, BAX. HE'S TOO... IMPORTANT TO DIE. AND SOLARITY CAN HELP HIM.

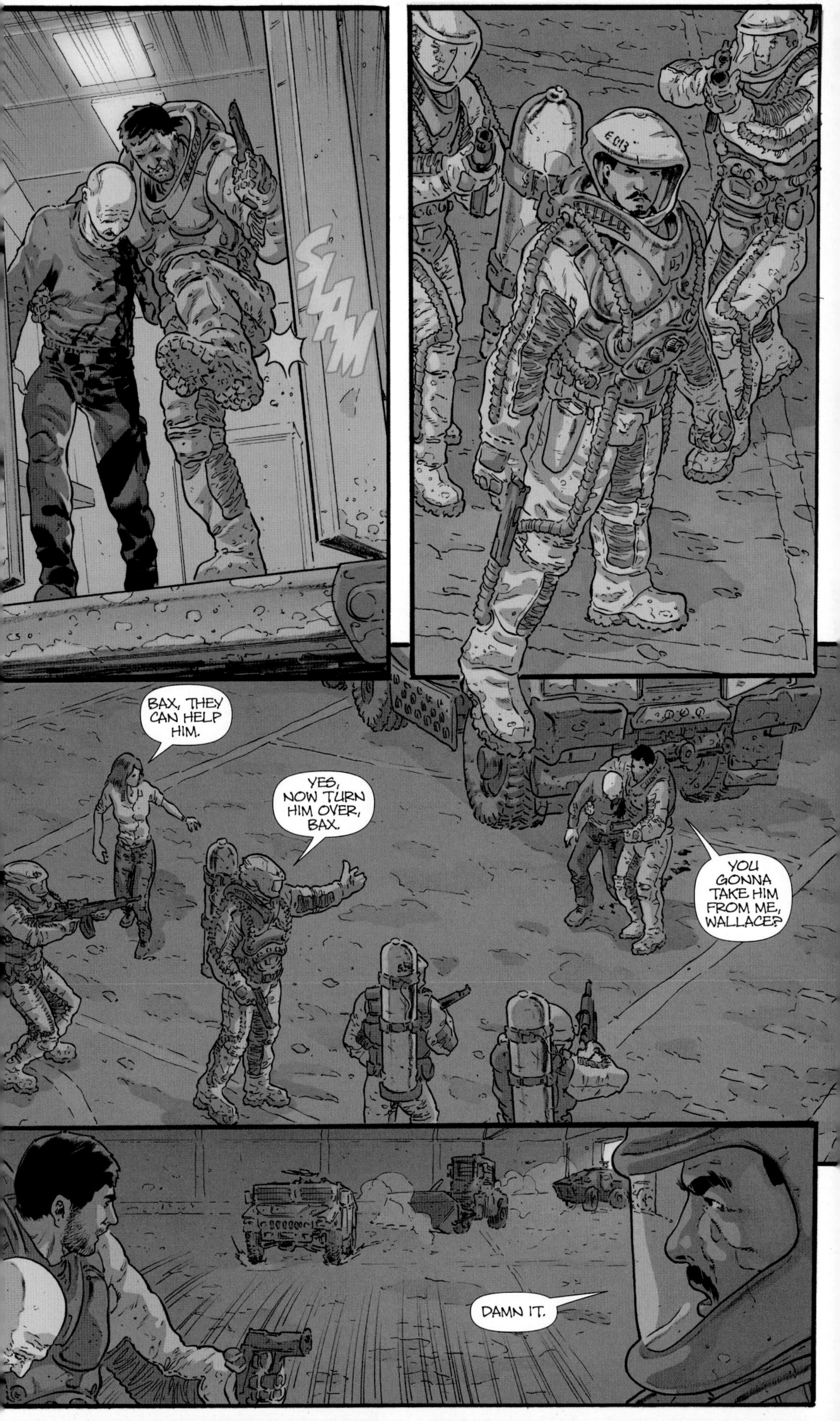
SLAM
BAX, THEY CAN HELP HIM.
YES, NOW TURN HIM OVER, BAX.
YOU GONNA TAKE HIM FROM ME, WALLACE?
DAMN IT.

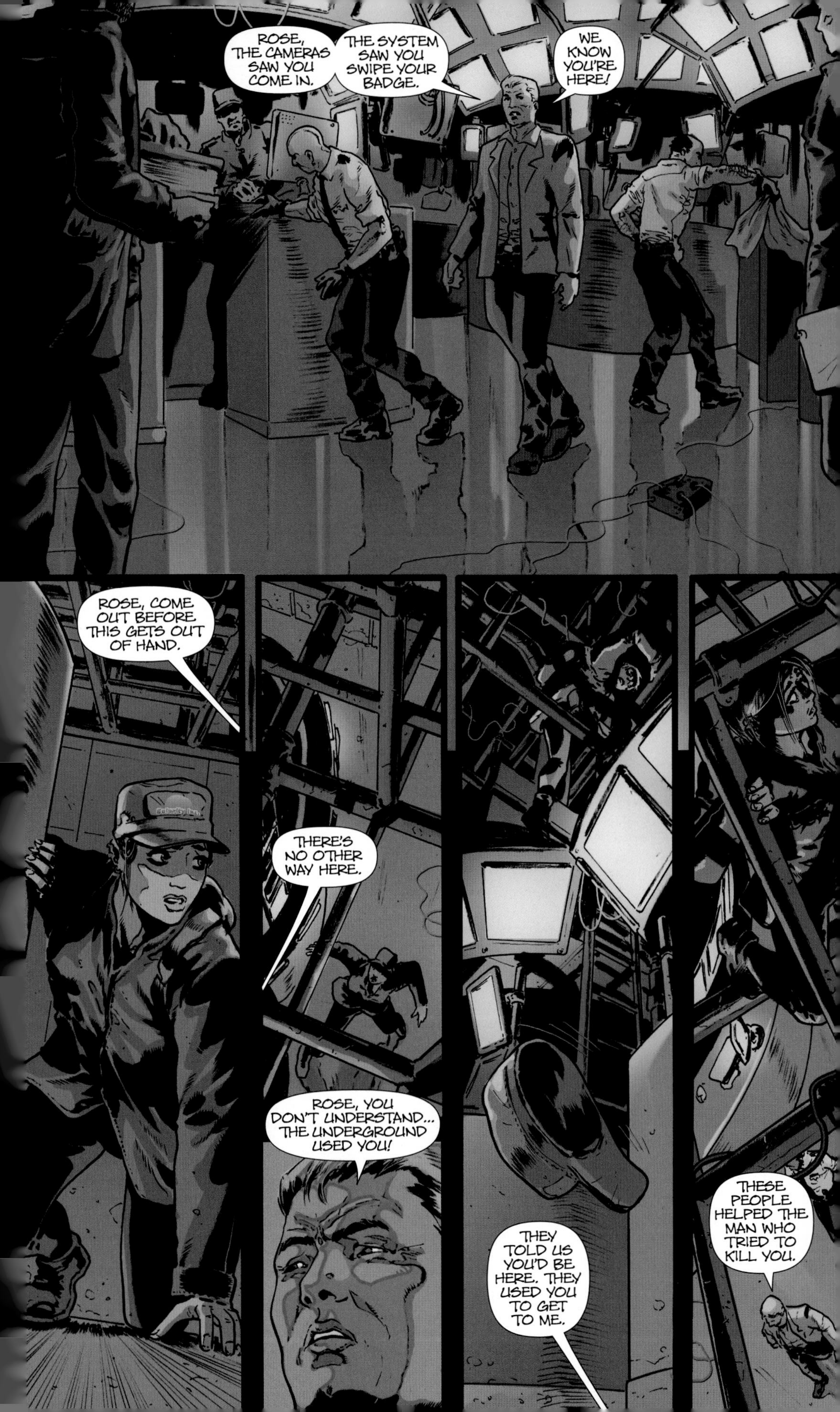
ROSE, THE CAMERAS SAW YOU COME IN.
THE SYSTEM SAW YOU SWIPE YOUR BADGE.
WE KNOW YOU'RE HERE!
ROSE, COME OUT BEFORE THIS GETS OUT OF HAND.
THERE'S NO OTHER WAY HERE.
ROSE, YOU DON'T UNDERSTAND... THE UNDERGROUND USED YOU!
THEY TOLD US YOU'D BE HERE. THEY USED YOU TO GET TO ME.
THESE PEOPLE HELPED THE MAN WHO TRIED TO KILL YOU.

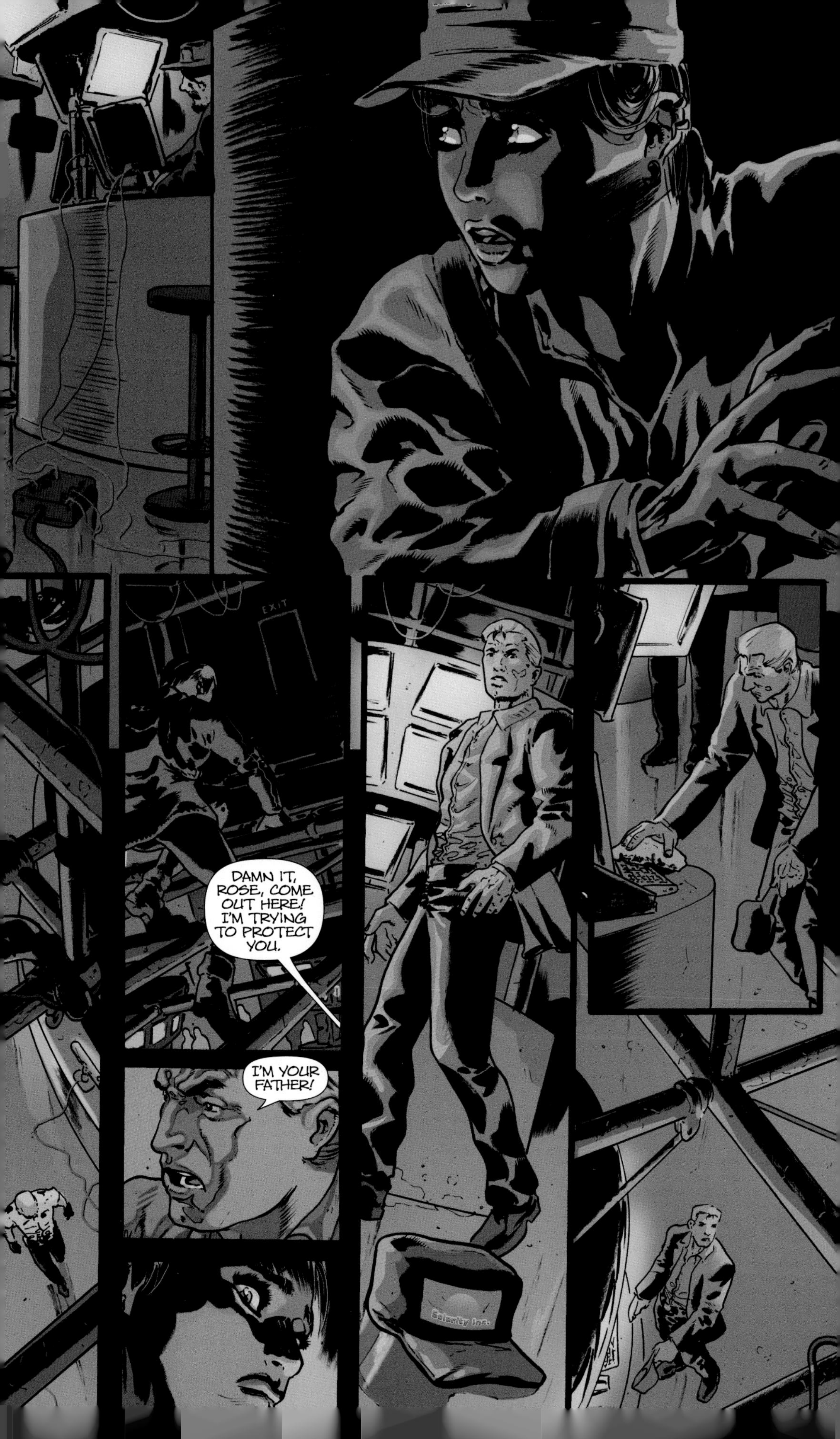
EXIT
DAMN IT, ROSE, COME OUT HERE! I'M TRYING TO PROTECT YOU.
I'M YOUR FATHER!
Solarity Inc.

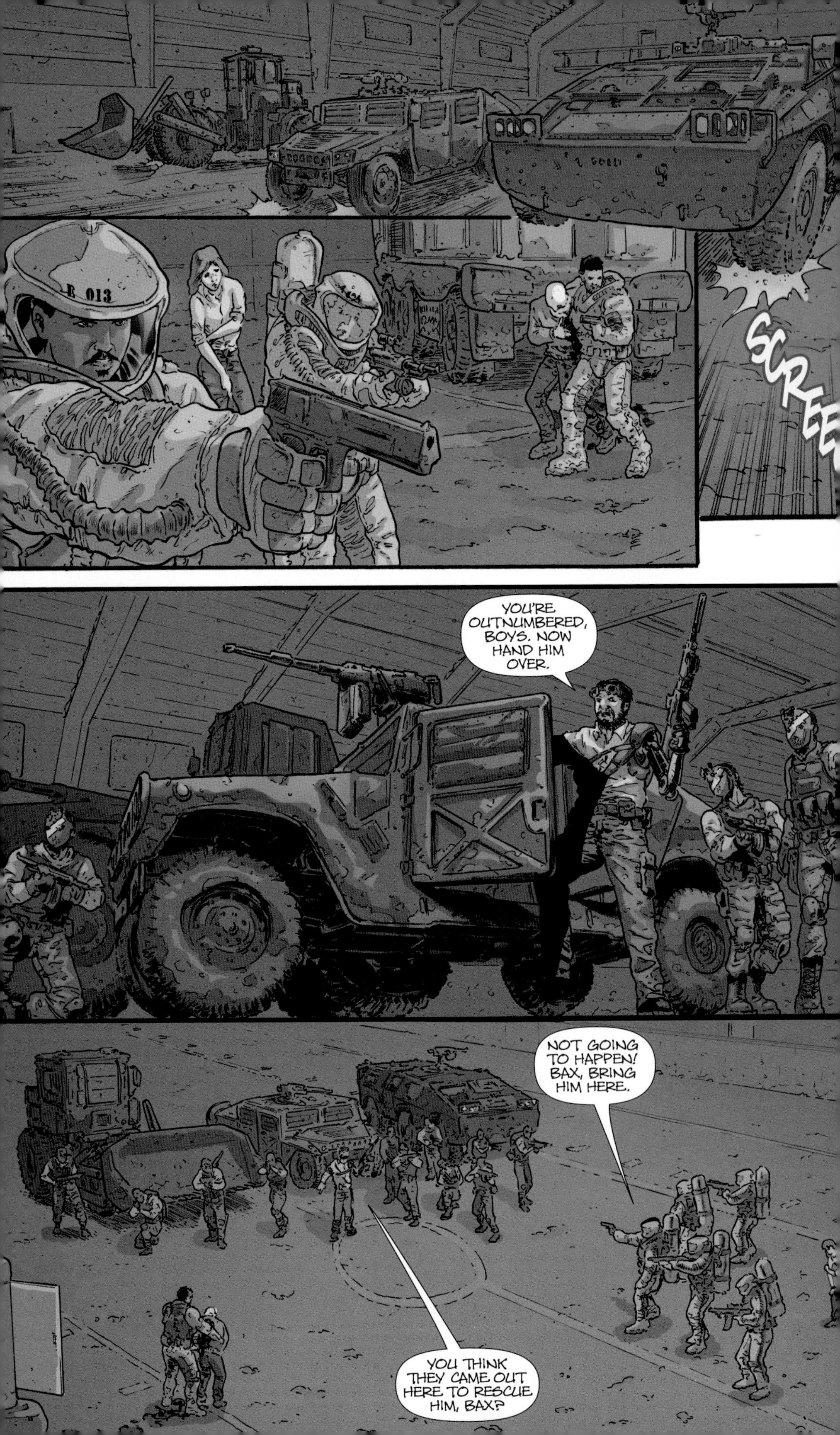
B 013
SCREEE
YOU'RE OUTNUMBERED, BOYS. NOW HAND HIM OVER.
NOT GOING TO HAPPEN! BAX, BRING HIM HERE.
YOU THINK THEY CAME OUT HERE TO RESCUE HIM, BAX?

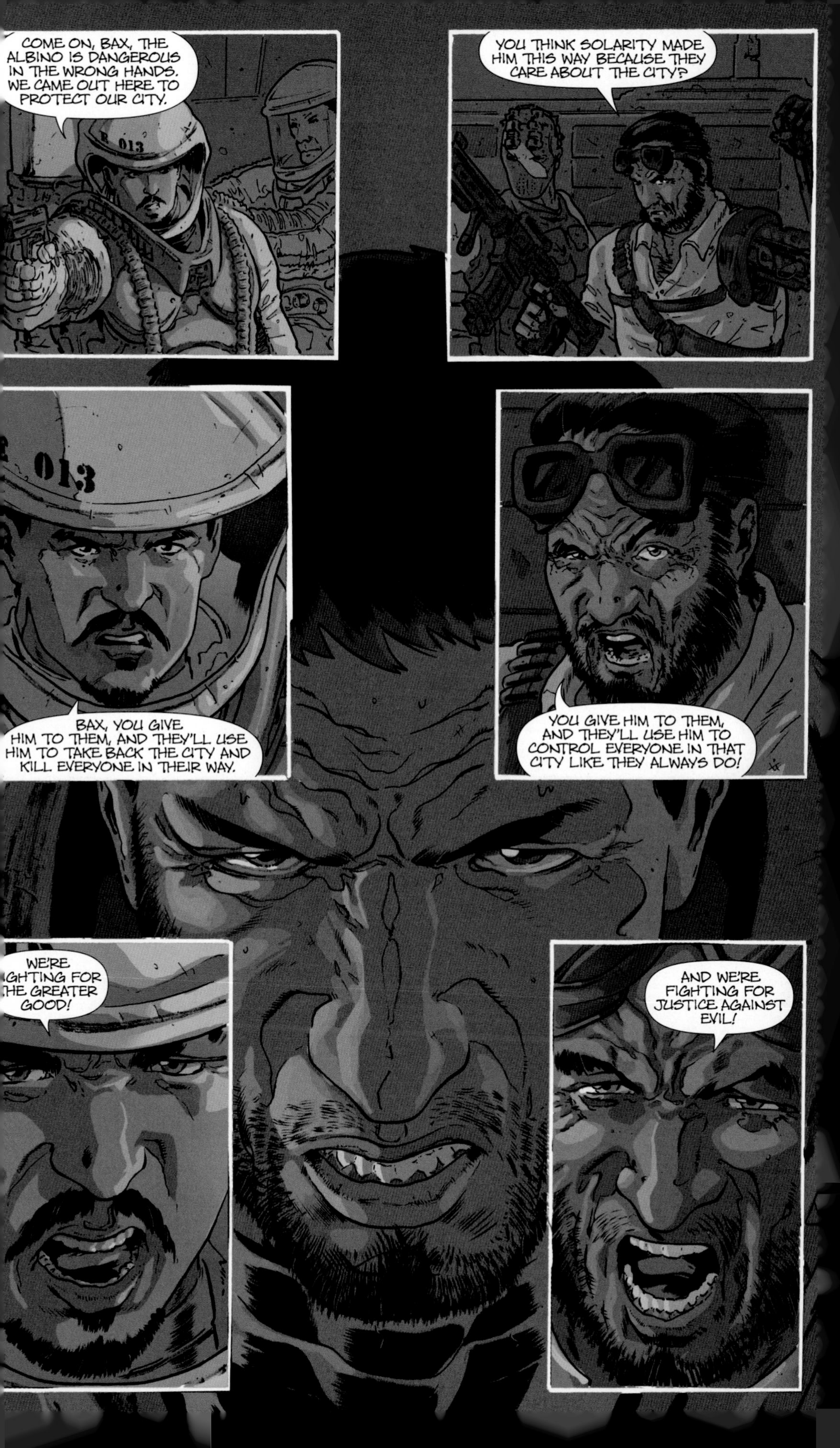
COME ON, BAX, THE ALBINO IS DANGEROUS IN THE WRONG HANDS. WE CAME OUT HERE TO PROTECT OUR CITY.
YOU THINK SOLARITY MADE HIM THIS WAY BECAUSE THEY CARE ABOUT THE CITY?
BAX, YOU GIVE HIM TO THEM, AND THEY'LL USE HIM TO TAKE BACK THE CITY AND KILL EVERYONE IN THEIR WAY.
YOU GIVE HIM TO THEM, AND THEY'LL USE HIM TO CONTROL EVERYONE IN THAT CITY LIKE THEY ALWAYS DO!
WE'RE GHTING FOR THE GREATER GOOD!
AND WE'RE FIGHTING FOR JUSTICE AGAINST EVIL!

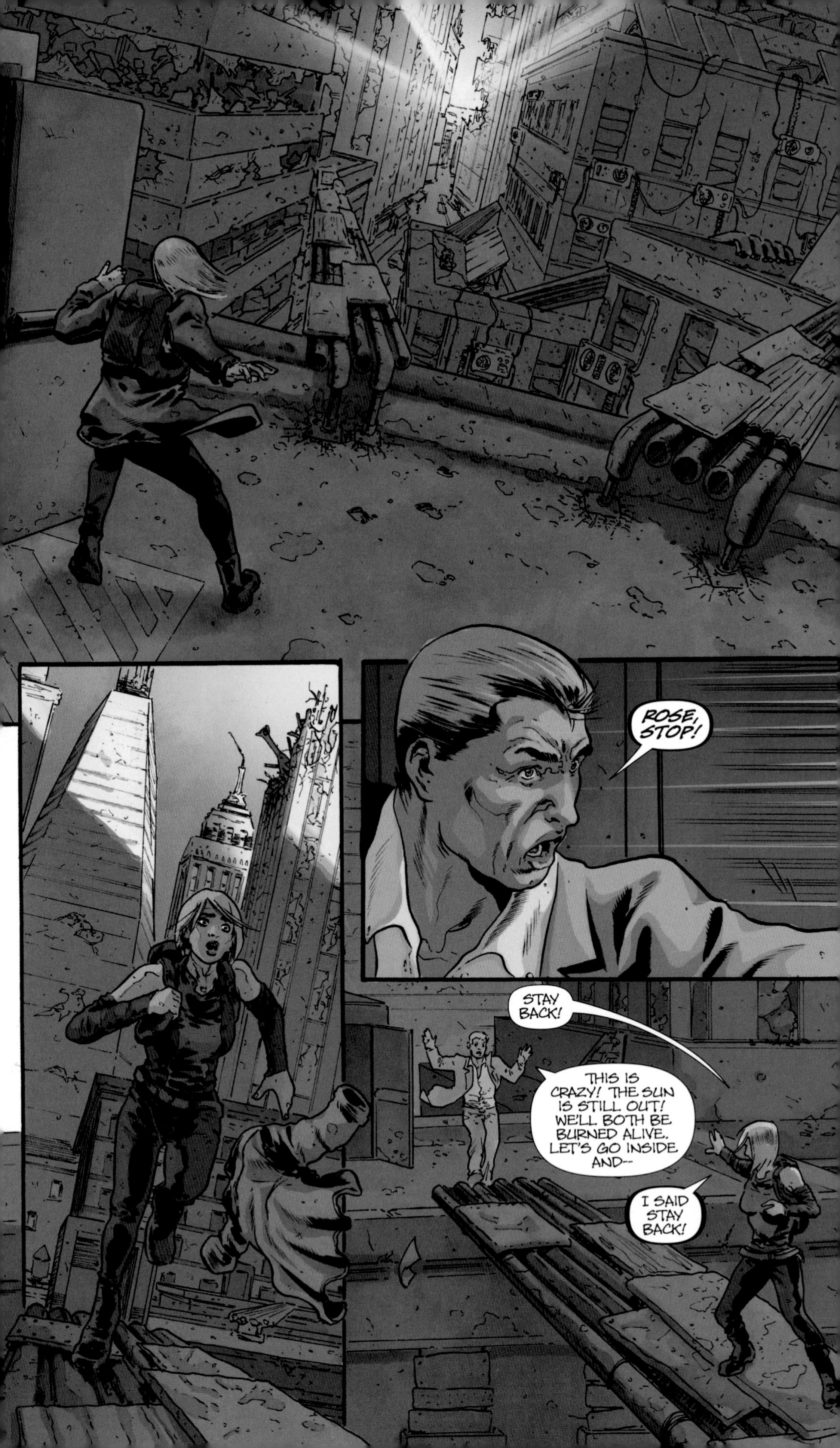
ROSE, STOP!
STAY BACK!
THIS IS CRAZY! THE SUN IS STILL OUT! WE'LL BOTH BE BURNED ALIVE. LET'S GO INSIDE AND--
I SAID STAY BACK!

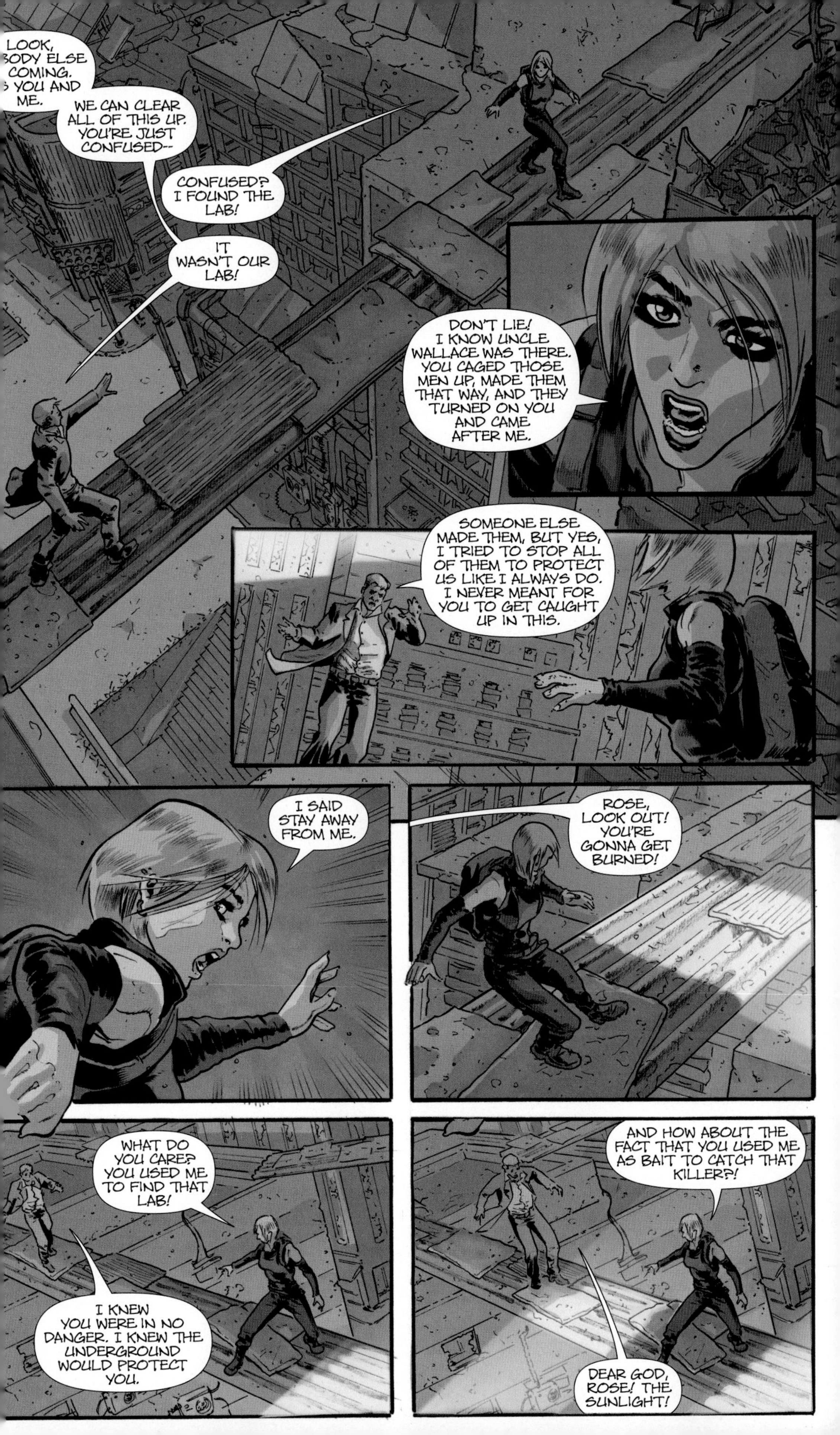
LOOK, BODY ELSE COMING. YOU AND ME.
WE CAN CLEAR ALL OF THIS UP. YOU'RE JUST CONFUSED--
CONFUSED? I FOUND THE LAB!
IT WASN'T OUR LAB!
DON'T LIE! I KNOW UNCLE WALLACE WAS THERE. YOU CAGED THOSE MEN UP, MADE THEM THAT WAY, AND THEY TURNED ON YOU AND CAME AFTER ME.
SOMEONE ELSE MADE THEM, BUT YES, I TRIED TO STOP ALL OF THEM TO PROTECT US LIKE I ALWAYS DO. I NEVER MEANT FOR YOU TO GET CAUGHT UP IN THIS.
I SAID STAY AWAY FROM ME.
ROSE, LOOK OUT! YOU'RE GONNA GET BURNED!
WHAT DO YOU CARE? YOU USED ME TO FIND THAT LAB!
I KNEW YOU WERE IN NO DANGER. I KNEW THE UNDERGROUND WOULD PROTECT YOU.
AND HOW ABOUT THE FACT THAT YOU USED ME AS BAIT TO CATCH THAT KILLER?!
DEAR GOD, ROSE! THE SUNLIGHT!

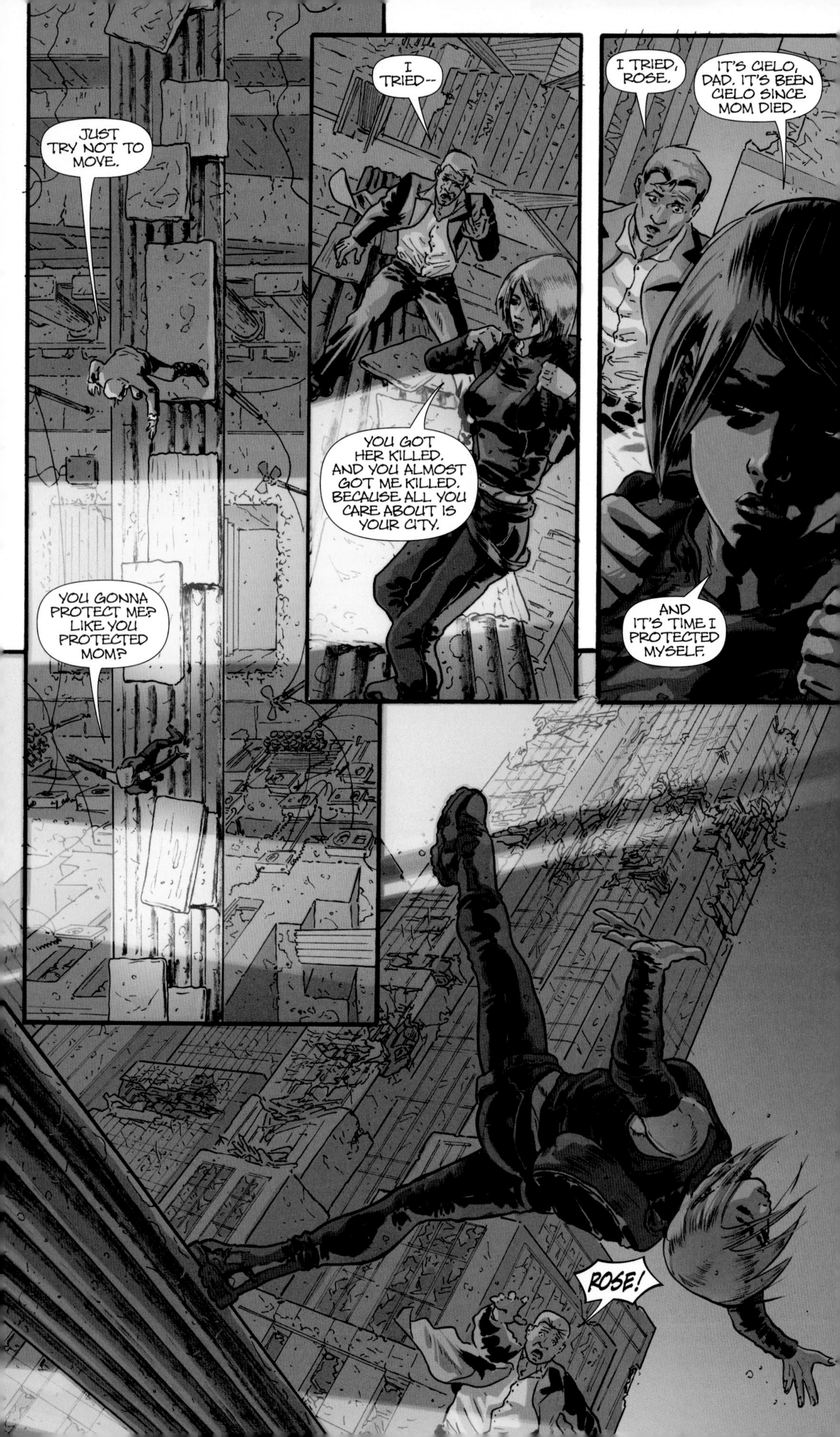
JUST TRY NOT TO MOVE.
YOU GONNA PROTECT ME? LIKE YOU PROTECTED MOM?
I TRIED--
YOU GOT HER KILLED. AND YOU ALMOST GOT ME KILLED. BECAUSE ALL YOU CARE ABOUT IS YOUR CITY.
I TRIED, ROSE.
IT'S CIELO, DAD. IT'S BEEN CIELO SINCE MOM DIED.
AND IT'S TIME I PROTECTED MYSELF.
ROSE!

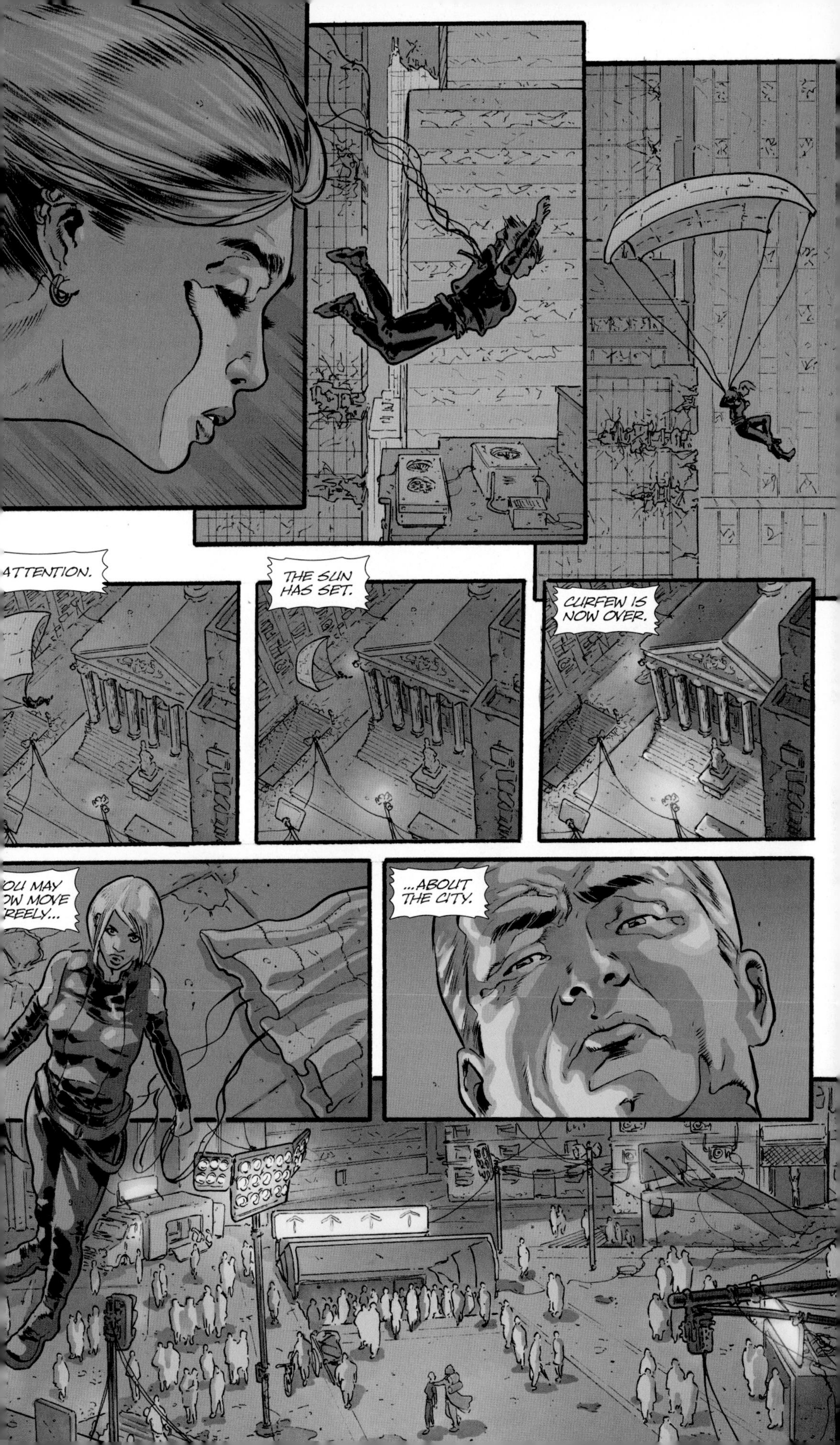
ATTENTION.
THE SUN HAS SET.
CURFEW IS NOW OVER.
OU MAY
OW MOVE
REELY...
...ABOUT THE CITY.

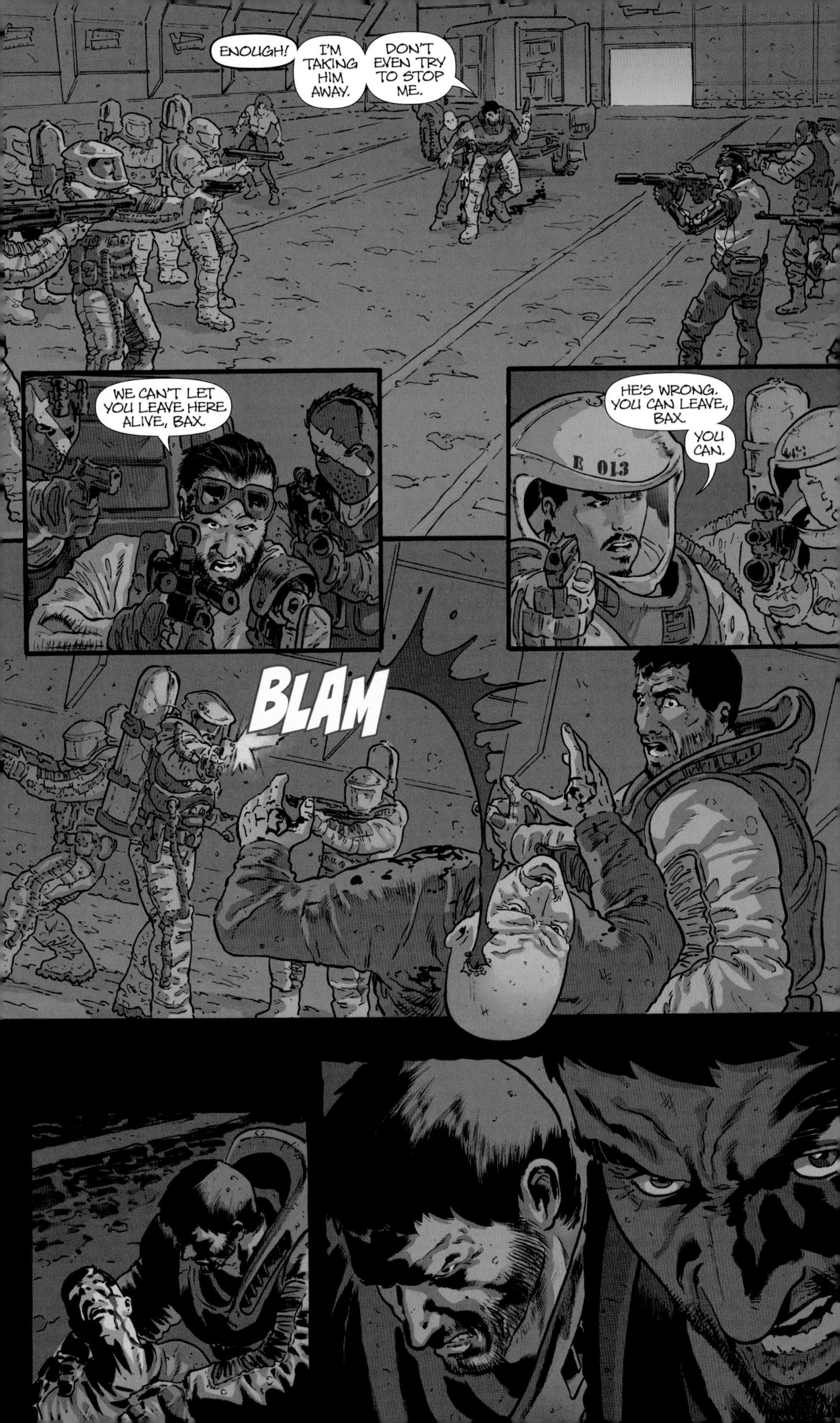
ENOUGH!
I'M TAKING HIM AWAY.
DON'T EVEN TRY TO STOP ME.
WE CAN'T LET YOU LEAVE HERE ALIVE, BAX.
HE'S WRONG. YOU CAN LEAVE, BAX.
YOU CAN.
E 013
BLAM

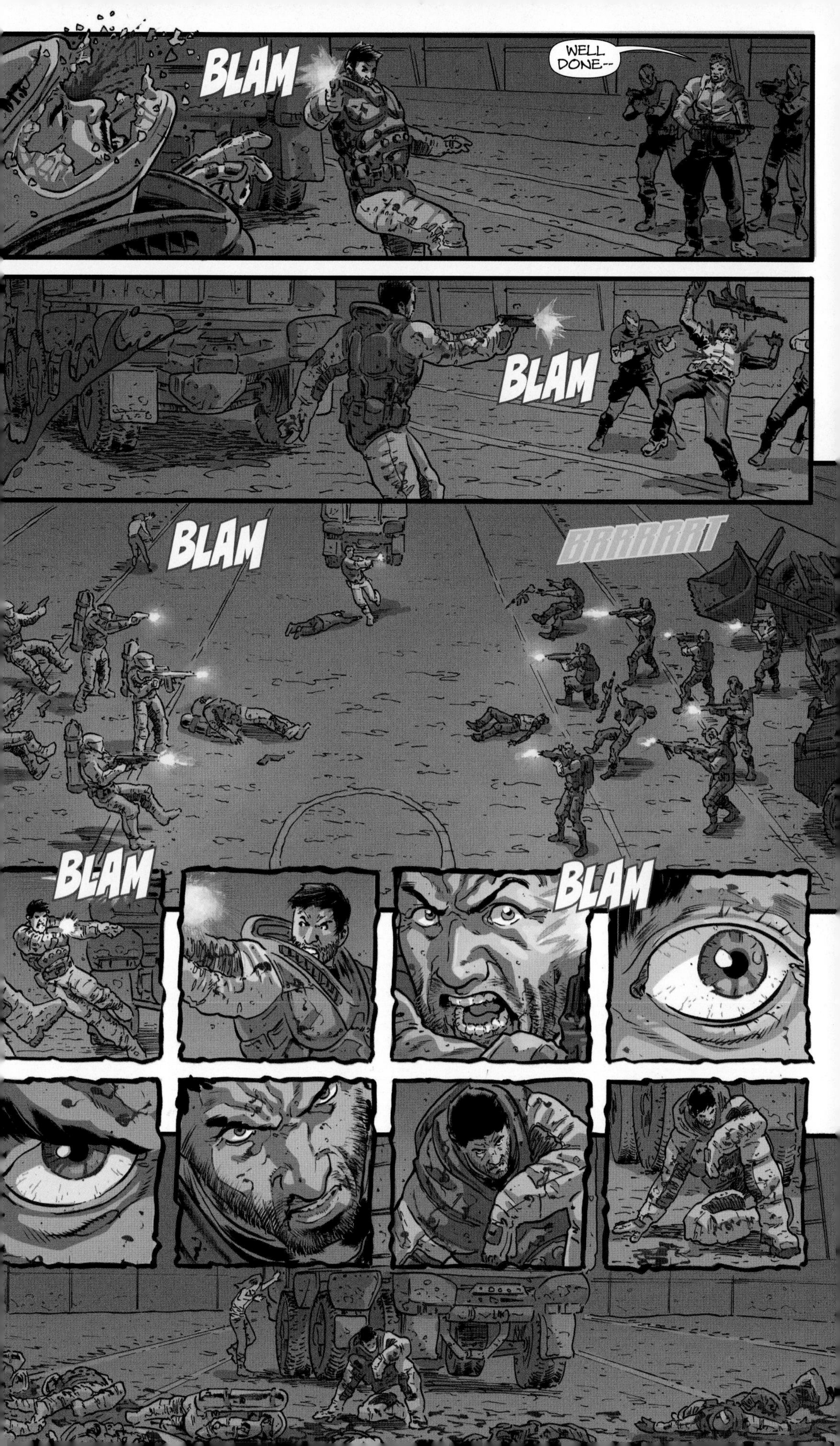
BLAM
WELL DONE--
BLAM
BLAM
BRRRRRT
BLAM
BLAM

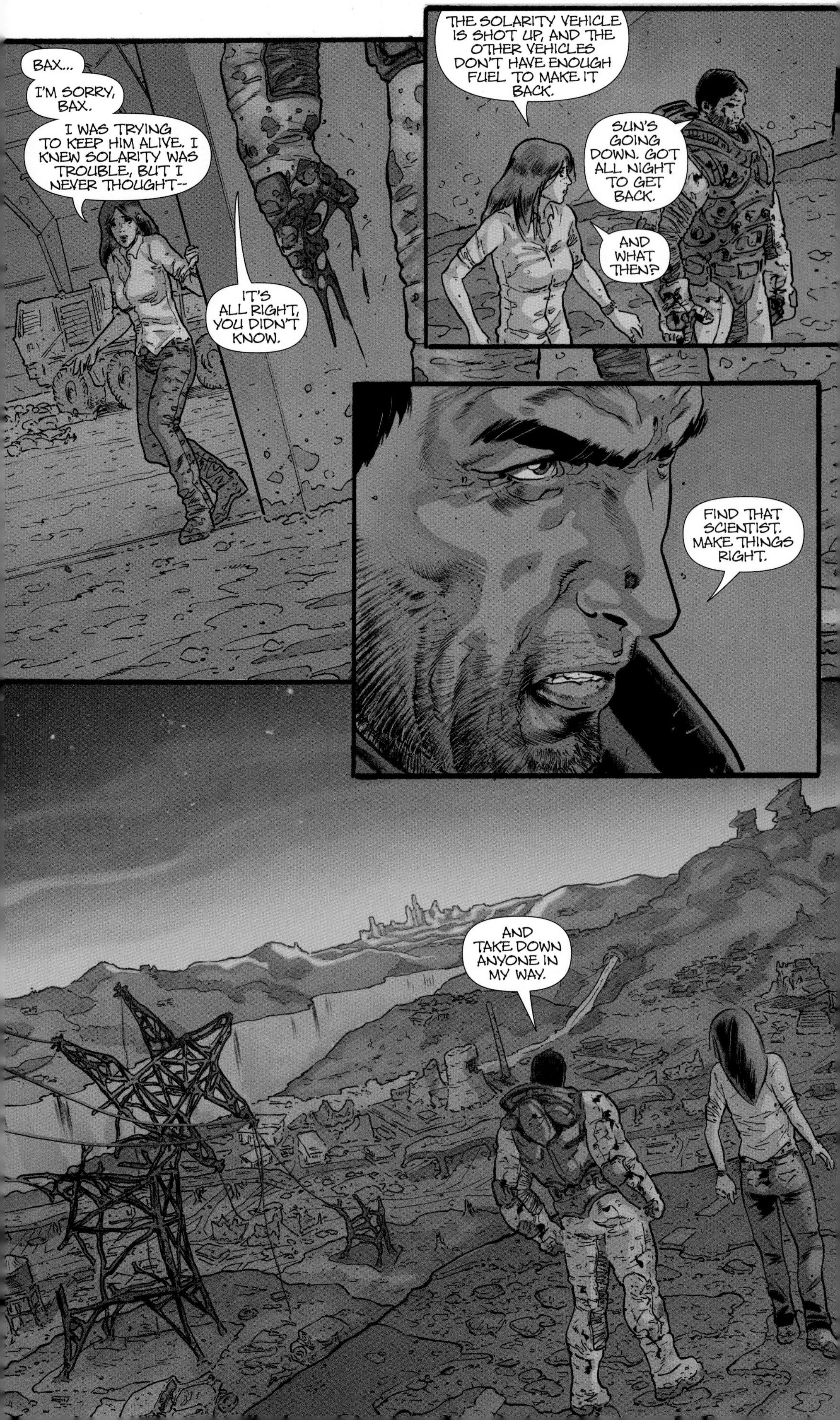

BAX...
I'M SORRY, BAX.
I WAS TRYING TO KEEP HIM ALIVE. I KNEW SOLARITY WAS TROUBLE, BUT I NEVER THOUGHT--
IT'S ALL RIGHT, YOU DIDN'T KNOW.
THE SOLARITY VEHICLE IS SHOT UP, AND THE OTHER VEHICLES DON'T HAVE ENOUGH FUEL TO MAKE IT BACK.
SUN'S GOING DOWN. GOT ALL NIGHT TO GET BACK.
AND WHAT THEN?
FIND THAT SCIENTIST. MAKE THINGS RIGHT.
AND TAKE DOWN ANYONE IN MY WAY.

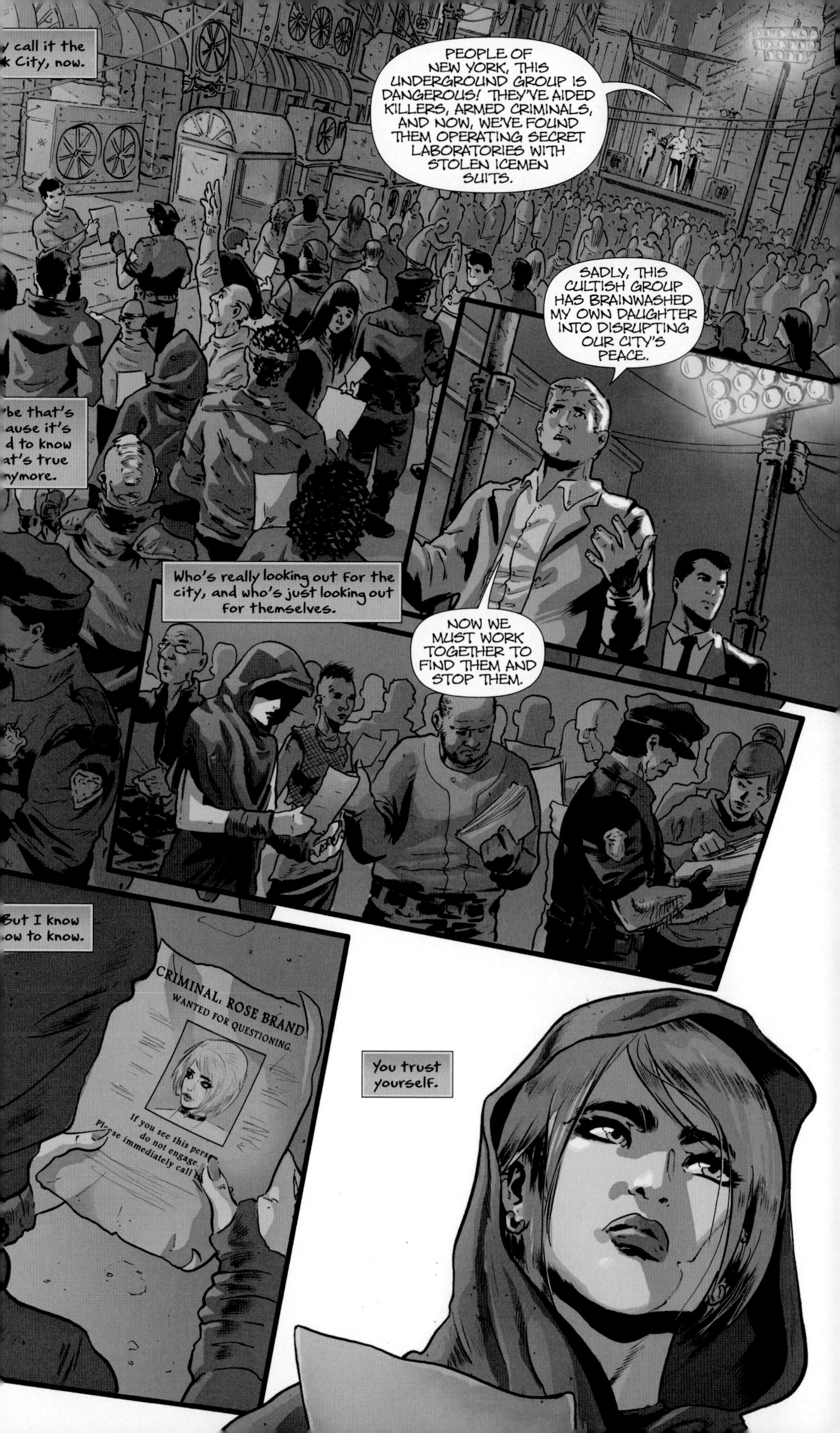

y call it the k City, now.
PEOPLE OF NEW YORK, THIS UNDERGROUND GROUP IS DANGEROUS! THEY'VE AIDED KILLERS, ARMED CRIMINALS, AND NOW, WE'VE FOUND THEM OPERATING SECRET LABORATORIES WITH STOLEN ICEMEN SUITS.
ybe that's ause it's d to know at's true nymore.
SADLY, THIS CULTISH GROUP HAS BRAINWASHED MY OWN DAUGHTER INTO DISRUPTING OUR CITY'S PEACE.
Who's really looking out for the city, and who's just looking out for themselves.
NOW WE MUST WORK TOGETHER TO FIND THEM AND STOP THEM.
But I know ow to know.
CRIMINAL, ROSE BRAND
WANTED FOR QUESTIONING.
If you see this pers
do not engage.
Please immediately call
You trust yourself.

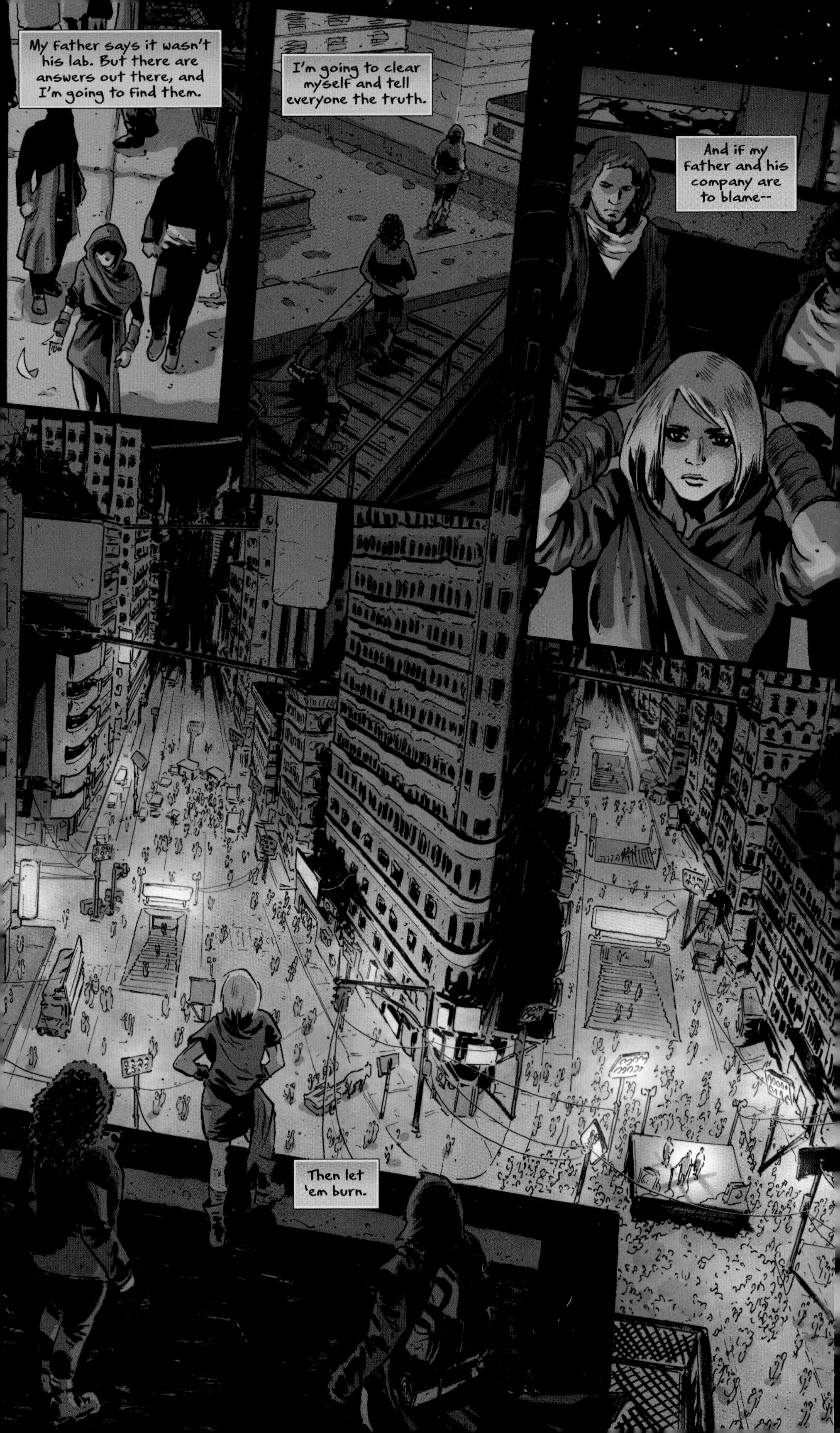
My father says it wasn't his lab. But there are answers out there, and I'm going to find them.
I'm going to clear myself and tell everyone the truth.
And if my father and his company are to blame--
Then let 'em burn.

PUBLIC NOTICE
IMPEACHMENT OF MAYOF

Attention New York City citizens,

Mayor Holden has been impeached and forcibly removed from his post. He an his office were engaged in over nineteen counts of authoritative and anti-democrati practices deemed illegal by our prevailing New York City court system. When face with his criminal acts, he attempted to circumvent our democratic institutions, dissolv our judicial system, and remove, without cause or right, all appointed members c government that opposed him. He ignored warnings from the New York Cit Emergency Task Force. His policies threatened our laws and civil liberties. Despite th collapse of our federal government, the New York City municipality maintains it authority and duty to uphold the laws and protect the citizens.

On Sunday, members of the New York City Emergency Task Force, consistin of New York Police Officers and Fire Department Officers, took control of the Mayor Office and City Hall. Newly appointed Police Chief Wallace Brandt accepted Mayc Holden's resignation. Mayor Holden is currently being held until a new sentencin hearing can be scheduled for his crimes.

Fire Chief Nicholas Brandt remarked, "With this action, we ensure that ou cherished American way of life is not lost. The people of New York City are strong an will never give up hope in the face of hardship." Brandt has served as the Fire Chie since the Day of the Flare, when he heroically helped Mayor Holden restore order t the city's emergency services and power grid. In addition to assisting the New Yor City Emergency Task Force in their efforts to provide food and shelter, Brandt company Solarity has been providing electricity to the entire city of Manhattan.

We face the light. We survive in the face of all. New mayoral elections will t scheduled as soon as possible, but until that time, the Emergency Task Force wi ensure the smooth operation of the Mayor's office and all of its said duties and publi services. Please direct all inquiries to Gregor Van Gorn of the Emergency Task Force now located in City Hall.

The New York City Emergency Task Forc

llo Nick,

You're about to have a bad day.

I have your science experiment. The man who doesn't burn in
unlight. Caught him traveling on the road. He's in my custody now.
Bravo, however you achieved this miracle. He told me all about
ow your scientist turned him into this abnormality. How did you do
t? You'll have to tell me when I come back to my city.

And when I do, if you want to live, you will tell the citizens
that you have discovered I am innocent of those crimes that you
framed me for, and you will allow me re-entry into the city.
Because if you don't right your wrongs, I will study this man, find
out this power, and then I will use it against you. I will have my
city back.

The true mayor of New York City,

Mayor Holden

Dear Readers,

ECLIPSE is my first comic book.

Eight years ago, I dreamed of writing a comic book.
I was also working a graveyard shift as a poker dealer.
I toiled at night and slept during the day. I had studied
writing in school, but not yet found success. I was living a
lifestyle different than most. I was disconnected from my
friends and family. Looking back, I can say...
...my life was facing darkness.

But I've always tried to see the bright side of things.

And that's what ECLIPSE is really about to me.
Being hopeful in dark times.

On behalf of the entire ECLIPSE Creative Team, we want to thank
Matt Hawkins and Top Cow for giving us the chance to tell this story.
We want to thank everyone at Top Cow and Image Comics for helping
us every step of the way. We want to thank every comic reviewer and
blogger and podcaster and fan who offered a kind word about ECLIPSE.

And we want to thank you, yes you, the reader, for picking up this comic
book and reading it! I buy a lot of comic books, but many land on the
shelf and wait to be read. It takes a commitment to read a comic book.
I hope you find ECLIPSE thrilling and entertaining, and maybe a little
thought-provoking. We hope you connect to it.

We'd love for you to stay connected. Reach out on social media!

The world and story of ECLIPSE are just getting started...

All the best,

Zack Kaplan

A PEEK BEHIND THE SCENES OF THE CREATIVE PROCESS OF ECLIPSE!

From the very beginning, we've tried to open up our process and give our readers a real glimpse into what goes on behind the scenes making a comic book. In Issues 1–4, we shared how a page goes from layout to ink, how we created our characters, how we did colors and letters.

So as we continue our exploration of the process and as we launch the second arc, what better topic could there be than how we went about building and expanding the world? When you do a second arc, you want to take the world places that it hasn't gone. But how do you magnify a world like ECLIPSE? We set out to see Bax take us beyond the city borders while Cielo explores deep into the city underground and Solarity itself.

Our team spent a lot of time discussing the new landscapes and that expanding world, so we wanted to share with you some excerpts from the script, some of Gio's amazing pencils and our comments on them all. Hope you enjoy!

A glimpse into the process behind

ECLIPSE

Solarity & The Border

ISSUE 5, PAGE 8, PANEL THREE

A very wide shot of the armored truck departing across the Marble Hill Bridge. (Google it. It's awesom The bridge has been transformed into a heavily fortified way in and out of the city. The shot is across t water, so we see New York City in the background, behind the bridge and its security. If any readers ha been wondering how isolated New York City is, we'll see it here. We may even see the coast with milita fortifications. The bridge towers will have harsh spotlights, maybe some police/security snipers. T vantage point will see the truck coming more towards us, but not entirely. The vehicle is probably small this shot.

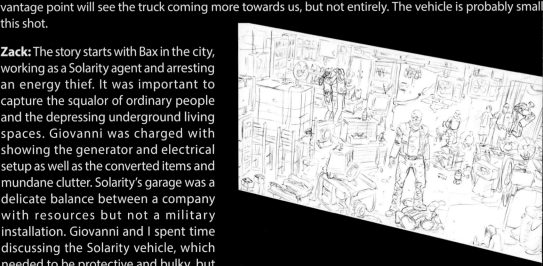

Zack: The story starts with Bax in the city, working as a Solarity agent and arresting an energy thief. It was important to capture the squalor of ordinary people and the depressing underground living spaces. Giovanni was charged with showing the generator and electrical setup as well as the converted items and mundane clutter. Solarity's garage was a delicate balance between a company with resources but not a military installation. Giovanni and I spent time discussing the Solarity vehicle, which needed to be protective and bulky, but not too aggressive or weaponized. The border was especially fun to explore. The city has been cut off, so security had to be represented. The border panel sparked a discussion about water, but the sun has not become hotter, it's just "changed", so while organic life is burned, water is unaffected.

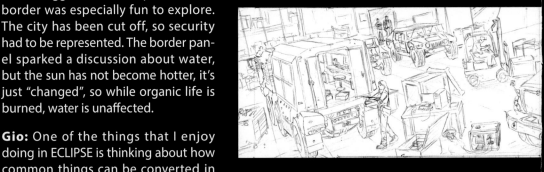

Gio: One of the things that I enjoy doing in ECLIPSE is thinking about how common things can be converted in this new world: so inside this energy thief's apartment I have drawn an old office computer used to direct the energy in the house, a power generator, car batteries used to keep a fridge turned on, industrial tanks for the drinking water, etc. Basically, it may seem like a whole mess, but it's not in a random order. There is reasoning behind it all, even if they are only simple details in a background. There is more order in the Solarity garage, but even there, things are converted and adapted, so you can see a laptop connected to a PC and then to a power generator. The water thing, yes, we knew readers would wonder about water in the ECLIPSE world, but we've made sure to consider it carefully and have a perfect answer.

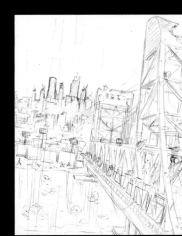

is our post-apocalyptic wasteland, as the little armored truck motors across the road, from one side of the page to the other. It's nighttime, but the moonlight should cast enough light to see some carnage. The traveling along a highway, but cars have been pushed to the side. We might see burnt corpses from the re, never cleaned up. We might also see more recent carnage. I don't think we see signs of life, so there's fires in the distance or people watching. But we can see crashed semi-trucks. We can see a building a biker gang might have adorned with skeletons and dark stuff before vacating the area. Maybe they took over a mini mart or gas station that we're passing. We don't see New York City anymore, that's for sure.

Zack: I think from the moment we got the second arc I knew we had to go outside the city and see what was out there. Creating the post-apocalyptic landscape was a fun challenge, because it needed to be unique. Of course, that wasn't hard. It just required a focus on the burnt bodies. We also wanted to capture the lawless nature of the world beyond the city. It helped to enforce the idea that despite the city's dystopian feel, there's a benefit to living there. We captured scenes of violence along the road, and one especially helpful device was seeing a barbaric outpost where someone has strewn their victims up along an oil truck and school bus to burn them alive. There had to be a whole little story in the detail of that sniper tower, and Gio did a great job with that.

Gio: I've waited all my life to draw a page like this: tens (or hundreds?) of rusted cars a desolate landscape, the contrast between the natural light of the moon, above the artificial cemetery of rotten, dead things created by the man. Every time I draw a new part of the ECLIPSE world, I always try to create something both alien and familiar at the same time, and I think that this came out very well. The little tower in the middle of the outpost a table, a chair, a sniper rifle and a little lamp. Yes, there is a little story behind that the story of the people who were living there, like the story behind every survivor in this new world.

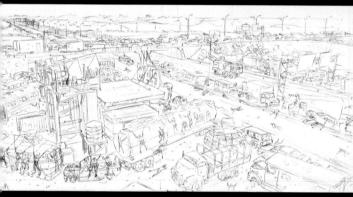

ax and Wallace stand on the edge of the hill, looking down at West Point's campus. The Gothic buildi
:and tall with towers in the air. There's little apocalyptic damage, but instead we see heavy modificat
o the campus to protect from sunlight, as well as heavy fortifications.

ack: I needed a compound for the x-Mayor of the city and his armed ang to live in, but it needed to be badass place to survive. It couldn't e mundane, because the sunlight as too dangerous for someone to urvive in a mundane location. It had to e special. Looking around the New ork City area, it didn't take long to ecide on West Point Academy. It had campus that could easily be converted nd protected from the sun. It would ave had a cache of food and weapons. he fortifications were easy to imagine long the walls and Gothic buildings, but : took some exploration to figure out the ate. Gio had some ideas and ultimately ve went with giant shipping containers eing raised and lowered by a military ehicle. That alone made Bax's arrival ave a real dangerous and suspenseful eel to it.

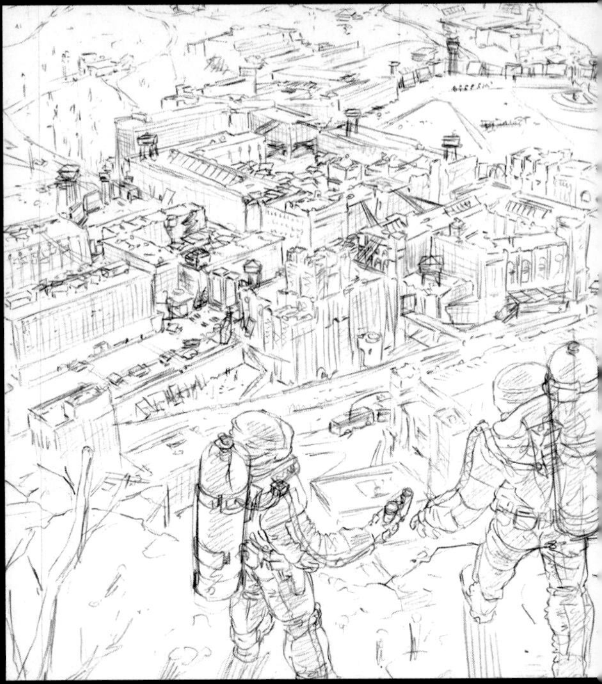

Gio: Looking at the pencils of the West Point panel, I find myself thinking about ny relationship with both pencils and nks. The pencils are the savage part of me. Sometimes they are very rough, not defined, un-rendered, and I'm never nappy when I stare at one of my penciled pages. For me, a penciled page is omething unfinished, not perfect. I use he inks to control that savage part of my art: my more precise ink lines apply order o the rough pencils ones. My brush and pens have the duty to maintain the order on the page. It's like the bad cop/ good cop thing. But I don't know yet which one between inks and pencils are the good and the bad. I loved creating the gate system of West Point. Again, we are talking about converted elements: containers and the truck used to create a safe barrier system, which is more visible in the next book.

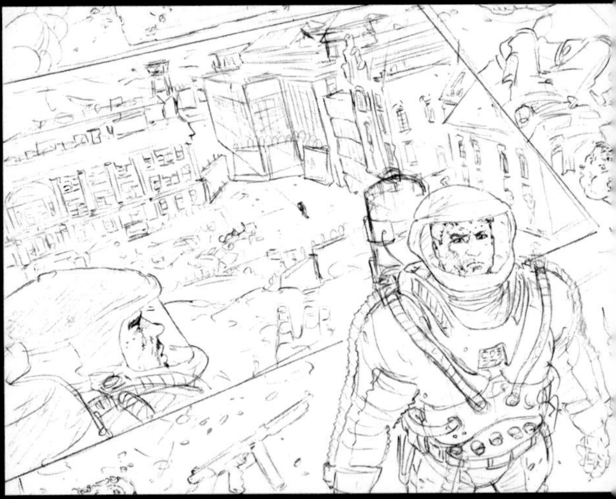

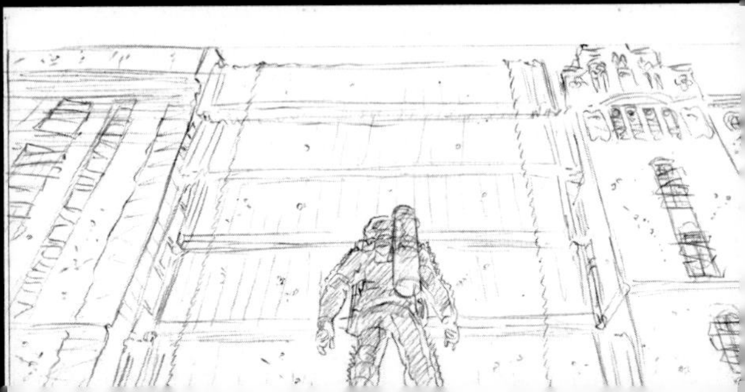

e wide shot of the tunnels. It should have a different feel than the tunnels we saw before, but similar
ner ways. There's a main crowd through the tunnel, and in the center of the crowd, walking through is Cielo. (This panel should be another one with lots to see, but if you can't fit all of these ideas in, don rry.) There's a marketplace for food with masses of lines. A manager barks at people to stay orderly, whil curity pushes to get the best produce. Elsewhere, we see a row of giant fish farm tanks, where salmo tter around. A man on a ladder reaches in to the top of the tank to retrieve fish for the iced display at h ll below, manned by his family. Elsewhere, a gang of children have stolen a fish and carve it up to eat i orner. There's a man spouting theories about the Flare, holding up a picket that might read: THE ALIEN STROYED OUR SUN AND THE GOVERNMENT KNEW. And a few people might stand there listening ybe there's a tunnel to housing and a landlord pushing out a family with everything they can carr cause they didn't pay their rent on time. There's still poverty and crime and disillusionment everywher we look. And there's a night club nearby, wit neon lights and tons of club kids getting read to go inside.

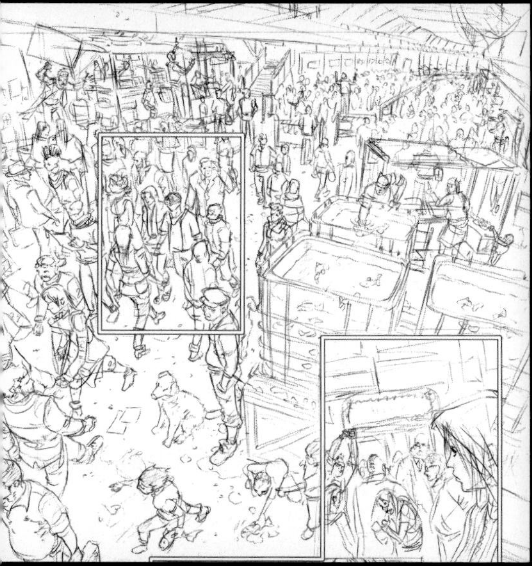

Zack: Cielo is on the move in the undergroun tunnels of ECLIPSE, and it gave us the chanc to use a lot of detail to see more of the worlc I asked myself what aspects of the world wer still unknown. Food? Let's see that there are fis merchants, along with street kids stealing tha fish. Theories on the sunlight? One man wit a picket sign thinks it was aliens who destroye our sun. Later, in the dark market, we see mor weapons and exotic items for sale. At ever turn, it was important to capture the feel c living under the surface, claustrophobic, tigh and dark, and Gio does an excellent job wit these never-ending tunnels of over-crowde masses trying to get through their day. Wit the police station, we were able t show people are using escalators an stairs to go in and out of buildings o the surface, while avoiding the stree entrances.

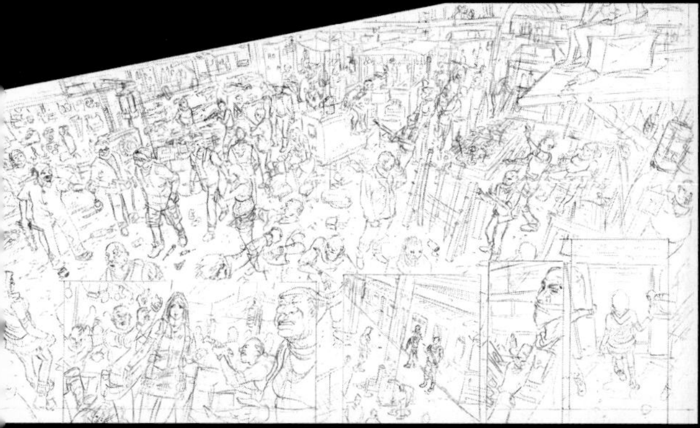

Gio: I'm pretty sure that ECLIPS readers have learned how much I lov to draw crowded scenes during th various issues of this series. Probabl a lot of artists hate when they fin out that there will be a crowde scene on a page. For me, it's lik Christmastime; Zack knows it very wel I especially enjoyed the black market i Issue #6. It had a different mood give by different people and stuff on sale This is one of the pages where yo can stare at every single person on i each one of them is doing somethin specific; they are not simply standin mannequins.

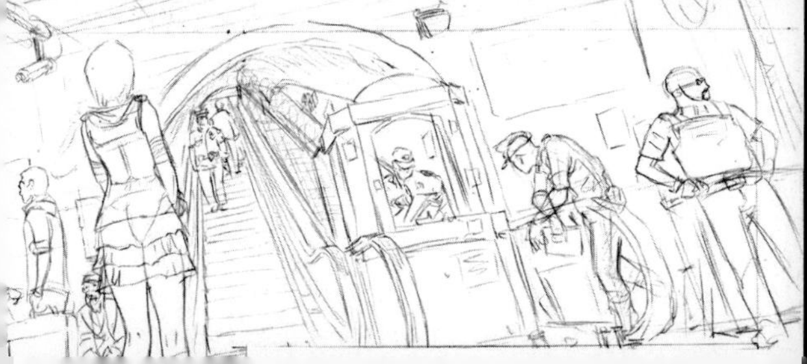

ISSUE 6, PAGE 16, PANEL ONE

Cielo races into a large, abandoned construction tunnel with giant, unfinished scaffolding holding up the tunnel. Some supports have been erected to hold up the tunnel, but further down, there was a cave-in and rays of light shine through from the street-level above. The scaffolding has different levels. And we can see empty sewer pipes here and there, coming out of the dirt walls. At the end of the tunnel lies a massive circular drill machine, left abandoned as well. These tunnels shouldn't have an archaeological feel too much. Large cavern with various metal/aluminum scaffolding at different tiers, abandoned construction materials, and sewer rivers flowing below, all need to feel ECLIPSE.

Jack: Cielo's investigation and journey take her to a construction area where new tunnels are being built. This was a chance to show how the city is creating living spaces underground, because they are expanding into new areas and tunnels. We have already seen that in the first arc with the residential communities being built, but now we get to answer the question as to how that was being done. The city has access to giant drills and machines, and crews are using scaffolding to install supports into these areas and then convert them. This particular area is abandoned, but it still effectively expanded the world. Gio and I spent time discussing the drilling machine, the orientation of the tunnel and the scaffolding area.

Gio: This whole sequence inside the tunnel was particular in terms of art: in the entire series, I never had to draw so many blacks and shadows like in this scene, and for me it was a strange sensation. Once I started ECLIPSE, I eliminated the heavy inks I was used to on my previous Dynamite pulp series like *The Shadow* or *Green Hornet*, and I was happy to make such a drastic change. But when I started this tunnel sequence, I knew that the best choice was to return to those heavy inks, with full blacks, big brushed (and less fine pens), the atmosphere deserved them. And now that I look at it, it seems so right: the contrast between the heavy black lines of the deeper underground places, and the more thin, dry pen lines of the surface world, hit by the sun. Yes, this is right.

As you all know, we love sharing our process with readers and this issue, we wanted to show you some more character designs. Any time you continue the story and expand the world one inexplicably meets new characters. As a writer, I always like to think about how the new characters will challenge our protagonists. I approach character in a variety of ways and ask myself many questions about a new character.

How do they see the world? What are they after? How do they confront conflict when their desires are challenged? Some characters see the world as a war and they must win every battle. Some see it as a battle for truth, lined with pitfalls of deceit. Some see it as a game of wits, where only the smartest can survive. Each character's worldview affects not just what they want, but how they speak and act. Without knowing a character's internal emotional engine, how they respond to anything, they drift and can be inconsistent. And of course, we're all victims of our own pasts, so a character's backstory is instrumental in informing how they are the way they are.

We set out to both grow our existing characters, Bax, Cielo, Nick and Everly, while creating new characters for our world: Etta the Conductor or our former Mayor Holden. As an artist, Gio takes a character description and transforms it into a living and breathing person that will take on many shapes throughout the story. We wanted to share with you the character descriptions, along with Gio's early character sketches, inks from the pages and his comments. We hope you enjoy the process.

DAVID BAXTER, aka BAX

Bax, our hero, hasn't changed too much since his last appearance, but we certainly might see him a bit more rugged. His new role with Solarity might be taking its toll. But he'll still exhibit the same gruff, withdrawn manner we've come to expect from him, despite his slow emotional growth.

Giovanni: Bax obviously has the same features that he did in the first four issues, but since he confronts different situations in this new arc than he did before, both in terms of action and emotions, you will discover new aspects of his character through his different expressions and body language. The Icemen suits are also the same, but I changed tiny details. For example, in issues #1–4, the front torso part was a big unique piece of metal. From issue #5, there are more action sequences, so I needed a more mobile version of the suit. That's why I divided the torso part into different pieces, in order to allow the wearer of the suit to be more agile. Icemen suits 2.0.

ROSE BRANDT, aka CIELO

Cielo will have changed a bit, as she slowly becomes more fraught by her recent experience with the killer. She's a bit traumatized, concerned for her safety and driven to find answers. Her outfit is a mix of her prior rich-girl look and a new, more street look, as she goes into the underground looking for answers.

Giovanni:
In the first series, Cielo was more of a victim, always finding a way to get into trouble, and always acting in a passive and defensive way in terms of body language. In this new arc, she shows a strong desire to act, transforming her into a far more active person. It's really a new way of life for her, and so drawing her required a totally different approach in terms of art. Sometimes I asked myself if I was drawing Cielo or Lara Croft! Zack had a clear idea for her clothing, and I worked off of that

a THE CONDUCTOR

ler of the Underground, is driven by She knows the world is full of ulterior o she takes care, plays her card close est and makes sure to avoid dangers. , she never lies or manipulates herself. a hard life before the Flare, but she opportunity to provide food to people termath, and when the companies, ity, tried to run the show, she went ound with her operation. She has no with death or violence or aggression, she believes it is better to give in to nature as self-interested killers. She deals with everyone, but she never t it. She's also deep and spiritual, as herself looking for the truth in life, the eaning in people.

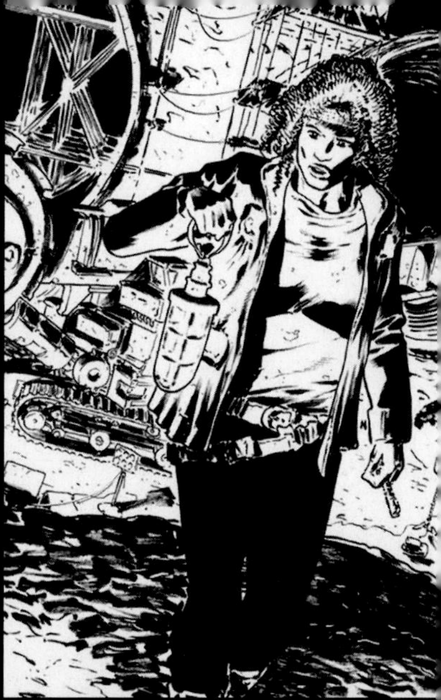

: I knew Etta the first time I read Zack's description of her. She is a woman w evere and merciless, but also so protective and right about what she believes o find the right look for a character that readers will see both as a "good" one ar n terms of facial expressions, as an artist, you always risk going too much in one r, and then you can lose the character altogether. Both aspects of the characte ted, and that was the challenge in drawing Etta. Zack likes to say often that th s are never totally good or totally bad, and Etta is a perfect example of ar

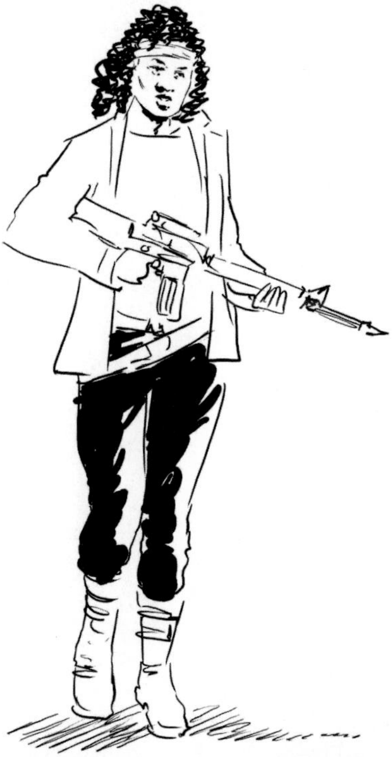

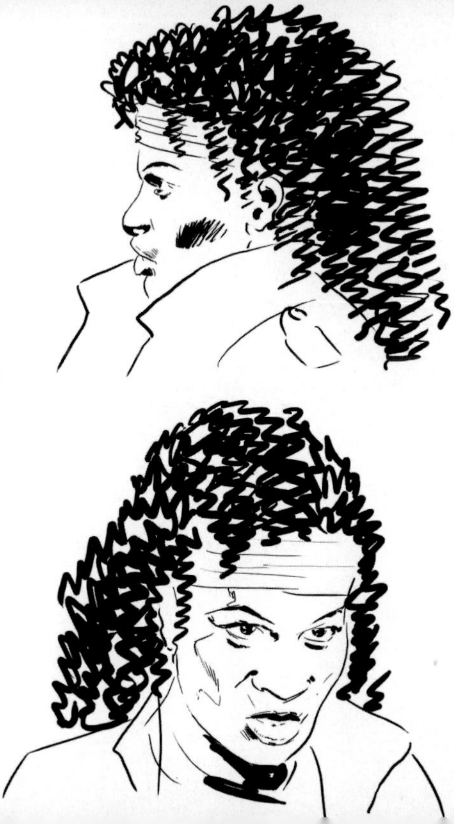

EX-MAYOR HOLDEN

Our former mayor from the flashback in Issue #2 has changed dramatically. He's been cast out of New York City by Solarity and the current powers that be. He's fallen on hard times, even lost his arm, which he's replaced with a new mechanical one, a third-world replacement with a shoulder strap. He's a darker shell of a man now. He always thought he was smart, but he feels that he lost control of his city because he wasn't strategic or strong enough. Never again. Now he leads the soldiers of West Point and he does so with a emphasis on order and control. He wants revenge and he's planning his takedown of New York City and Solarity.

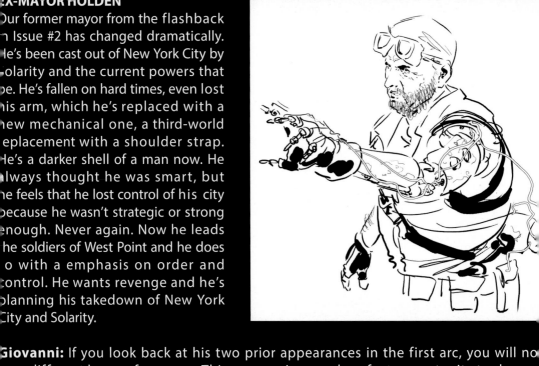

Giovanni: If you look back at his two prior appearances in the first arc, you will no how different he was from now. This was a unique and perfect opportunity to show w happens to the characters of this world before the Flare and after. I assure you that under beard, the same man exists, but the world around him has changed. Zack and I discussed artificial arm a lot, and whether to have it be something fully artificial or something less dr like an injured arm. Ultimately, Zack stressed how hard Holden's time had been outside the so the completely artificial arm worked best.

e men are former West Point cadets and
y soldiers, but also just refugees from
nd the Northeast. Holden leads about
men here. They have access to military
and weapons, but they wear uniforms
n attempt to maintain order. The
orms are military in style, but ECLIPSE
more post-apocalyptic. There is also a
ass looking Sergeant that Holden leans
There should be some distinguishing
k that perhaps represents their new order.

vanni: It was important that these soldiers
e weapons and gear that was not too
icular. In the world of ECLIPSE, it's important
emember that other than the Icemen suits,
e are not really "new" things, so the weapons
dn't be new. Also, many of these soldiers
e army men, so I realized they would want to
ntain that soldier look. I tried to give them
mask, because I didn't want to distract the
der with a lot of different faces. That's why I
ded for the classic ballistic mask, but with a
ue detail, a sword painted over it from the
st Point Academy logo (similar to the white
d over the Uruk-hai from LOTR).

SCI-FI   SCI-FI/SPLINTER CELL   SWAT/SCI-FI

PAINT BALL   TACTICAL   HOLDEN'S now

ON

on is another albino able to go out into the sunlight. Orson was always a
onsible man, a carpenter who never thought about his place in the world.
-Flare, he worked on the Underground Farms. Unknown circumstances
e brought him to be immune to the deadly light rays, but rather than be
trolled by others or help society in anyway, he would prefer to have
hing to do with it all. He feels the world is void of morality and the best
g he can do is disconnect from it. He has no interest in using his gift to
o any group or person. In short, he has lost hope.

vanni: Zack and I searched for a guy with
peration in his facial features. In the first series,
antagonist, the albino priest, was using his
wers" of sunlight immunity to do bad things,
he was sure of himself and his capabilities
e he knew he was unique to normal people.
Orson was a character that even with his
cial, unique capabilities, wasn't inspired
n the desire to take advantage of people.
doesn't seem to care that he's got this gift. I
k after some tries, we totally found him. It'd
ike if someone lived in the normal world with
perman powers, but they were always sad.
t might be impossible, but that was exactly
t we were looking for with Orson.

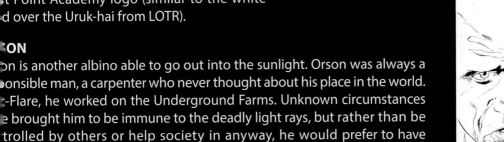

Coloring comics definitely doesn't get the credit it deserves. Gio's lines and artwork are stunning, but colors bring atmosphere, style and life into the images. It's an integral part of the story-telling, which is why we can't explore it enough!

During the first arc of ECLIPSE, we were blessed with two great colorists, but the nature of comic books is that creative teams are not always able to stay together. For the second arc, we brought on newcomer Flavio Dispenza as our colorist, fresh out of Italy's Scuola Internazionale di Comics. That's comic book art school! Can you believe that? This is his first American comic book! Talk about talent!

However, it was challenging because we quickly were thrust into a monthly series, and Flavio was given the near impossible task of blending his style to match the previous style of the book while making the next arc his own. Some series can explore entirely different looks from arc to arc, but with ECLIPSE, the sun itself is a character as is the city of New York. The story's look required a level of consistency.

Flavio rose to the challenge and crushed it. The colors are unbelievable! Whether the story takes us into the gritty underground tunnels or the sun-baked wasteland, the environments come to life. Along with the help of his flatter, Francesca Cittarelli, he captures a cinematic feel with lighting, texture and other coloring techniques.

Gio and I pour our hearts and souls into this series, and we are not sure Flavio knew what he was in for when he signed on, but he matched our enthusiasm, our tireless work ethic and our attention to detail. I knew we had reached a true nirvana when Flavio asked us for more notes so he could really nail it. Consider it nailed, Flavio! Well, without further ado, Flavio will share his comments with you as well as some of the stunning works-in-progress from the coloring process. Enjoy!

impse into the process behi d

ECLIPSE

vio: I'm Flavio Dispenza, the colorist for the second arc of ECLIPSE. Pleased to meet you all! I'
I to have the opportunity to share with you my experience during the coloring of ECLIPSE an
work process I developed for the series.

nwork is one of the keys to making ECLIPSE the comic it is. As I started the second arc, I had t
cohesion to what had been done before without compromising my own style. The solutio
nis challenge was to create a way for everyone to share their input in a constructive way b
wing everyone to view the roughs.

gh colors are my way of planning ahead so that in the final days before a deadline, when I hav
ork faster, I won't have to deal with thinking about atmosphere or finding solutions to an issu

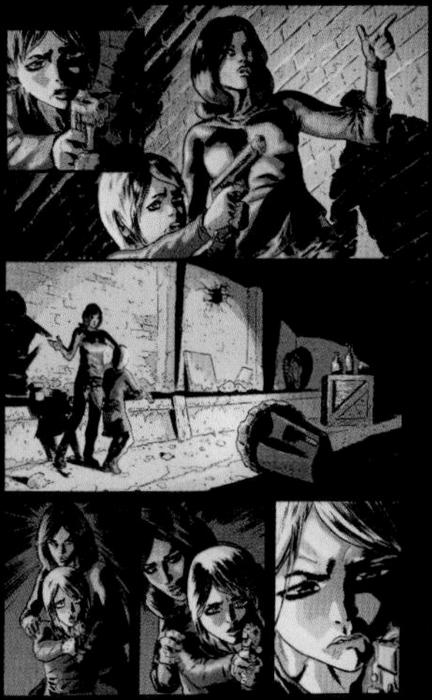

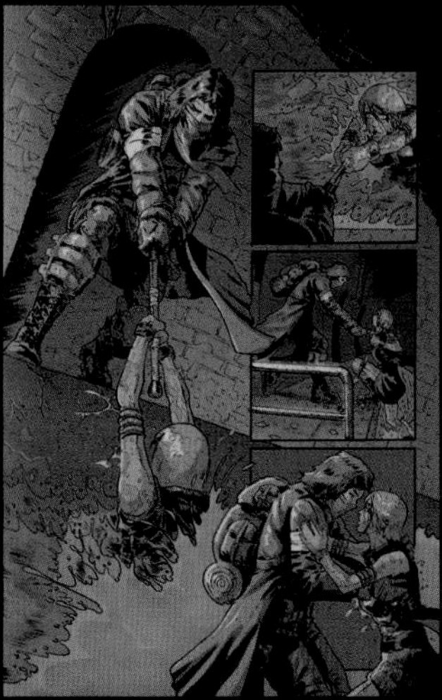

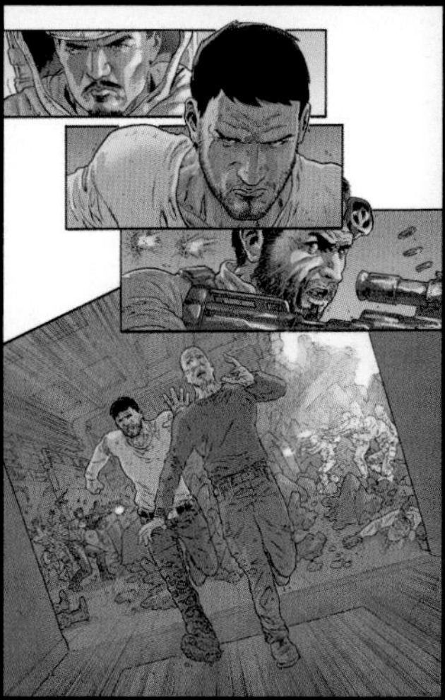

changes or adjustments are discussed at this rough stage, and that gives me time to rethin
choices for the whole book and avoid needing to "patch" something at the last minute.

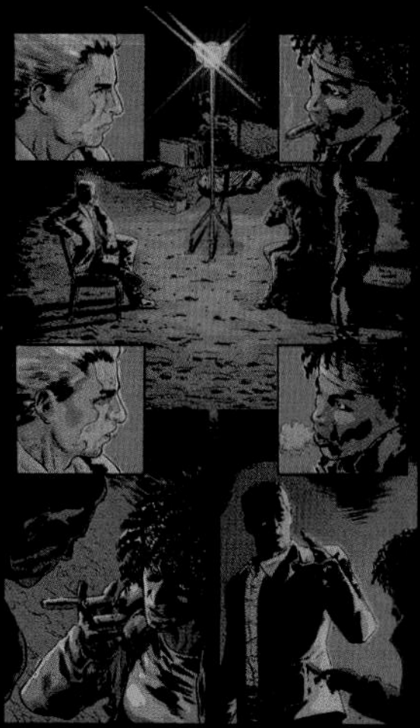

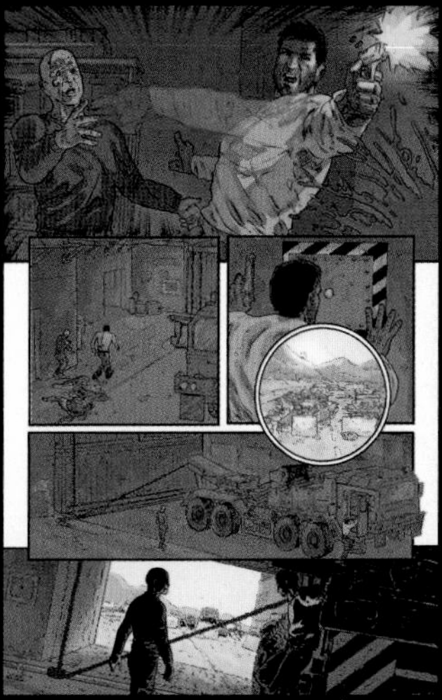

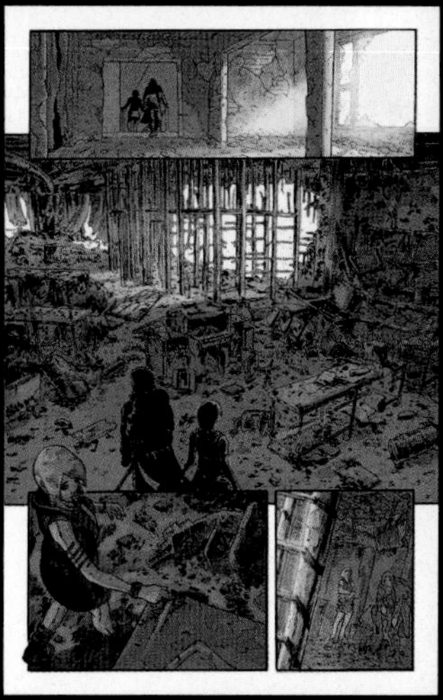

MO: Once the roughs get approved, I move on to the second step: the flats. My flatter, France
tarelli, proceeds to do the clean selections of the different elements on the page, and using
ughs as a reference, she reproduces the correct palette for the base.

th these kind of flats, I can go straight to the next step: the modeling.

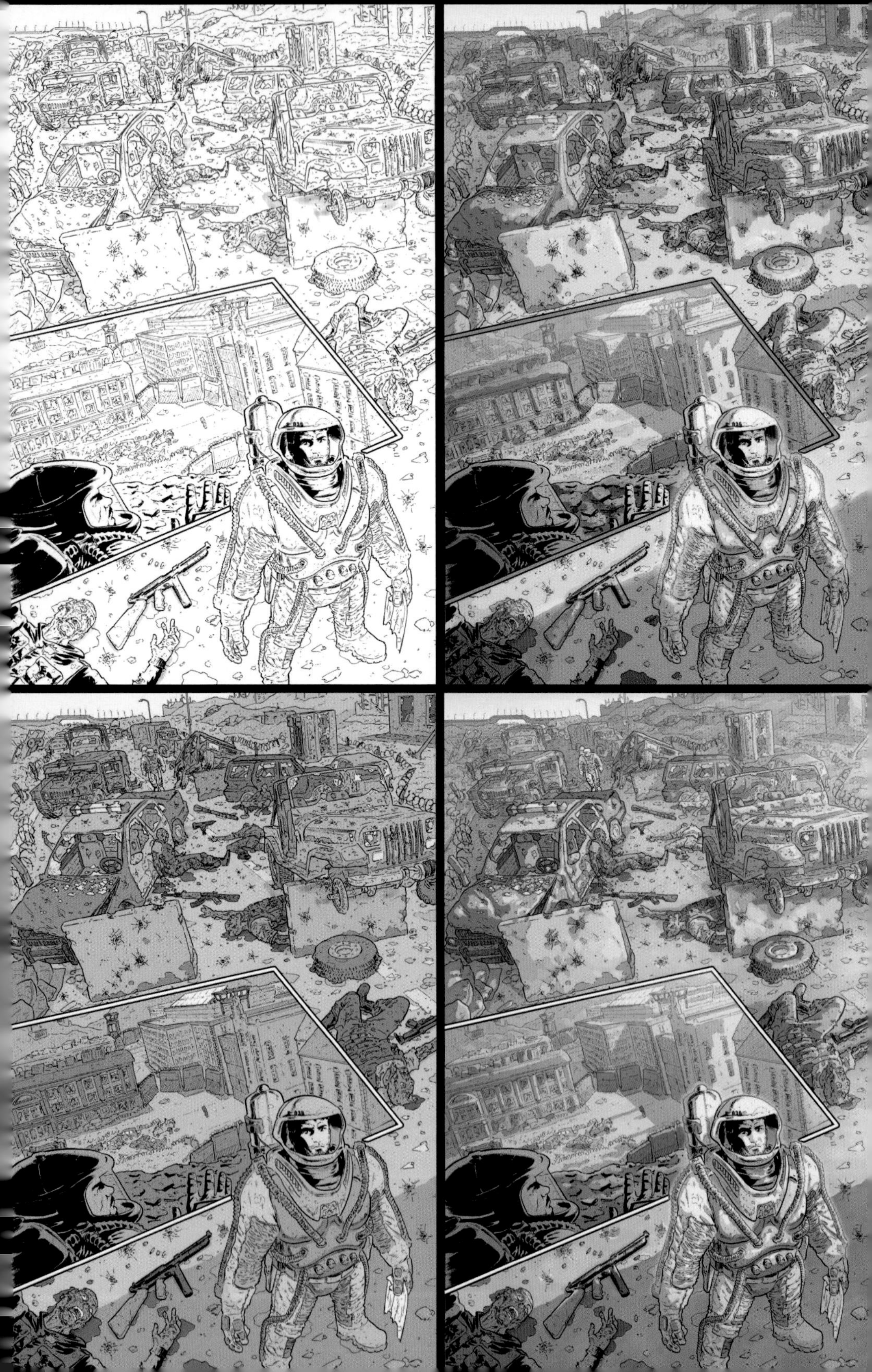

ues, it's important to respect the style of the lines. Otherwise
or can become a barrier between the art and the reader, rather than an integral element
roves immersion. Consistency between color and line art helps to create a believable wor

n characters usually have heavier inks, which I like to render with simple, clean shadows, tr
ere I can to mimic Gio's style. I try to limit the shading to a single multiply layer, avoiding ad
ng light layers on top of it when I can, saving lights only to dramatize scenes.

his scene with Bax burning the soldier, I looked for a way to render the effect of sun on hu
h. At first, I thought about cooked meat, but then I realized that a fried meat effect was r
at I was looking for. Flesh and skin frying in their own fat show through bright orange
ow with some small white spots on them, like grease. I think it worked really well.

egards to the backgrounds, they are already so rich and detailed that I try to avoid using text
gradients. I work manually with my own brushes to enhance Gio's clear lines without ris
ering them.

these pages, we thought to create a bazaar-like atmosphere. That's how Zack imagined it,
ved the idea. I tried to picture this scenario through the use of warm, dirty tones and str
rescent lights to give the reader the idea of a lively, exotic underground market. It's shady
of life, and you could get your throat sliced open at any time. I love these pages!

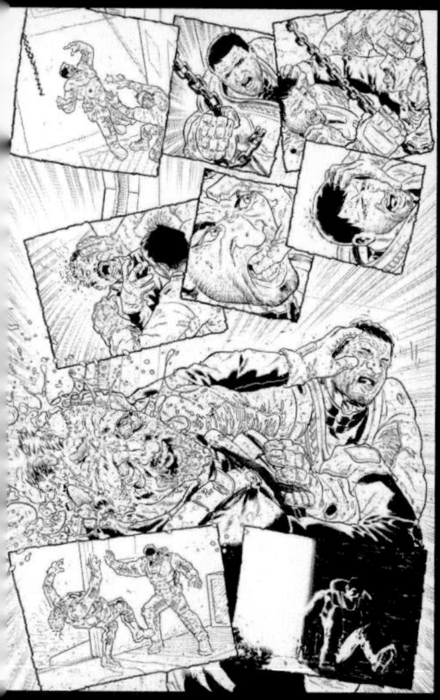

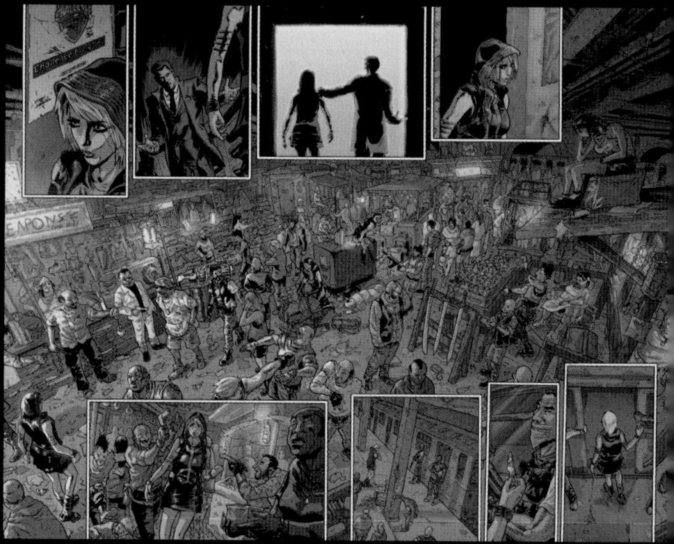

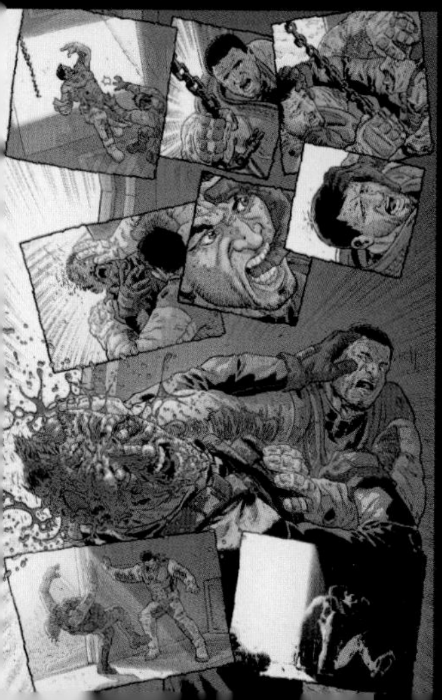

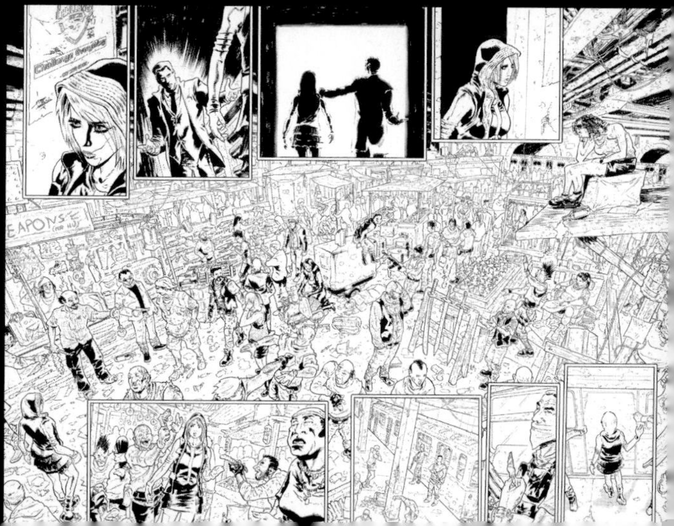

. One exception are the sunlight effects. To create the right intensity for the deadly r
o work over the ink, burning the lines and coloring over them.

o many details, it's important to guide the reader through the page. A few basic color
adows help create a sort of spotlight effect to direct the reader's eye to where I want

thank you to Zack and Giovanni for giving me the opportunity to share my thought
nd of course, for the chance to break into the American market!

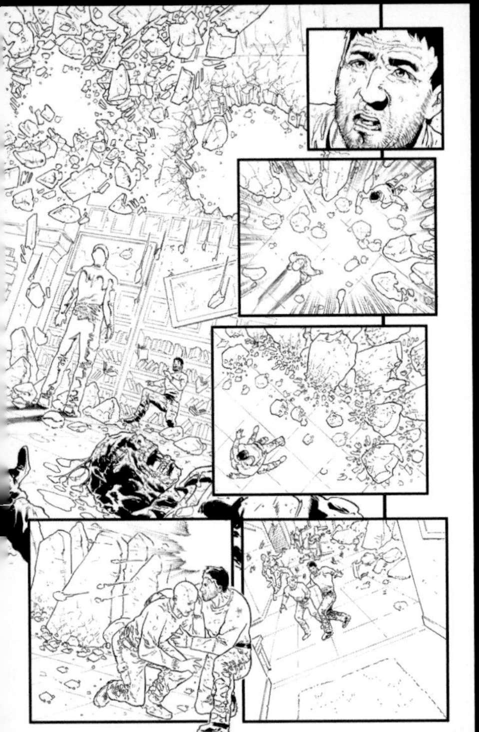

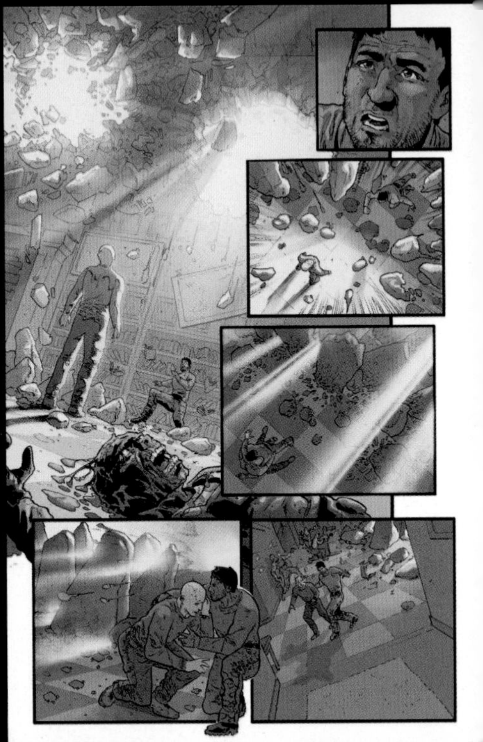

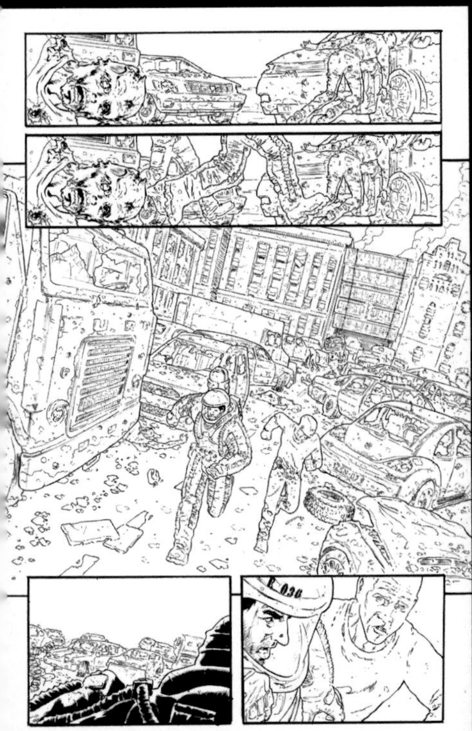

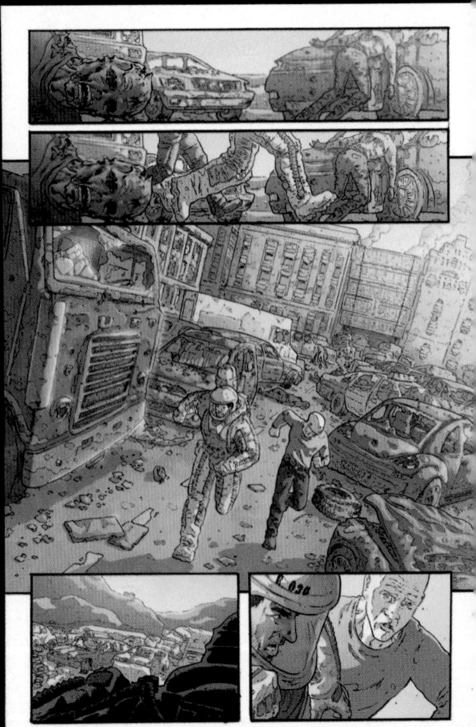

ECLIPSE was the first creator-owned book for both Giovanni and I, and it was Flavio's first US book, so we were all motivated to use the back pages of the series to let readers behind the scenes. So far, we've explored the process of transforming Giovanni's layouts into inks, designing characters from scratch for both arcs of the story, coloring the art by both colorists Chris and Flavio, lettering the pages by Troy, and world-building for the second arc. However, there is one area we have yet to discuss: the writing!

Every day I aspire to chart out a solid story, create an interesting world and dynamic, engaging characters, and put it all into a script, so that the artists may transform it into the pages you see. So I'd love to share that process with you!

A glimpse into the process behind

ECLIPSE

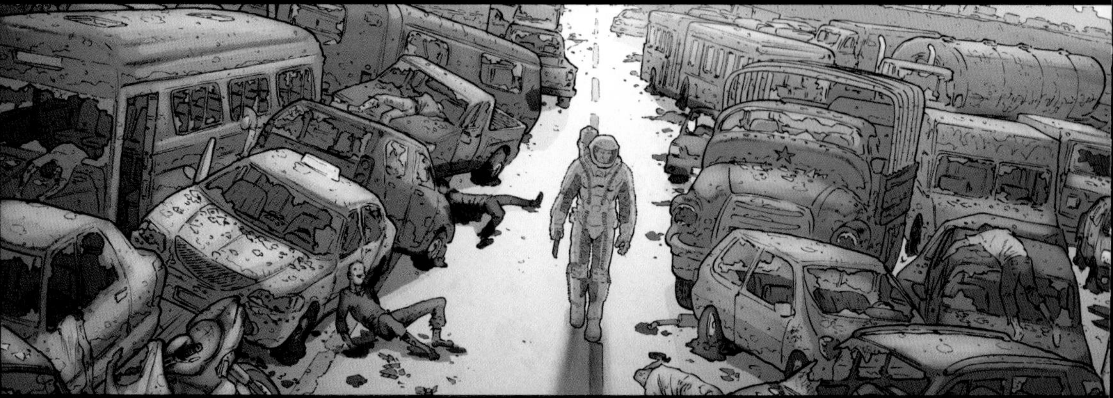

Zack: People always ask me if I know where the story is going with ECLIPSE.

Of course I do! Kind of.

I always had a vision for how ECLIPSE might continue past the first arc. I certainly knew how might end. But the in-between was something I had to work out. I think a storyteller usually h an idea for a beginning and ending, but writing is a process of discovery.

One of the most difficult challenges I faced was determining just how much story to do in t second arc. When ECLIPSE had a successful debut, it was promoted to an ongoing series. Howev this just meant it would be more than a 4-issue mini. But would we get to go 12 issues or issues? Could it end at only 8 issues? How would I write the next chapter if I didn't know how ma chapters I would have?

And how much story was there? I didn't want to end ECLIPSE with readers desperate for more, a I didn't want readers to become exhausted with a never-ending story either. The second arc h to stand on its own to be fulfilling, but I would be gambling to leave the story unresolved wit cliffhanger. If the series ended due to circumstances beyond our control, the risk was the story wo be forever incomplete. I took the risk. It's the same risk I took in the first arc. I leaped and hoped.

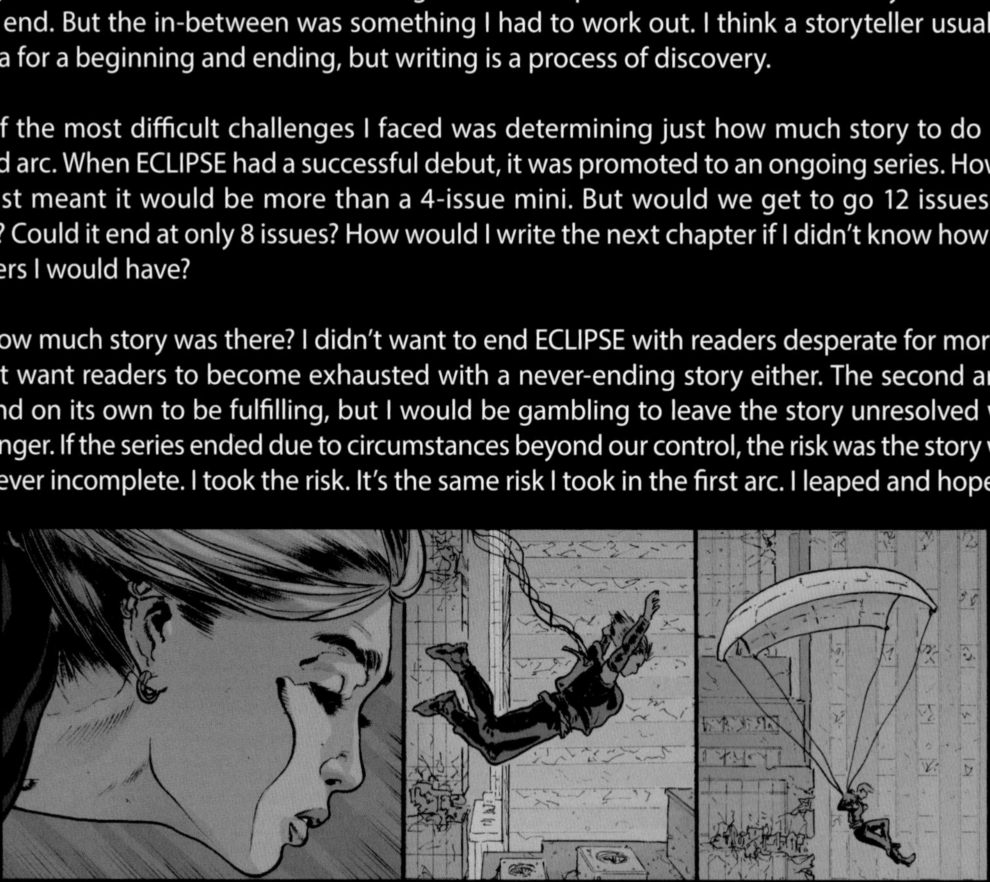

After that decision, I knew the second arc was simply the next chapter. Time to chart that chap out. Some writers may have set pieces or plot ideas in mind when they craft story. And th things do shape the story beats. But I always look to my characters to determine what will happ next. The first character I wanted to truly look at was Cielo.

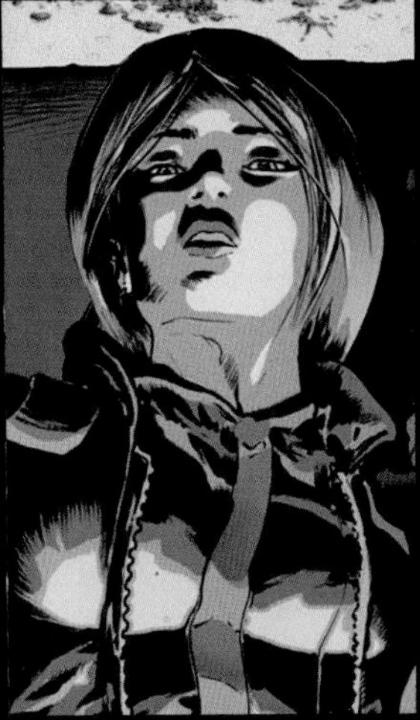

Zack: Cielo is a rebellious and active character in the first arc, but the first four issues were Bax's story. I knew in the next arc that she would become a detective herself and find answers. But if I teamed her up with Bax, then she would be in his shadow. His goals would eclipse hers (sorry, couldn't resist the pun). She had to be on her own.

Cielo's central relationship is with her father, Nick Brandt, who is at the center of everything in ECLIPSE. And despite Nick's motives, he has continually put his daughter in jeopardy. So Cielo had to face that brutal realization. How does one deal with the fact that their own parent would risk their life for the city and the greater good? Once Cielo learned the truth, she would have to become empowered and confront her father. And in the end, she is transformed into a rebel against her father's company.

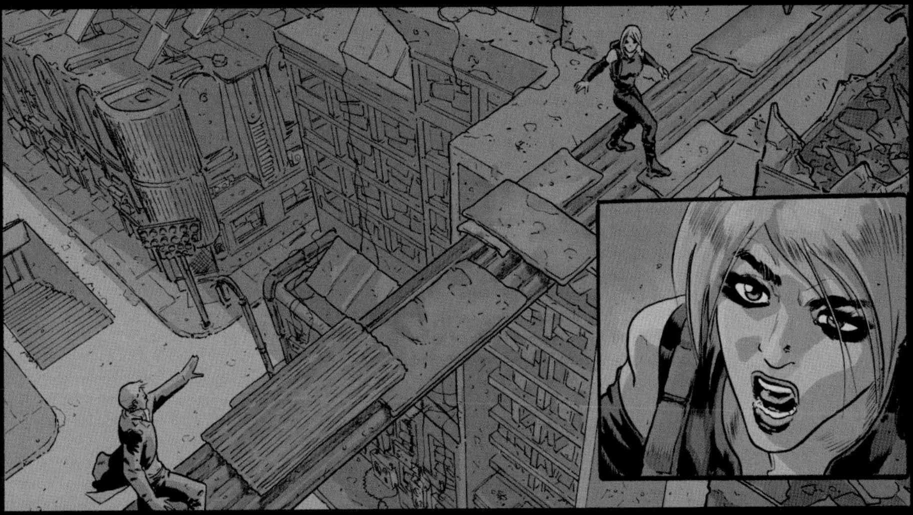

ch issue of ECLIPSE uses flashbacks to explain the emotional state of the character in their present. it was with great pleasure that I devoted the second arc flashbacks to Cielo. But how could ose flashbacks emotionally exacerbate Cielo's issues? Well, I had always thought Cielo's mother d died, but what if Cielo's father had gotten his wife killed during his conflicts against the city's ayor? What if Cielo finds that her father is risking her life just like he risked her mother's life? That eated a real emotional complication that made the final confrontation even more satisfying.

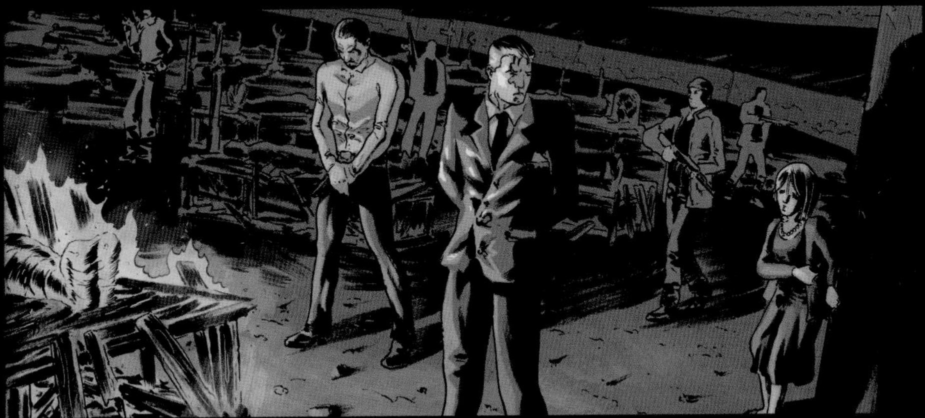

Zack: In the first arc, Bax transforms from a reclusive, cynical man to a hero once again willin to risk his life for others. At the beginning of the second arc, he doesn't entirely trust Nick ar Solarity, but how can he help the city, when it's run by a company that uses people? He mu challenge Solarity. And so, his second chapter sees him transform from a complicit man acceptir of Solarity's immoral necessities to a man following his own morality at any cost.

Solarity sacrifices the well-being of the weak and poor for the overall success of the city. B the reason Solarity had resorted to this way of life was because the former fascist may had sought to use force and create a military state of civilian soldiers. That was how I cam to the location of West Point Academy and the soldiers.

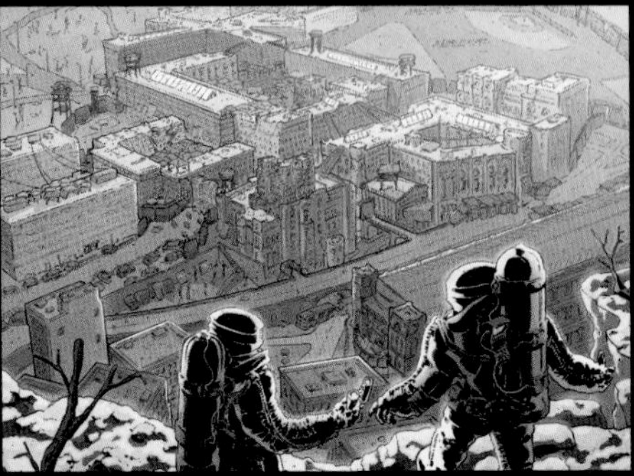

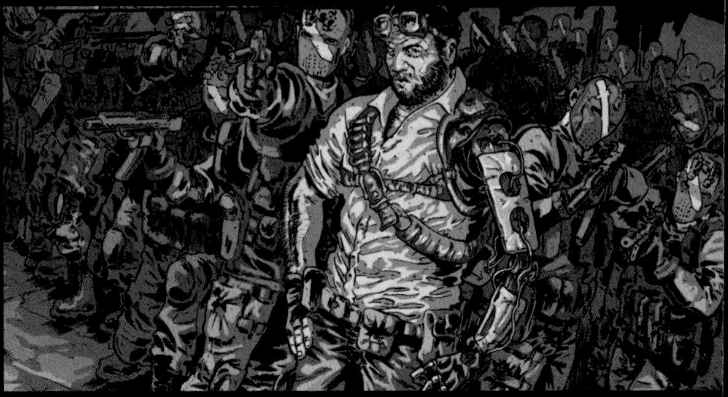

In this arc, Bax would face two different factions and their worldviews. But how would Bax respo when he found another albino immune to the sunlight? Both Mayor Holden and Solarity seek control this man and his gift, and so Bax immediately must decide what is he going to do abo the bigger picture here. There are people who can survive sunlight. How will Bax handle that? W he side with Mayor Holden or Solarity? Or will he chart his own path?

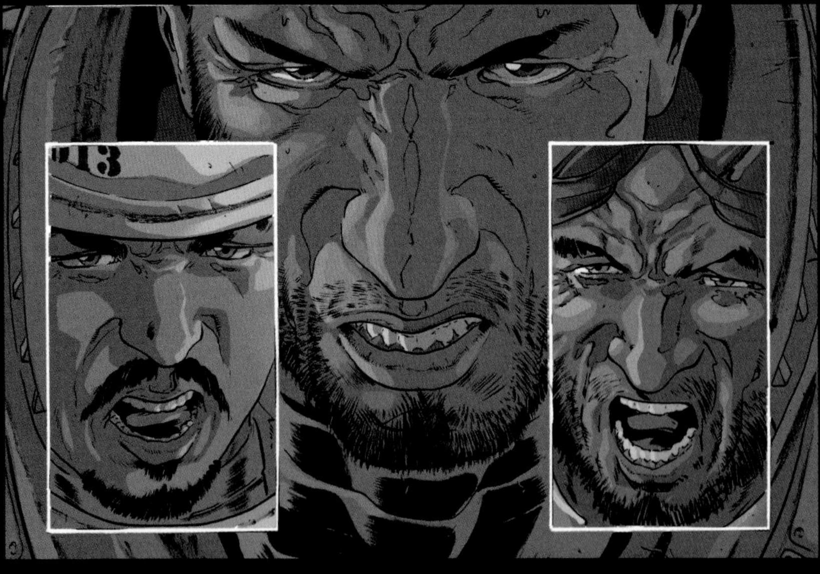

I love climaxes in which the character picks a direction that doesn't seem obvious to us a essentially orders off the menu. And of course, while Bax makes the right decision and follows own moral code, the results are tragic for the world once again. The albino is killed. But I never vi this simply as a story about the world. It's about the characters, and each arc is a chance for Bax become more prepared to ultimate deal with the next conflict and perhaps truly right the wo for good.

erall story's direction, but then I turn a bulletin board to chart out the major ›ry beats. I actually have six boards in / office that can be hung and removed m the wall depending on my current iting project (thank you French cleat nging systems). I use flash cards to art out the major beats, and then I fill he gaps until I have every scene nailed wn. I'll go to the keyboard to write out details and work out the kinks. In the d, I have a board that shows a scene- -scene breakdown of the entire arc.

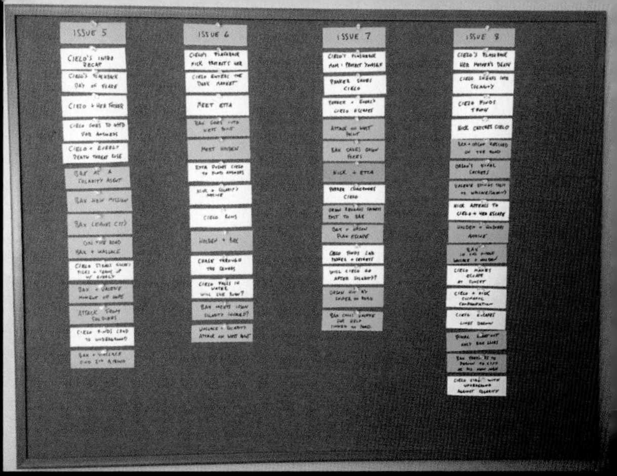

m there, I use another board with cards to determine the page breaks. Flash cards make it eas nove things around to make changes, and it's helpful to look at everything in a physical order ny writers use this technique in Film/TV writing too.

en I outline. Yes, another step before I actually write the script! I have to capture the scene nflict, the rising tension, character choices, dialogue subtext and clean transitions. This is the writing of the story, focusing on the essentials before I think about panels.

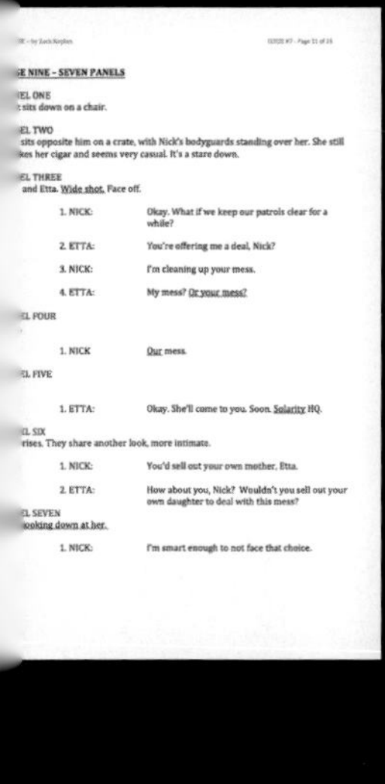

E NINE – SEVEN PANELS

EL ONE
sits down on a chair.

EL TWO
sits opposite him on a crate, with Nick's bodyguards standing over her. She still kes her cigar and seems very casual. It's a stare down.

EL THREE
and Etta. Wide shot. Face off.

1. NICK: Okay. What if we keep our patrols clear for a while?

2. ETTA: You're offering me a deal, Nick?

3. NICK: I'm cleaning up your mess.

4. ETTA: My mess? Or your mess?

EL FOUR

1. NICK Our mess.

EL FIVE

1. ETTA: Okay. She'll come to you. Soon. Solarity HQ.

EL SIX
rises. They share another look, more intimate.

1. NICK: You'd sell out your own mother, Etta.

2. ETTA: How about you, Nick? Wouldn't you sell out your own daughter to deal with this mess?

EL SEVEN
ooking down at her.

1. NICK: I'm smart enough to not face that choice.

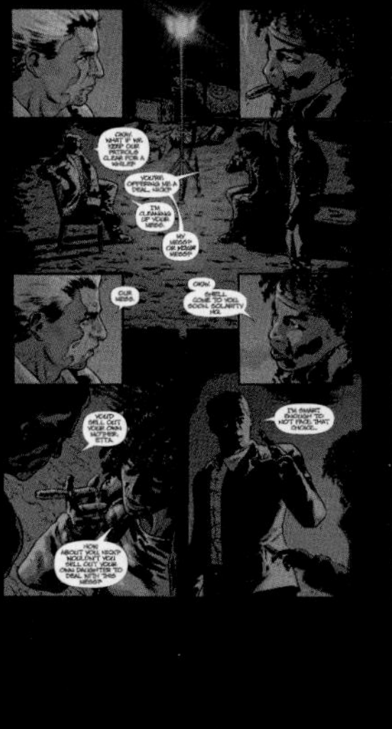

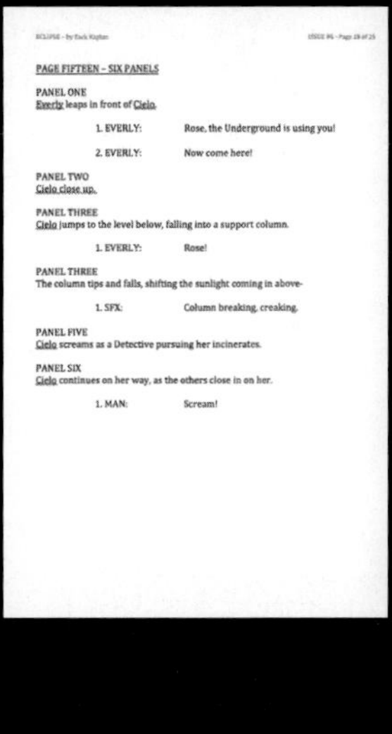

PAGE FIFTEEN – SIX PANELS

PANEL ONE
Everly leaps in front of Cielo.

1. EVERLY: Rose, the Underground is using you!

2. EVERLY: Now come here!

PANEL TWO
Cielo close up.

PANEL THREE
Cielo jumps to the level below, falling into a support column.

1. EVERLY: Rose!

PANEL THREE
The column tips and falls, shifting the sunlight coming in above-

1. SFX: Column breaking, creaking.

PANEL FIVE
Cielo screams as a Detective pursuing her incinerates.

PANEL SIX
Cielo continues on her way, as the others close in on her.

1. MAN: Scream!

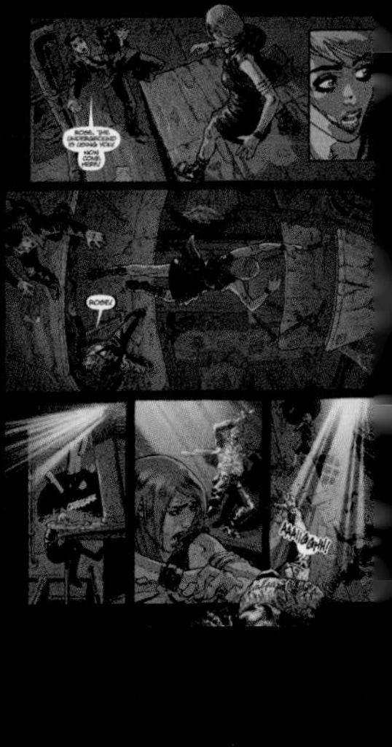

e I have a detailed outline, then I go to paneling in the script. For dialogue-heavy scenes, the dialogue down on the page and then assess the good panel breaks for the dialogue. I as ›se scene it is and what emotion they are feeling. Can I emphasize that emotion with a pane key character with a close-up?

on is similar. I chart out the basic beats. Cielo runs. She jumps. Agents get burned. She leaps falls. Etc. Those beats become panels. Sometimes a jump or a punch requires many panels fo beginning and end of that action. For complex action sequences, I have to determine the speed of the ments, and I'm always looking for the musicality of the paneling. Pacing is extremely important to me.

Zack: During my collaboration with Giovanni, my focus on paneling has become mo
relaxed, simply because Giovanni is so good at panel storytelling. I would rather give hi
the freedom to shine. My earlier scripts were far more rigid with a panel count. Now, I wri
5–7 PANELS for one page or I write PANEL TWO (might be 3 panels separating action). I al
add all sorts of artist notes in my script to explain my goals and offer Gio choices for ho
to panel.

One sequence that truly shows off our collaboration is the Issue #8 climax between Cie
and Nick on the rooftop walkways at sunset. I gave Giovanni a tremendous amount
freedom here. I had plotted out the story and determined the confrontation would ta
place over 4 pages. I knew the core beats. It would start with Cielo coming outside. Ni
follows her, and their confrontation occurs as Cielo becomes trapped by sunlight. The
as their argument comes to a head, she expresses that she no longer trusts him. Then sl
jumps, coasting safely to the ground. Those were the beats, but the way in which th
played would depend a lot on the physical design of the space. So, I left the writing op
without page breaks.

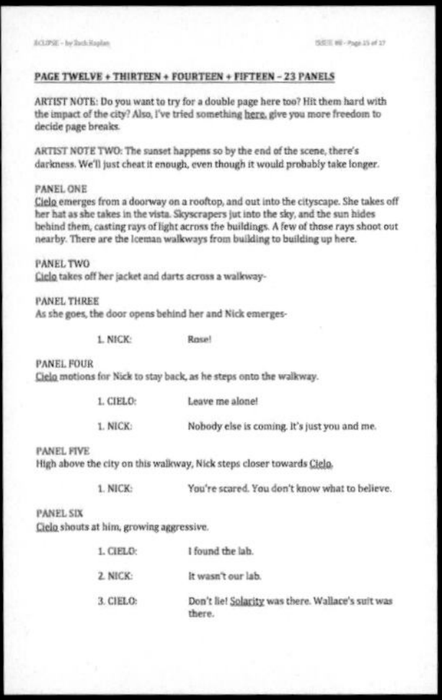

ECLIPSE – by Zack Kaplan ISSUE #8 – Page 15 of 17

PAGE TWELVE + THIRTEEN + FOURTEEN + FIFTEEN – 23 PANELS

ARTIST NOTE: Do you want to try for a double page here too? Hit them hard with the impact of the city? Also, I've tried something here, give you more freedom to decide page breaks.

ARTIST NOTE TWO: The sunset happens so by the end of the scene, there's darkness. We'll just cheat it enough, even though it would probably take longer.

PANEL ONE
Cielo emerges from a doorway on a rooftop, and out into the cityscape. She takes off her hat as she takes in the vista. Skyscrapers jut into the sky, and the sun hides behind them, casting rays of light across the buildings. A few of those rays shoot out nearby. There are the Iceman walkways from building to building up here.

PANEL TWO
Cielo takes off her jacket and darts across a walkway-

PANEL THREE
As she goes, the door opens behind her and Nick emerges-

1. NICK: Rose!

PANEL FOUR
Cielo motions for Nick to stay back, as he steps onto the walkway.

1. CIELO: Leave me alone!

1. NICK: Nobody else is coming. It's just you and me.

PANEL FIVE
High above the city on this walkway, Nick steps closer towards Cielo.

1. NICK: You're scared. You don't know what to believe.

PANEL SIX
Cielo shouts at him, growing aggressive.

1. CIELO: I found the lab.

2. NICK: It wasn't our lab.

3. CIELO: Don't lie! Solarity was there. Wallace's suit was there.

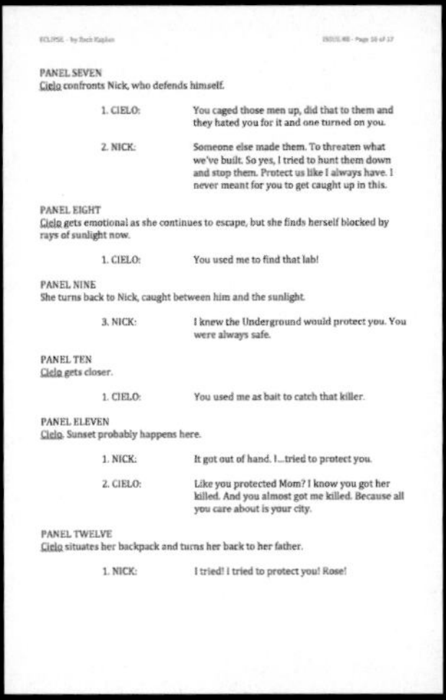

ECLIPSE – by Zack Kaplan ISSUE #8 – Page 16 of 17

PANEL SEVEN
Cielo confronts Nick, who defends himself.

1. CIELO: You caged those men up, did that to them and they hated you for it and one turned on you.

2. NICK: Someone else made them. To threaten what we've built. So yes, I tried to hunt them down and stop them. Protect us like I always have. I never meant for you to get caught up in this.

PANEL EIGHT
Cielo gets emotional as she continues to escape, but she finds herself blocked by rays of sunlight now.

1. CIELO: You used me to find that lab!

PANEL NINE
She turns back to Nick, caught between him and the sunlight.

3. NICK: I knew the Underground would protect you. You were always safe.

PANEL TEN
Cielo gets closer.

1. CIELO: You used me as bait to catch that killer.

PANEL ELEVEN
Cielo. Sunset probably happens here.

1. NICK: It got out of hand. I…tried to protect you.

2. CIELO: Like you protected Mom? I know you got her killed. And you almost got me killed. Because all you care about is your city.

PANEL TWELVE
Cielo situates her backpack and turns her back to her father.

1. NICK: I tried! I tried to protect you! Rose!

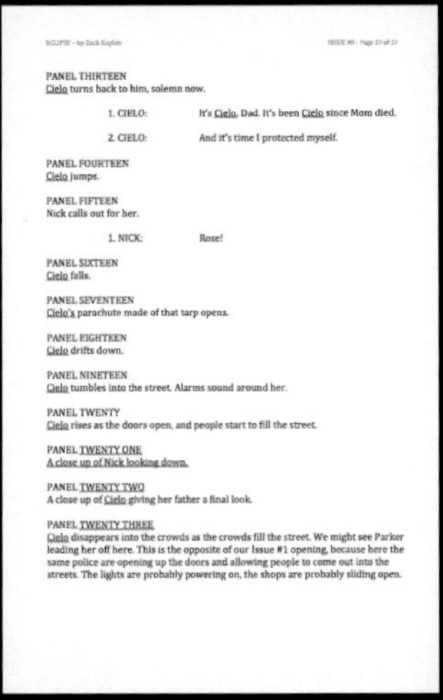

ECLIPSE – by Zack Kaplan ISSUE #8 – Page 17 of 17

PANEL THIRTEEN
Cielo turns back to him, solemn now.

1. CIELO: It's Cielo, Dad. It's been Cielo since Mom died.

2. CIELO: And it's time I protected myself.

PANEL FOURTEEN
Cielo jumps.

PANEL FIFTEEN
Nick calls out for her.

1. NICK: Rose!

PANEL SIXTEEN
Cielo falls.

PANEL SEVENTEEN
Cielo's parachute made of that tarp opens.

PANEL EIGHTEEN
Cielo drifts down.

PANEL NINETEEN
Cielo tumbles into the street. Alarms sound around her.

PANEL TWENTY
Cielo rises as the doors open, and people start to fill the street.

PANEL TWENTY ONE
A close up of Nick looking down.

PANEL TWENTY TWO
A close up of Cielo giving her father a final look.

PANEL TWENTY THREE
Cielo disappears into the crowds as the crowds fill the street. We might see Parker leading her off here. This is the opposite of our Issue #1 opening, because here the same police are opening up the doors and allowing people to come out into the streets. The lights are probably powering on, the shops are probably sliding open.

Gio had the freedom or responsibility, however you see it, to map out the various pan
and actually determine the page breaks. Gio nailed it in the first pass. It's a good exam
of how giving an artist freedom while still having some paneling structure can lead
great results.

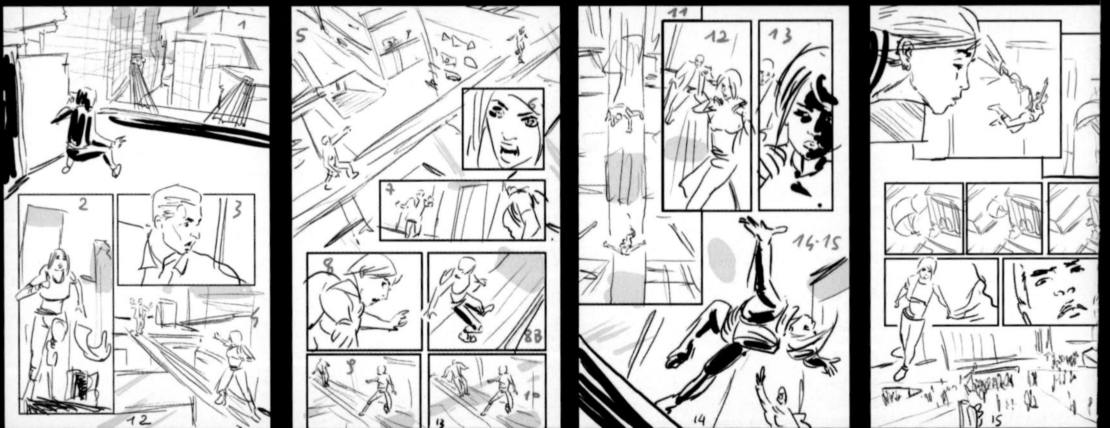

k: Sometimes during the layout process, Gio and I discuss the page when the scrip
always specific. When laying out Issue 8, Page 17, Gio and I explored Bax's import
ax and how to fit the action and character into one page in a satisfying way.

cript page offered options. Gio opted to combine Holden's response to Wallace's de
Bax's shooting of Wallace. Then Bax kills Holden in the next panel. That worked wel
some space! But then, how were we to do a massive shootout in less than half a pag
submitted two brilliant layouts, and after discussion, we came to a third layout versi
above. The small panels a zoom-in on Bax's eyes and then a zoom-out help pass t
and get us to the shootout's aftermath.

PAGE SEVENTEEN – SIX OR MORE PANELS

PANEL ONE
(Or two panels)
A two shot as Bax shoots Wallace dead, right through the glass helmet.

PANEL TWO
Holden grins, thinking Bax has chosen his side.

1. HOLDEN: Well done-

PANEL THREE
(or two panels)
Another two shot as Bax shoots and kills Holden. Or maybe over the shoulder of Holden, getting shot through the head, with Bax in the background. Or reverse, over Bax's shoulder, as Bax holds the gun out, firing, so we see Holden's face as he's shot.

PANEL FOUR
A wide shot. Both leaders lie dead, or perhaps Wallace lies dead on the ground, and Holden is still falling. The henchmen on both sides are shocked, but Bax is already firing on them as well. We should also see one or two of the henchmen with their guns up already starting to fire. Basically, the gunfight is erupting here. (Maybe in the background we see Valerie ducking behind the vehicle)

PANEL FIVE
(Or many panels)
Bax FIRES, shooting the henchmen. It's a blood bath, and Bax should be covered in blood at the end of this. He's also becoming an animal in a way. He's full of emotion.

PANEL SIX
The aftermath. Everyone is dead. A strew of bodies. The Solarity vehicle is shot up badly, steaming from the engine. (important because they can't use it again) Bax stands there covered in blood. Cinematic moment. And we might see Valerie ducking out from her cover behind the vehicle, but while she is focused on Bax, and she's a little afraid of him, he's just lost in the carnage, still reeling from all this killing.

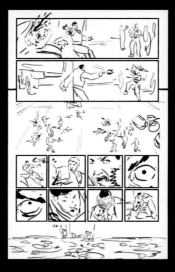

ourse, after the inks, I get one last chance dit the dialogue before Troy, the letterer, s his work. I like to print out every page, read through the script while looking at art. The beauty of comics is that the script change several times before it goes to the ter, allowing a writer the chance to make the story and art and dialogue all work d in hand.

pite that entire process of writing, I still find rve-wracking to send a comic to the printer. n the end, it must be done. And while I off with a clear vision, I often find that I've ed up in a different place than I thought I'd And yet, it's still in larger ways exactly what I nded. It's still ECLIPSE!

said from the beginning, writing, especially mics, is a process of discovery.

COVER GALLERY
ALL COVERS BY GIOVANNI TIMPANO

ISSUE FIVE

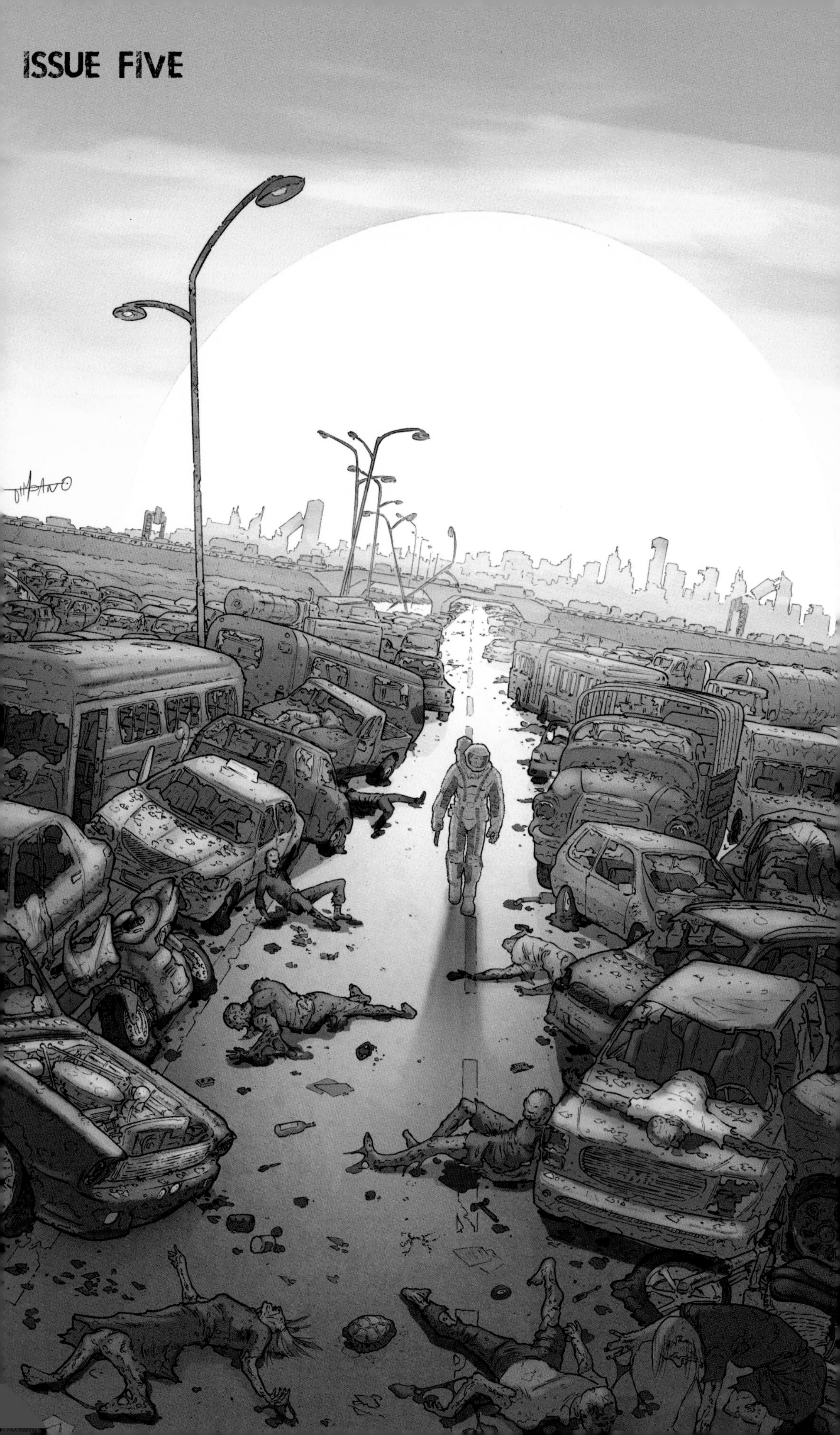

ISSUE SIX

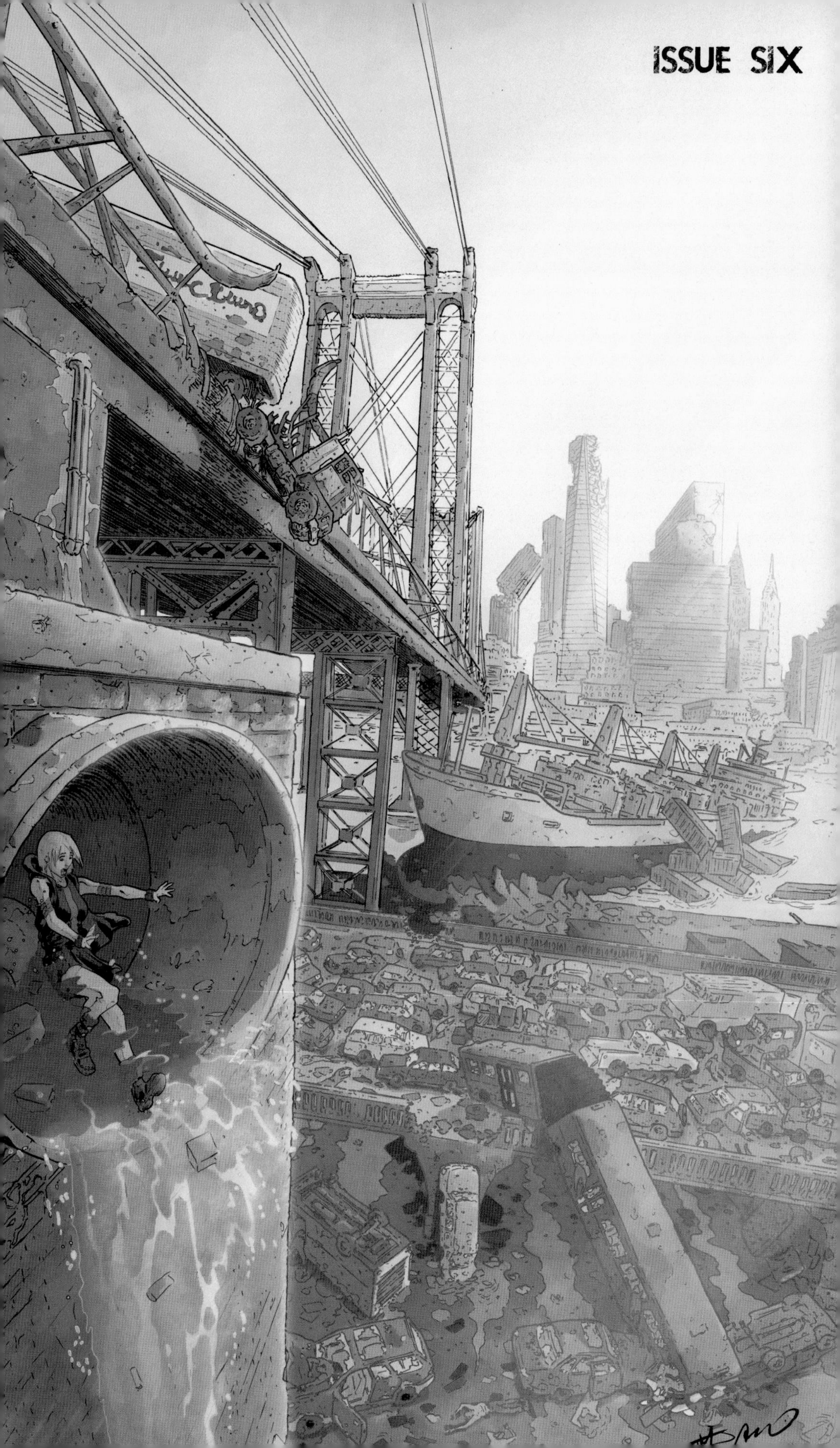

ISSUE SEVEN

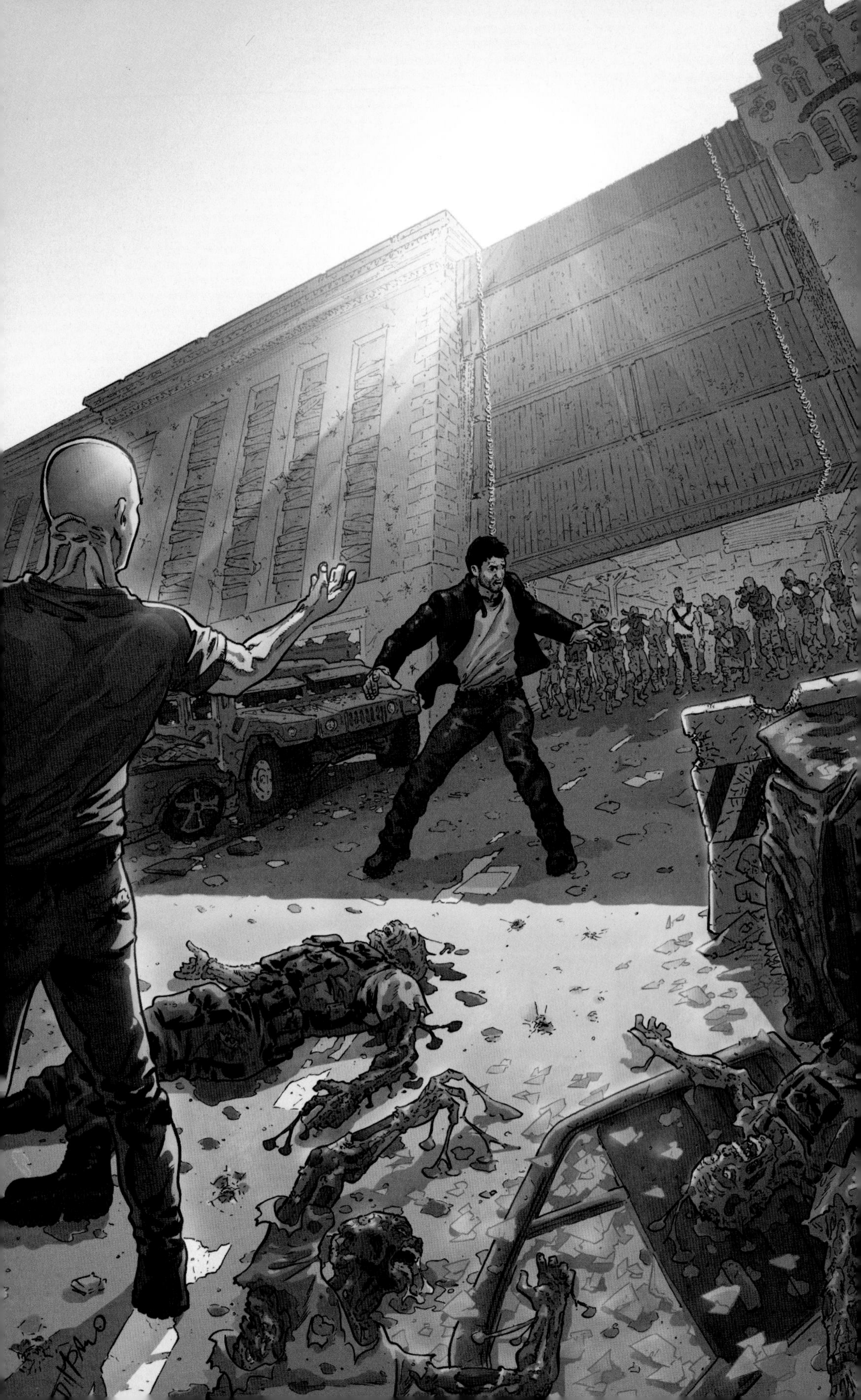

ISSUE EIGHT

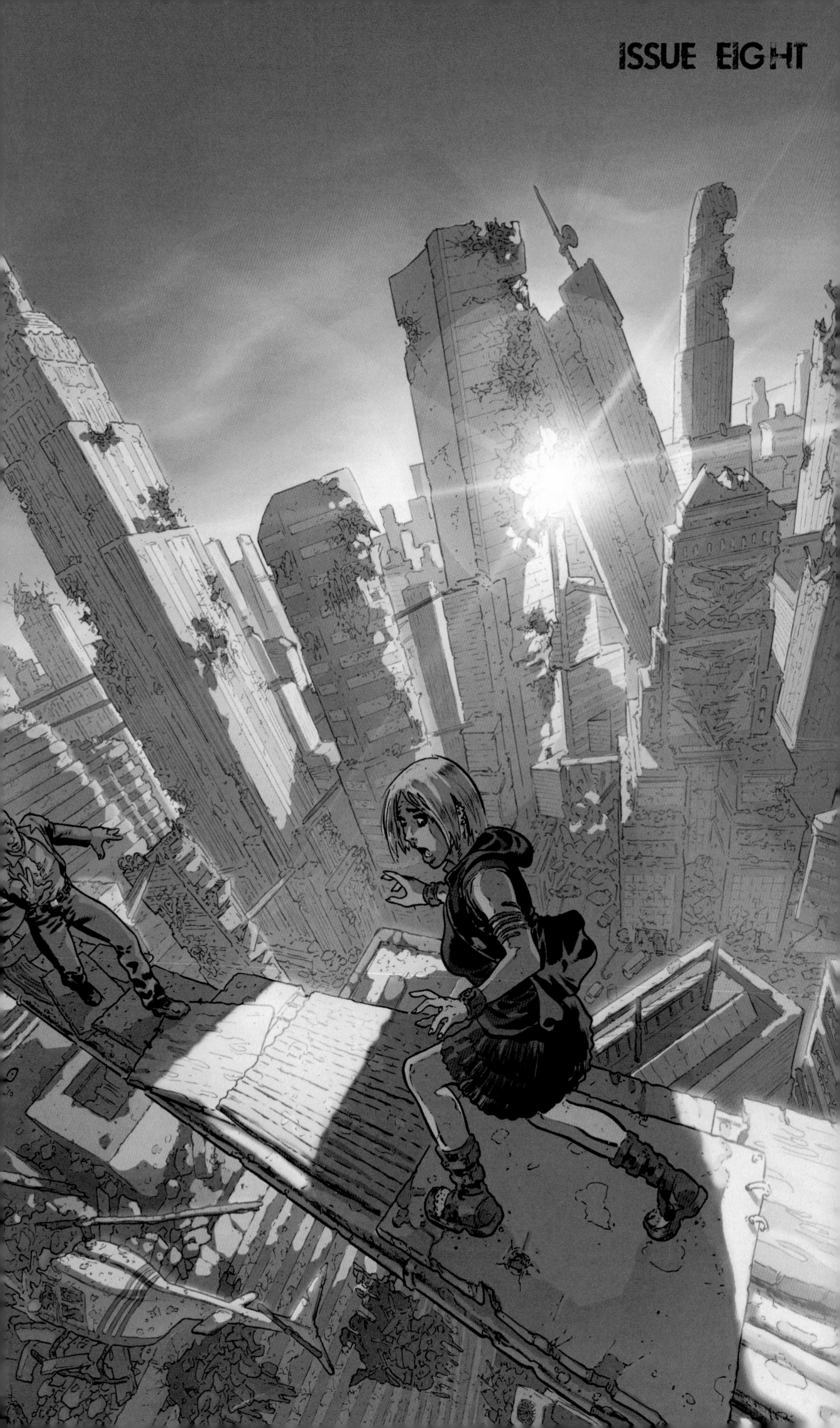

The Top Cow essentials checklist:

IXth Generation, Volume 1
(ISBN: 978-1-63215-323-4)

Aphrodite IX: Complete Series
(ISBN: 978-1-63215-368-5)

Artifacts Origins: First Born
(ISBN: 978-1-60706-506-7)

Broken Trinity, Volume 1
(ISBN: 978-1-60706-051-2)

Cyber Force: Rebirth, Volume 1
(ISBN: 978-1-60706-671-2)

The Darkness: Accursed, Volume 1
(ISBN: 978-1-58240-958-0)

The Darkness: Rebirth, Volume 1
(ISBN: 978-1-60706-585-2)

Death Vigil, Volume 1
(ISBN: 978-1-63215-278-7)

Eden's Fall Volume 1
(ISBN: 978-1-5343-0065-1)

Postal, Volume 1
(ISBN: 978-1-63215-342-5)

Rising Stars Compendium
(ISBN: 978-1-63215-246-6)

Sunstone, Volume 1
(ISBN: 978-1-63215-212-1)

Symmetry, Volume 1
(ISBN: 978-1-63215-699-0)

The Tithe, Volume 1
(ISBN: 978-1-63215-324-1)

Think Tank, Volume 1
(ISBN: 978-1-60706-660-6)

Wanted
(ISBN: 978-1-58240-497-4)

Bloodstain, Volume 1
(ISBN: 978-1-63215-544-3)

Witchblade: Redemption, Volum
(ISBN: 978-1-60706-193-9)

Witchblade: Rebirth, Volume
(ISBN: 978-1-60706-532-6)

Witchblade: Borne Again, Volum
(ISBN: 978-1-63215-025-7)

For more ISBN and ordering information on our latest collections go to:
www.topcow.com
Ask your retailer about our catalogue of collected editions,
digests, and hard covers or check the listings at:
Barnes and Noble, Amazon.com,
and other fine retailers.

To find your nearest comic shop go to:
www.comicshoplocator.com

ECLIPSE™

Published by Top Cow Productions, Inc.
Los Angeles

ECLIPSE

Created by Zack Kaplan

Zack Kaplan
Writer

Giovanni Timpano
Artist

Flavio Dispenza
Colorist

Elena Salcedo
Editor

Troy Peteri
Letterer

Francesca Cittarelli
Flatter

For Top Cow Productions, Inc.
For Top Cow Productions, Inc.
Marc Silvestri - CEO
Matt Hawkins - President & COO
Elena Salcedo - Vice President of Operations
Henry Barajas - Director of Operations
Vincent Valentine - Production Manager
Dylan Gray - Marketing Director

Production by Carey Hall

Cover by Giovanni Timpano & Flavio Dispenza

To find the comic shop nearest you, call:
1-888-COMICBOOK

Want more info? Check out:
www.topcow.com
for news & exclusive Top Cow merchandise!

IMAGE COMICS, INC.
Robert Kirkman—Chief Operating Officer
Erik Larsen—Chief Financial Officer
Todd McFarlane—President
Marc Silvestri—Chief Executive Officer
Jim Valentine—Vice-President

Eric Stephenson—Publisher
Corey Murphy—Director of Sales
Jeff Boison—Director of Publishing Planning & Book Trade Sales
Chris Ross—Director of Digital Sales
Jeff Stang—Director of Specialty Sales
Kat Salazar—Director of PR & Marketing
Branwyn Bigglestone—Controller
Sue Korpela—Accounts Manager
Drew Gill—Art Director
Brett Warnock—Production Manager
Leigh Thomas—Print Manager
Tricia Ramos—Traffic Manager
Briah Skelly—Publicist
Aly Hoffman—Events & Conventions Coordinator
Sasha Head—Sales & Marketing Production Designer
David Brothers—Branding Manager
Melissa Gifford—Content Manager
Drew Fitzgerald—Publicity Assistant
Vincent Kukua—Production Artist
Erika Schnatz—Production Artist
Ryan Brewer—Production Artist
Shanna Matuszak—Production Artist
Carey Hall—Production Artist
Esther Kim—Direct Market Sales Representative
Emilio Bautista—Digital Sales Representative
Leanna Caunter—Accounting Assistant
Chloe Ramos-Peterson—Library Market Sales Representative
Marla Eizik—Administrative Assistant
IMAGECOMICS.COM